LJB

W9-AMT-454

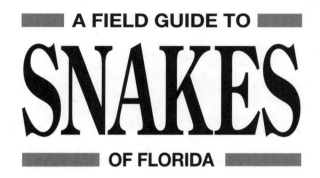

A FIELD GUIDE TO

SNAKES

OF FLORIDA

Gulf Publishing Company

Houston, Texas

A FIELD GUIDE TO

SNAKES

OF FLORIDA

ALAN TENNANT

In Collaboration with Kenneth L. Krysko

Introduction
Richard D. Bartlett

Range Maps
Kenneth L. Krysko

For Helen
Who, with intelligence, dedication, and love
Pulled it all together.

Gulf Publishing Company
Book Division
P.O. Box 2608 □ Houston, Texas 77252-2608

10   9   8   7   6   5   4   3   2   1

Library of Congress Cataloging-in-Publication Data

Tennant, Alan, 1943–
    A field guide to snakes of Florida / by Alan Tennant ; in collaboration with Kenneth L. Krysko ; introduction, Richard D. Bartlett ; range maps, Kenneth L. Krysko.
        p.   cm. – (Gulf's field guide series)
    Includes bibliographical references (p.   ) and index.
    ISBN 0-87719-291-X
    1. Snakes—Florida—Identification.   I. Krysko, Kenneth L. II. Title.   III. Series.
QL666.06T456   1997
597.96'09759—dc20   96-36403
                                                      CIP

Contents

Brown-blotched Terrestrial Snakes

Large Kingsnakes

Red-and-black-banded Snakes

Elapidae

Coral Snakes

Viperidae

Moccasins

Rattlesnakes

Acknowledgments

Authors frequently acknowledge that they could not have completed a particular work without the help of colleagues. Rarely, I think, is this as true as is it is with *A Field Guide to Florida Snakes,* where my indebtedness is deep to all those who helped. In roughly the chronological order in which they joined this project, these people are: Craig and Linda Trumbower, who went out of their way to re-involve me with a large part of Florida's herpetological community. Among the leaders of this very generous community of enthusiasts are Dick and Patti Bartlett, whose kindness and hospitality were a godsend. The depth of herpetological understanding and breadth of experience Dick brought to his Introduction and the *Storeria, Rhadinaea,* and *Farancia* species accounts he wrote for the book—as well as his familiarity with the state's academic and scientific communities—are matched by the excellent photographic work that produced his color plates. The same generosity characterizes Bill and Kathy Love, who offered both excellent photographs and the sort of hospitality and encouragement that only comes from people who share one's lifelong fascination with reptiles and amphibians.

Early in the project Len Krysko provided an enormous boost by opening his diverse collection of Florida snakes for photography, then arranging the volume's central collaboration between his son, wildlife biologist Kenneth L. Krysko, and myself. Without Kenney's energy and enthusiasm, backed by years of field collecting in Florida's marshes and pinewoods, sawgrass prairies, cypress domes, and offshore Keys (from which much of the material for his excellent distribution maps is drawn) this volume would have been infinitely poorer. Kenney led us to David Alan Zlatkin—who offered specimens for photography, searched Mt. Trashmore, and courteously advised passers-by to avert their jogging trajectories to avoid a large eastern diamondback—and to John Decker. Decker is one of those rare naturalists motivated only by a love of the subtropical world of the lower Florida peninsula, which they see rapidly vanishing and who devote themselves to the study and conservational propagation of its vanishing reptiles and amphibians.

The same is true of Kevin Enge. His familiarity with Florida's myriad natural community types and their ophidian populations (from which much of the *Habitat* section is drawn), combined with his familiarity with herpetological literature, provided a great deal of the research and collaborative editorial input upon which this volume relies. Moreover, Enge's position as monitor of the state's commercial trade in reptiles for the Florida Game and Freshwater Fish Commission gives him the authority to address "Snakes and the Law."

Equally at home in the field is Dick Bartlett's colleague, ace wildlife photographer Barry Mansell. Barry's ability to come up with superlative color plates of snakes so rare, like *Tantilla oolitica* and *Nerodia clarkii taeniata*, that they have almost never been found in the wild—let alone photographed—is supported by his broader skills as woodsman and photographer of birds and mammals, including the phantom black bears of Jacksonville.

As administrator of the Wildlife Research Laboratory of the Florida Game and Freshwater Fish Commission, Paul E. Moler is a busy guy with great responsibilities. Yet, with enormous generosity he took a tremendous amount of time to meticulously examine this text and using both his long experience in the field and his comprehensive knowledge of the pertinent scientific literature—as well as great patience—he carefully steered an early draft of this manuscript onto firmer herpetological ground.

Other important contributors to this volume are Billy Griswold, whose photographic skill resulted in several excellent color plates, and Billy's dad, Bill Griswold, who provided most of the information on the southern hognose snake, *Heterodon simus*. David Auth gave all of us access to the collection of the Florida Museum of Natural History in Gainesville, where Kenney Krysko spent weeks of research. Kenny Wray and Brice Noonan were invariably quick to offer help with field notes, library research, digging up fossorial snakes in the midst of rainstorms, and poking fun at undue seriousness. Tim Walsh of the Central Florida Zoo shared his notes on one of the state's rarest snakes, *Lampropeltis calligaster occipitolineata,* and William B. Montgomery offered slides and both esthetic and herpetological perspective. My longest-time field-trip partner, book collaborator, and critic, Craig McIntyre, also contributed slides, extensive journal and literature references, precise notes on his long-term captive maintenance of rare species such as *Cemophora coccinea copei,* and great snake-hunting lore.

Jon Hall read part of the manuscript and offered suggestions on lapses in logic, as did Tom Doerr in syntax. My researcher, Melody Lytle, did a job so much better than I expected that I am still astonished at her competency in the library and on the computer networks.

And, finally, my editor, Tim Calk, of Gulf Publishing, has proven to be the most patient, fair, and supportive publishing executive with whom I have had the pleasure of working.

Alan Tennant
Lexington, Texas

I would like to dedicate my portion of this book to my parents, Len and Barbara Krysko.

I would also like to express my appreciation to the following people who provided information for this text: Billy Griswold, Paul E. Moler, F.W. King, Kevin Enge, David Auth, Kenny Wray, Dick and Patti Bartlett, John "Rosy" Decker, David "Piercer" Zlatkin, Doug Riesco, Richard Franz, Steve "Pickle-barrel" Johnson, Clive Longden, Brice Noonan, Maria Camarrillo, Barry Mansell, Greg Lepera, Bill Cope, Sanford Boye, George Dalrymple, Naushad Vadsaria, Doug Barker, and Corey and Casey Kullman.

Kenneth L. Krysko
Gainesville, Florida

Preface

In the end
We will preserve only what we love
We will love only what we understand
We will understand only what we have learned
Baba Dioum
Senegalese Conservationist

Paleontologist Robert T. Bakker once observed that only with considerable difficulty had he been able to perceive a thecodont—a stubby little Jurassic reptile—to be as beautiful as a cheetah. The thecodont just had a different environment—an environment to which it adapted by squatting on the shores of ancient mud pans, gobbling down other reptiles and amphibians, and living in the same workable give-and-take with its neighbors. That environment, infinitely extrapolated across the panoply of living beings, reveals a system of balances so intricately poised and delicately counterweighted that only a bit of its circuitry is yet available to our understanding.

The system's essence, however, is clear: Cosmologically complex sets of opposing hungers and wills-to-live suspend each life form in a tenuous balance between dominance over its environment and extinction. In this unconscious genetic struggle, each species' individual capacities and élan contribute to the natural forces massed against its prey, its predators, and many of its neighbors. Collectively asserted, the efforts of those neighbors/competitors oppose the creature's own drive for biological success just enough to allow all of them to exist, at least momentarily balanced, in communities ranging from those living in a drop of water to those carpeting the Great Plains. Over the aeons, these communities are far from stable, for their long-term equilibrium is in constant flux. Over short spans of time, however, this system of opposing interests generally maintains a sort of slightly-varying stasis, quickly replacing dropout species with immediate efflorescences from neighboring life forms that venture evolutionary tendrils into every newly-vacated environmental space.

As little more than blinking spectators to the process, we can only respect the contenders. Yet, nothing could be further from our historical record, for respecting these contenders requires shedding the dark opacity of a great many biases. That's not easy. As Bakker recognized, the first and most difficult step in learning anything meaningful about the natural world is overcoming the human cultural perspectives that limit our biological empathies.

This is especially true concerning snakes. We generally don't eat them, some of them can kill us, and in the prevailing cultural context many are so scary and repugnant that (even to people who would hesitate to harm any other vertebrate) it has long seemed proper to kill a serpent. Yet, with the passing of so many animals that threatened first our lives, then our livestock, that viewpoint is changing. Recently we have come to see how much we have lost in ridding our lives of the bears and wolves, mountain lions and rattlesnakes that we formerly saw only as villains.[1] Too late, for the most part, awareness is dawning of the fundamental ignorance of filtering the actions and appearances of these erstwhile competitors through our provincial human perspectives of good and evil, beauty and ugliness, as though such narrow criteria could set standards for a system of harmonies that preceded our existence by billions of years and will certainly outlast us by an equivalent span.

Culturally ingrained as it is, to choose certain striking beings—cheetahs, swallows, or redwood trees—to grace with our eccentric aesthetic value is to ignore how meager this recently-acquired cultural concept is when judged against a cosmic order whose structure binds the stately parade of stars and planets, shapes the flow of tectonic currents that mold the continents, and has wrought the symmetry of serpents no less than that of tigers. Meeting our cultural need to assign malfeasance to creatures we perceive as psychologically alien traps us within the illusion that our species is a separate entity—an illusion that hides from us our essence as no more than another minuscule thread in the planet's organic tapestry. In this infinitely complex matrix, every single species of us is inextricably bound to the others by myriad, dovetailing pacts not of our own making but on which, nevertheless, our joint survival ultimately depends.

This book is an attempt to bridge, in a single small area of natural history, the gap between the data of the professional research journals—how some-

---

[1]The first book dealing solely with the conservation of a snake – and a venomous one at that – has recently appeared: *Biology, Status, and Management of the Timber Rattlesnake* (Crotalus horridus): *A Guide for Conservation,* William S. Brown, Society for the Study of Amphibians and Reptiles, Lawrence, Kansas, 1993.

one found out what we scientifically "know"—and the general, popular awareness of the natural world that largely determines our role in preserving or destroying it.

The common and scientific names used here follow the nomenclature established by the Society for the Study of Amphibians and Reptiles in Joseph T. Collins, et al., *Standard, Common, and Current Scientific Names for North American Amphibians and Reptiles* (Lawrence, Kansas: Society for the Study of Amphibians and Reptiles, 1991). I am also indebted to Conant, Roger, and Collins, Joseph T., *A Field Guide to Reptiles and Amphibians,* Houghton Mifflin, 1991, for several of the record lengths cited for various snake species.

The species accounts groups the snakes in sections that reflect (1) A snake's resemblance to other similarly sized and patterned serpents; (2) Its occupancy of similar habitat—aquatic snakes, for example; and/or (3) Its taxonomic/evolutionary relatedness to other members of the same section.

Every species and subspecies that occurs in Florida is described. (The number assigned to each animal in the text is also used in the photograph captions and the index.)

The range maps accompanying the text are an attempt to define the distribution of these animals. The dark-shaded portion of each map represents the approximate distribution of a particular species or subspecies. Because, even in well-studied areas, the geographical range of most species and subspecies has not been determined with precision—in part because human intervention is constantly altering so many of Florida's natural ecosystems—range demarcations are necessarily generalizations. The more lightly shaded regions on some of the maps indicate zones of intergradation; areas where the ranges of two or more subspecies overlap. Genetic crosses found in these areas generally exhibit characteristics of each of the neighboring subspecies. Yet, because the boundaries of intergradation zones between adjacently ranging subspecies are even more variable than the distribution boundaries between full species, specimens occurring in intergradation zones may (1) exhibit any combination of the characteristics of either of the subspecies involved; or (2) closely resemble the non-intergraded form of either race.

Snakes, moreover, are not found everywhere within their geographic ranges. In general, they occur only where suitable environmental conditions and habitat exist. Many of these species and subspecies may be quite common in some parts of their ranges, for example, yet rare or absent in other places well within their overall geographic distribution. Because the environmental conditions determining their presence are in constant flux, range maps for all forms of wildlife are best thought of as slowly altering cartographic kaleidoscopes: kaleidoscopes which in the future will surely continue to rearrange the range boundaries offered here as habitat alteration causes extirpation of many animal and plant populations while allowing others to expand their occupied territories.

Introduction—Paradise Almost Lost

When naturalists talk about habitats in Florida, rather than speaking of traditionally-used biotic divisions such as coastal plain, Piedmont and mountain provinces, in lowland Florida they refer to pine-oak sandhills, cypress domes, trash piles, disturbed areas—and even to a category called human habitations. Yet, bizarre as some of these categories may seem, to the naturalist Florida is nevertheless paradise—but paradise now almost lost.

Lost because, to the developer, Florida's few remaining wild lands remain a coveted target. This trend is exasperating for native Floridians, because control of their destiny has long since been wrested away by throngs of emigrants who now control the political reins, hence the destiny, of this state. Their effect has been most extreme in the southern coastal areas of the peninsula, and the natural Florida I began visiting in the mid-1950s, and even the Florida to which I moved in the early 1960s, is gone forever.

Yet, I consider myself fortunate to have come to know the state as it was in mid century for, during the '50s, '60s, and '70s, acre by acre and mile after mile, changes to the land occurred. Take the border of US 27, south of Clewiston.

Already modified in the '50s by a drainage canal, beyond that canal and to the west of 27 the Everglades still stretched away to the horizons. There were few farming lands between Clewiston and Andytown then, and the tips of the sawgrass that covered those vast, wet prairies waved in unison when the wind was light. In more tumultuous weather the sedges would lay flat, tips pointed away from the tempest, their serrate blades notching the water's surface. In the distance there were always the isolated hummocks of subtropical and tropical hardwoods; trees that were home to wonderfully-colored tree snails, birds, amphibians, and reptiles.

But even then bureaucrats were detailing plans for the draining of the Everglades, which when completed would make the great wetland "truly of use to the people of Florida." Today, you need only drive south from Clewiston on US 27 to see how successful the federal and state governments have been in taking a national treasure and turning it into a gigantic farm.

One of the first, and cheapest, things they did was to introduce exotic species of trees, such as the Australian paper bark, or melaleuca. This tree more than fulfilled its intended role, because besides being incredibly efficient at transpiring water and thus drying up wetlands, the seeds of melaleuca are broadcast aerially, and the invader immediately took off on its own. Not that this bothered the agricultural interests; after all, you can't grow cabbages, sugar cane, or sod on land that is naturally seasonally submerged. Not all of the introduced trees were a scourge, however. Australian pines provided refuge for many native serpents: corn snakes sought seclusion behind shards of their peeling bark, or took the sun by lying lengthwise along their larger, lower limbs. Everglades rat snakes climbed higher, seeking the highest crotches at midday, then positioning themselves in loose coils to bask on the lower branches in the rays of the lowering afternoon sun. Scarlet kingsnakes also found Australian pines to their liking, and followed the ascending stems of Virginia creeper and poison ivy upwards into moisture-retaining pockets beneath the trapped and decomposing needles, where they would quietly coil and remain for long periods of time. The larger rat snakes would eventually leave the security of the trees to seek smaller prey, but the resting scarlet kings' prey, in the form of anoles and skinks, came right to them, and they only had to leave the pines if they chose.

Even in the face of the conversion of South Florida to agricultural uses, some herpetofaunal species—corn snakes, yellow rat snakes, and scarlet kings in particular—proved remarkably resilient. After decades of environmental modification, these habitat generalists remain abundant—as recently as a year ago I found several corn snakes in small patches of weedy vegetation and construction rubble behind warehouse complexes in downtown Hialeah—and they continue to be common "backyard snakes" in many areas throughout the state.

But the Everglades rat snake is now even rarer than the few remaining patches of the habitat in which it evolved. Rat snakes are still abundant in the Everglades, but few retain the suite of colors that characterized the Everglades rat snake, *Elaphe obsoleta rossalleni*. Originally, while rat snakes throughout the periphery of the Everglades were clad in scales of yellow, those that evolved in and were adapted best to the isolated, perpetually wet tropical hammocks deepened in color and took on shades of orange. Orange suffused not only their brightly colored dorsums, but spread to the venter and the chin—even the eyes. (Rather than black, like those of surrounding races, even the tongue of *E. o. rossalleni* was red.)

The subspecies Everglades rat snake, described in 1949 by Wilfred T. Neill, was named after one of Florida's premier reptile showmen, E. Ross Allen. Since then, the validity of the race has been questioned, but the Everglades rat snake was at the very least a well defined color variant with a circumscribed range.

What happened to it? As roads were forged through the Everglades, and as its swamps were drained, the yellow rat snake, a race that prefers drier conditions, slowly expanded its range inward from the periphery to the very heart of the 'Glades. As they went, the racially dominant yellows intergraded with the Everglades rats, and one by one the characteristics of the orange *E. o. rossalleni* were genetically swamped.

When I first started visiting Florida in the '50s, Everglades rat snakes were remarkably common from Clewiston south to Homestead. During that time, I could go out into the 'Glades or even just follow US 27 southward and come up with a dozen or more of those big orange snakes in the course of a night's hunt. I can even recall being excited when my companions and I found the occasional yellow rat snake. But by the late '60s and early '70s, a change could be seen in the rat snakes we were finding. The body color was less orange, the tongue was black and red or entirely black, and the chin, more often than not, was white. By the late '70s we had come to realize that, even in the old hunting areas, we were no longer catching true Everglades rat snakes. We were catching intergrades, with characteristics skewed heavily towards the yellow rat snake; by the mid '80s, for anyone to find a phenotypically pure Everglades rat snake was cause for celebration among the entire herpetological/herpetocultural community.

Other things were equally memorable before the Everglades were opened to roads and agriculture—things like being able to walk along the old Tamiami Trail Canal on nearly any warm spring evening and see a hundred or more water snakes, cottonmouths, and mud snakes; things like being brought to tears by the hundreds of snakes and frogs crushed by speeding traffic on rainy nights along that same stretch of canal (see Note at end of Introduction), things like being able to walk along what was then called Krome Avenue, the southern end of Route 997 between the Tamiami Trail and Homestead, and see a dozen or more big corn snakes draped in the Australian pines that bordered that canal, as well as more ribbon and garter snakes along the canal's edges than you could count. All this while the sawgrass prairies stretched off into the distance. Today, the pines are gone, the traffic streams by in a never-ending line, and the sawgrass prairies are truck farms. So many tens of thousands of snakes have been crushed, collected for the pet trade, or dispossessed by land modifications that to see 20 to 50 snakes of all varieties combined in the course of several days is an event worthy of notice.

Other habitats have been modified as well. One that is particularly important is Florida's dry, central north-south ridge. Much of this sandy highland has been converted to citrus groves and other agricultural endeavors, trailer parks, and subdivisions. The few areas of sandy scrub that do remain continue to provide ideal habitat for some magnificent snake species, among them eastern diamond-backed rattlesnake, the eastern indigo, and the rare, endemic crowned and secretive short-tailed snakes. (At the moment, private conservation groups and the federal government are collaborating to purchase and protect as much as possible of the little remaining sandhill scrub in what will perhaps one day become a national wildlife refuge. Consisting initially of many disjunct land parcels, with time, additional land purchases may lessen this proposed preserve's checkerboard effect.)

But not *all* is bad about the citrus groves that are now so prevalent in Florida's sandy midlands. At least, not groves with surface irrigation canals, because the canals provide habitat for southern leopard and other frogs, which draw racers and water snakes. These, in turn, are fodder for indigo snakes. Until they were afforded both federal and state protection, indigos were one of the US's most coveted serpents. (Try as I might, I'm unable to understand this. They are smelly, parasite-ridden captives prone to voiding feces every time they are handled, but indigos were once so popular with hobbyists and so common in the wild that more than one Florida collector made his entire livelihood capturing indigos for the pet trade.) Such heavy hunting greatly diminished Florida's indigo population, but with protection the indigos would probably have rebounded by now were it not for the fragmentation of their habitat.

Indigo snakes are big, wide ranging animals that might use as much as 250 acres of suitable habitat. Unfragmented tracts of such size are increasingly rare, and in their extensive wanderings indigos come in contact with unsympathetic humans and congested roadways. Tracts of land like the huge Merritt Island National Wildlife Refuge or the Gulf Hammock Preserve on the opposite side of the state still offer ample amounts of suitable indigo habitat, however, and with the educational programs now being offered it really does seem that more Florida residents are beginning to value the few remaining urban indigos. One immense agricultural entity in the central part of the state exhorts its employees to protect indigo snakes and carefully screens outsiders who wish to study the animals living on their landholdings.

Besides native forms, individuals (or occasionally populations) of snake species that don't belong in Florida at all are now routinely encountered, particularly in the southern part of the state where freezes are a rarity. Some, such as the minuscule, now firmly-established Brahminy blind snake, apparently do not adversely affect any native reptile or amphibian. The potential impact of others, such as the common boa, remains unknown. These South American constrictors have been established in a small breeding colony in Dade County for more than a decade, but this population does not seem to be expanding beyond its present, circumscribed location.

For years, other big tropical constrictors such as Burmese and occasional reticulated pythons have been found in Florida, but it is thought that all have been escapees or deliberate releases, for no wild breedings have been documented. I have recently learned, however, that the aquatic Australasian elephant trunk snake has been present in one or more small ponds in South

Florida for well over a decade, and neonates have reportedly been seen; their effect on the area's indigenous wildlife remains unknown.

What does the future hold for Florida's wildlife? Pressures adverse to its continued well being will continue to accelerate as, with less and less land available, more and more people continue to settle here. This will probably lead to the demise of certain habitat specialists, yet conservation groups are becoming more vocal, and land use restrictions are now stronger and more environmentally conscious than ever. It is difficult to tell a landholder, however, who initially made his/her purchase in the long ago days of few restrictions, that the property he/she has been holding on speculation can no longer be developed. As a result, animosities between landholders and conservationists/regulators invariably develop.

Fewer wild areas also means more reptiles concentrated in the diminishing tracts of wilderness that remain. Such abnormally concentrated ranges adversely impact the more territorial varieties like the big eastern indigos, while, under these conditions, disease is more easily transmitted and can become epidemic.

Concentrations of snake species also draw "market hunters" collecting for the pet and snakeskin trade. (You'd be surprised how readily an otherwise obscure species can be marketed when it becomes available in numbers.) For example, the commercialization of its hide has caused Florida's "flagship rattlesnake," the eastern diamondback, to dwindle in numbers and—because of the early mortality caused by this hunting—to decline in overall size as well. Once a commonly seen snake of sandy pine-palmetto woodland from the lower Keys to the Georgia border, the eastern diamondback is now uncommon in the southern three fifths of the state as well as in the Keys.

More recently, depredation by a third major force has begun to affect a huge proportion of Florida's wildlife. The culprits are the two species of introduced Latin American fire ants which, small though they may be, are among the earth's most efficient predators. With no natural predators of their own in Florida, and few effective chemical controls available, the spread of fire ants through the sunbelt is rampant. As they increase and broaden their range, fire ants are everywhere radically reducing the numbers of ground-dwelling mammals, ground nesting-birds, and terrestrial reptiles. Size of prey means little to these insects; it simply takes more of them longer to overcome the fawn of a white-tailed deer than a cottontail.

Reptiles are especially vulnerable to fire ant predation, and the almost complete disappearance of one of the largest concentrations of kingsnakes in North America, long attributed by conservationists to overcollecting for the pet trade, may in fact be the direct result of fire ant predation on the kings' eggs and slow-moving hatchlings.

It wasn't until the early '80s that I began to hear grumblings from herpers about a reduction in the numbers of snakes, kings in particular, on Payne's Prairie, and I wondered whether their decline might have been brought about by overcollecting for the pet trade. When I moved to a house right on the edge of the prairie in the mid-90s I set out to talk with local researchers about the reduction in kingsnake numbers, and was distressed to learn that few snakes of any kind were seen on Payne's Prairie anymore: when my friend, Carl May, caught and released a single kingsnake on the shoulder of 441 in 1994, his find brought expressions of incredulity from both researchers and herpetoculturists.

A mere 25 years ago 20 to 30 kings could be seen on almost any spring afternoon's walk across that prairie. The prairie was still there, it was now a well-protected state preserve, but the snakes were gone. It was baffling.

Then, at the November 1995 meeting of the Gainesville Herpetological Society, a program asking "Where Have All the Kingsnakes Gone?" was given by fire ant researchers (and herpetologists) Don Jouvenaz and Craig Allen. In their presentation, Jouvenaz and Allen offered clear data correlating the reduction in numbers of kingsnakes, and many other wildlife species, with the increasing presence of fire ants. Although recognized as one of the most destructive insects to have ever invaded the United States, it seems that fire ants' full destructive potential has yet to be realized.

In 1983, *The Ecological Impact of Man on the South Florida Herpetofauna* by Larry David Wilson and Louis Porras was published jointly by the University of Kansas and the World Wildlife Fund-US. The authors, both with decades of herpetological experience in South Florida, declared that "South Florida is approaching eco-collapse." Wilson and Porras based their conclusion on the burgeoning human population, continuing untenable land management practices, and an ever-increasing number of established species of alien herpetofauna. Because of our collective failure to correct these problems, entire ecosystems in South Florida have been effectively eradicated, and the lack of prudent stewardship is steadily working its way northward up the peninsula.

While we can never return to the days that were, we in Florida can hope to learn to manage our lands and conserve our wildlife more wisely. Many among us feel that additional safeguards must be provided for our wildlife, of which snakes are an important component, and proper habitat management and restoration, as well as safeguards against overcollecting, would help assure the continuance of all species.

A solution to the fire ant problem must also be found.

Rather than following the path of reticence that characterizes the environmental protection departments of most other states, the state of Florida, custodian of the greatest herpetological diversity in the southeastern United States, should forge and implement new and effective protective programs for, although ravaged and imperiled, the "wild Florida" that does remain continues to support a remarkable biodiversity. With enlightened stewardship, it can continue to do so.

R.D. Bartlett
Gainesville, Florida

Note: Soon after the two Everglades-bisecting highways, US 41, or the Tamiami Trail, and Interstate 75, known as Alligator Alley, were completed, they became avenues of destruction for the huge population of snakes living in southern Florida's marshes. Now, when sea-turtle migrations are the subject of major television documentaries and the seasonal journeys of herd-living dinosaurs have become common knowledge, reptilian migration no longer seems strange. But during the late 1940s no one knew that thousands of reptiles and amphibians would periodically try to cross those newly completed causeways—because nobody had any idea that reptiles in Florida or anywhere else undertook mass migrations. Earlier population shifts by Everglades herpetofauna were hidden in the depths of the flooded sawgrass that stretched for miles across the marshes, so it was a great surprise when, every few years, across Alligator Alley and the Tamiami Trail came a few alligators, hordes of frogs, sirens, and—sometimes every few feet for miles—thousands of snakes.

Periodically moving from dryer to wetter areas—as these animals had done for millenia—meant crossing the newly-engineered roadway dikes, however, and the presence of so many snakes right out on the pavement triggered quick reprisals. One such migration I came upon in June 1953 had spawned a grisly carnival atmosphere, drawing carloads of young men out from Miami and Ft. Myers—men who walked up and down both road shoulders in the rain, shooting snakes with pistols and .22s until their ammunition was gone, then pounding other reptiles to death with their tire tools.

Nearly forty years later, despite the conversion of much of the Everglades/Big Cypress wetland to agriculture, mass reptilian migrations were still taking place. As junior author Kenneth L. Krysko observed:

> On 30 May 1992, my father, Len Krysko, and I witnessed a mass migration of snakes along a two mile stretch of the Tamiami Trail near the northeastern border of Everglades National Park at Shark Slough. Between 8 and 11 am, approximately 800 individuals of a total of 11 species including *Thamnophis sirtalis, T. sauritus, Nerodia fasciata, N. floridana, N. taxispilota, Coluber constrictor, Farancia abacura, Opheodrys aestivus, Regina alleni, Seminatrix pygaea,* and *Agkistrodon piscivorous,* were observed either dead on this road—about 30% of the species recognized had already been run over—or moving slowly along the south road shoulder (there was little vegetation on the north side of the pavement). Walking along the road caused most of the snakes to flee back into roadside vegetation, but they soon made another attempt to cross.

Frank Bernardino and George Dalrymple of Florida International University have found a strong correlation between water level and snake migration: as water levels decrease, Bernardino and Dalrymple have observed that large numbers of snakes in the Pa-hay-okee wetlands of Everglades National Park migrate toward the wetter periphery of the Shark River Slough.

Alan Tennant

Florida Snake Habitats

Many of us think Florida's natural environment is one of a subtropical peninsula that gradually richens as one moves southward, from the ordinary southern pine woods of the northern part of the state into the lush, wetland paradise of the Everglades. This impression is fostered by the constant commercial presentation of southern Florida as a mecca for tropical wildlife (especially alligators and flamingos), offered by the seedy roadside zoos that for decades have characterized the area, and by the presence of Everglades National Park at the southern tip of the state.

Yet that image, that notion of southwardly increasing tropical diversity, is approximately the opposite of the truth. Instead of a gradual richening of the biotic community toward the peninsula's southern end, the most diversely speciated part of Florida for birds, mammals and herpetofauna is the north. Located on the continent's Gulf Coastal rim, within a short distance of a very old, biologically well-developed mountain region and the lowlands bordering two different oceans, the state's Panhandle receives species from four geographic areas of endemism: the southern Appalachian highlands, the Atlantic Coastal Plain, peninsular Florida, and the Gulf Coastal Plain. This overlapping of faunal groups is also reflected in the area's herpetological diversity. Within continental boundaries (that is, until one reaches a peninsula or offshore islands) the number of reptile and amphibian species in the northern hemisphere increases as one moves southward. In the eastern United States, that means a peak along the upper Gulf Coast—this area boasts the third-richest turtle fauna in the world—

where the highest herpetofaunal species diversity north of Mexico occurs in the Apalachiacola River Basin.

This continental margin-area is followed in herpetofaunal variety by Northern Peninsular Florida's dry central ridge of sandhill scrub. Known biologically as "Island Florida" because during interglacial periods it was periodically cut off from the mainland by elevated sea levels, this silicaceous upland is home to remnant members of a desert-adapted fauna that, during the Pleistocene, occupied an arid Gulf Coast corridor stretching from the Southwest to the Florida peninsula. That left a group of rare serpents—the state's endemic crowned and short-tailed snakes, as well as threatened species like the Florida pine and eastern indigo snakes—more or less confined to the peninsula's geologically-ancient central sandhills.[1] Among these animals, some of the old desert-forged ecological relationships also remain, with many species benefitting from the labors of the soil-excavating gopher tortoise, whose humid burrows function as desiccation-mitigating moisture sinks in time of drought, and offer refuge from fire and predators, as well as provide shelter from winter cold and summer heat. In "Island Florida," fire is an important environmental factor, for the state has one of the highest frequencies of lightning strikes in the United States. Habitats that under natural conditions regularly burn here include sandhill, upland pine, pine rockland, mesic flatwoods, wet flatwoods, dry prairie, wet prairie, depression marsh, basin marsh, and swale. Where fires are frequent, many wildlife species have evolved to cope with it, and those whose limited mobility prevents them from fleeing typically burrow deeply below ground, or take shelter in water. Fires can even be beneficial, for some xeric-adapted snakes such as the southern hognose and crowned snakes benefit from the more open conditions created by fire, and attain their highest population densities in early successional habitats created by vegetative disturbances such as fires, hurricanes, and logging. Yet fires that occur during drought conditions may cause extensive mortality because marshes lacking water provide few refuges, while the reduced plant cover left by such fires can lead to increased predation by raptors.

Southward from the sandhills, the number of herpetofaunal species declines. At odds as this is with the common image of Florida, biologically it's not surprising: everywhere on earth peninsulas extending from continental land masses support less varied floral and faunal communities toward their extremities.

A similar "peninsular effect" of reduced species diversity versus equal-sized mainland regions has also been observed in Florida for mammals and land birds. The reduction in avian species-richness along the Florida peninsula is believed to be the result of a progressive decrease in habitat diversity from the peninsula's base to its tip. Many birds reach their southern range limits because suitable habitat is lacking, and decreasing herpetofaunal species richness along the same corridor is a result of the same reduction in topographic and habitat variation.

---

[1]Most of this xeric habitat-adapted herpetofauna could not recolonize northward when the glaciers retreated because a mesic southeastern woodland environment had replaced the earlier arid terrain to which it was adapted.

As David Auth of the Florida Museum of Natural History has demonstrated, despite the vastness of the Everglades wetlands, Southern Peninsular Florida is comparatively depauperate of reptile and amphibian species.[2] Intense human development of southern Florida has also decimated its natural plant and animal communities, but even before European settlement the Everglades-Big Cypress region south of Lake Okeechobee was the most herpetologically species-poor part of mainland Florida. Nevertheless, despite the paucity of species, until recently this area was incredibly rich in absolute numbers of reptiles and amphibians. (See Note on page 7.) Part of the reason is that the longer growing season available in southern Florida means that many snake species remain active throughout the year. Because foraging success is the main factor controlling clutch frequency in snakes, greater annual food intake contributes to higher population densities, especially among aquatic serpents such as the water snakes, mud snakes, crayfish snakes, and black swamp snakes.

Species paucity, however, is due largely to the absence of upland areas and the consequent lack of varied topography that creates more numerous habitat niches. For example, the diversity of tree species decreases in southern Florida (tropical hardwoods occur only in scattered stands), the lack of acid wetlands and divided-drainage streams results in less-varied aquatic habitats, and the winter dry season (a time of high stress for both amphibians and aquatic reptiles) is more pronounced in the southern peninsula than in northern Florida. Aquatic and marsh-living herpetofauna in southern Florida is also subjected to more pronounced seasonal fluctuations in the water table than that living further north: marshes in northern peninsular and panhandle Florida receive high winter precipitation, which means that water often remains in low-lying areas through early summer. Water levels in southern Florida marshes typically decline throughout the fall and winter and often disappear entirely by spring.

Adding to this ecological stress is the fact that little of the natural water flow of the Everglades remains. An elaborate hydraulic management network of canals and levees south of Lake Okeechobee has so altered the lake's natural outflow that, even where wetland remains, native plant communities in the Everglades/Big Cypress area have been significantly degraded. Comparatively little original wetland remains, for between 1936 and 1987 Florida's natural marshland declined by 56%, mostly because so much of the overflow from Lake Okeechobee that formerly kept the Everglades wet was diverted to agriculture. The loss of these wetlands has both significantly diminished aquatic and semi-aquatic snake populations and impacted adjacent terrestrial herpetofauna that depends on nearby marshes for food and moisture—upland serpents such as racers, eastern diamondback rattlesnakes,

---

[2]Some features of southern Florida's subtropical plant life are beneficial to herpetofauna, however. Many small anurans, lizards, and snakes such as corn snakes and scarlet kingsnakes that feed on these smaller creatures take refuge in the axils of the dead leaf fronds of cabbage palms, especially during drought. Similarly, the abundance of epiphytes, particularly bromeliads, in tropical Florida provides arboreal herpetofauna with hiding places containing food and water, and gives them some protection from the infrequent episodes of cold weather.

and eastern and southern hognose snakes regularly venture into wetland habitats in search of prey, as well as seek refuge there from grassfires.

The tendency for species-richness to decline from the base to the tip of the Florida peninsula is especially pronounced as one approaches the southern end of the mainland: fourteen herpetofaunal species disappear between Volusia and Brevard counties. This diminution is most extreme in the Florida Keys. Because for thousands of years these tiny islands were largely biologically isolated from the mainland, their herpetofauna is different from and has long been significantly more depauperate than that of peninsular Florida. Although nearer the mainland, the upper Florida Keys are even less species-rich than the lower Keys. This is a result of the closer geologic relationship between the lower Keys and the mainland because, during periods of lowered sea level, along with the islands of Florida Bay the lower Keys were a dry land extension of the mainland. At this time the upper Keys, whose foundation is a more recently developed coral reef that grew in the Pamlico Sea, had not yet been formed.

During historical times, in fact, the Keys have never had more than a third as many herpetofaunal species as the mainland—a situation to be expected from small islands without reliable sources of fresh water whose rocky, periodically storm saline-overwashed interiors offer few habitat niches.

Moreover, just as in the Everglades, the region's naturally-low species richness is exacerbated by human habitat alteration. Besides appropriating most of the land area of these small islands for residential and commercial development, human alteration of the fragile Keys ecosystem has included the introduction of Brazilian pepper—a supremely aggressive plant that has displaced most of the islands' native vegetation—subsequently establishing other exotic plants and animals, and inadvertently bringing in gene-pool-diluting mainland races of scarce Keys endemics like the rosy rat snake.

Within these three natural regions—the Panhandle, Northern Peninsular Florida, and Southern Peninsular Florida (which includes the Keys)—the Florida Natural Areas Inventory has developed a series of *natural community groups*. Determined by both their plant and animal components, these include Xeric Upland, Mesic Flatland, Mesic Upland, Floodplain, Wet Flatland, Southern Florida Limestone Rocklands, and Coastal.

Each community group is made up of two or more smaller and more precisely delineated Habitat Areas, whose number of resident species generally increases with the structural complexity of the habitat. *Microhabitat* is the localized area within the Habitat Area where (due to variables such as the accessibility of shelter, food availability, soil moisture and permeability, light, temperature, and relative humidity) a species tends to spend most of its time.

· **Xeric Upland Communities** are typical of well drained sandy terrain covered with xeric-adapted vegetation, and include the following habitats:

Sandhill habitat occurs on rolling sandhills and consists of widely spaced longleaf pines and deciduous oaks above a ground cover of wiregrass and herbs.

Scrub habitat also occurs on sand ridges or old dunes, but has deeper, finer sand. Its vegetation consists of sand pines and scrub oaks interspersed with patches of barren sand and ground lichens.

- **Mesic Upland Communities** consist of a diverse mixture of broad- and needle-leaved trees, and include the following habitats:

Mixed hardwood forest is a climax hardwood forest of magnolia, hickory, sweetgum, southern maple, chestnut oak, and spruce pine.
Upland pine forest is composed primarily of mature longleaf pine; it occurs on rolling hills in the panhandle and north-central peninsula.

- **Mesic Flatland Communities** have flat, often silicaceous soils interspersed with organic material, and include the following habitats:

Prairie is a poorly-drained treeless plain with a dense ground cover of grasses, herbs, saw palmetto, and shrubs.
Pine flatwood is an open-canopy forest of widely-spaced pines with little or no understory but a dense ground cover of herbs and shrubs.

- **Wet Flatland Communities** have poorly-drained sand, marl, or limestone substrates, and include the following habitats:

Wet marl prairies are treeless, seasonally inundated plains covered with a hydrophytic ground cover of wiregrass, toothache grass, maidencane, and spikerush.
Wet prairie hammocks are slightly elevated groves of stunted cypress or mangroves widely scattered among the sedges and grasses of marl prairies.

- **Floodplain Communities** are periodically flooded, but not permanently inundated by rivers; their soil is alluvial sand or peat. They include the following habitats:

Bottomland forest consists of low-lying, closed-canopy woodland made up primarily of tall, straight trees such as water oak, red maple, sweetgum, loblolly, and spruce pine. It is flooded for up to 50% of the growing season.
Floodplain cypress swamp is flooded most of the year. Its vegetation consists of buttressed hydrophytic trees like bald cypress and tupelo.
Everglades swale consists of marshland grass and sedges growing in a broad, shallow channel with water flowing through it for most of the year. In Florida, this means the outflow of Lake Okeechobee into the Everglades-Big Cypress region's "river of grass."

- **Southern Florida Limestone Rockland Communities** are low, flat limestone outcrops covered with tropical vegetation, and include the following habitats:

Pine rockland is the sparse, slash pine woodland with a patchy understory that occurs along the oolitic Miami limestone ridge and also forms the base material of the lower Keys.

Rockland hardwood hammocks are slightly elevated mots of tropical hardwoods—live oak, gumbo limbo, wild tamarind, pigeon plum, false mastic, and poisonwood—and palms widely scattered among the sedges and grasses of Everglades swale.

· **Coastal Communities** are environments that border salt water, and include the following habitats:

Coastal strand is salt-tolerant shrub thicket made up of saw palmetto, live oak, cabbage palm, myrtle oak, yaupon, sea grape, and Spanish bayonet, which occurs on stabilized sand dunes.

Maritime hammock is the narrow band of hardwood forest growing on old coastal dunes that often parallel marine shorelines. It consists of live oak, cabbage palm, and red bay, and is characterized by a dense, wind-pruned canopy.

Tidal marsh is open expanses of grasses, rushes, and sedges along coastlines and river mouths. Black needlerush, smooth cordgrass, and sawgrass are their most prevalent vegetation.

Tidal mangrove swamp is the dense stands of red, black, and/or white mangroves and buttonwood that occur along tidally inundated shores in southern Florida.

Because wildlife habitats are constantly changing, so do their herpetofaunal assemblages. Reptiles' use of any given habitat will vary depending on individuals' sex and reproductive condition, their foraging and digestive state, degree of ecdysis, disease, or injury, social relationships,[3] and even learning. Therefore, like the range maps that accompany the species accounts, the Habitat Table that follows is necessarily an approximation.

Further, compared to other herpetofauna, snakes are far more likely to partition the environment by prey-species choices rather than by habitat preferences. Many Florida serpents such as the crayfish snakes (which feed almost exclusively on crustaceans), rainbow and mud snakes (which prey on eels), hognoses, (which take anurans), pine snakes (gophers), and the crowned snakes (centipedes and termites), are extreme food-species specialists whose prey orientation, rather than any affinity for a given soil or plant community, usually determines their whereabouts. Because snakes' prey animals are themselves most often habitat specialists however, they generally link serpents to specific habitats.

Much of the data from which the following table is drawn were generously provided by Kevin Enge, author of *Habitat Occurrence of Florida's Amphibians and Reptiles,* Florida Game and Fresh Water Fish Commission Technical Report of December, 1996.

---

[3]Some snake species are periodically territorial. During the breeding season males may antagonistically dominate rivals, thus limiting their access to otherwise available habitat. At this time males also often engage in long-distance movements in search of mates, during which they are likely to enter unexpected habitats.

Panhandle

Northern Peninsula

Southern Peninsula

Habitat Table

P indicates the Florida Panhandle, N indicates northern peninsula Florida, and S indicates southern peninsula Florida. See map on previous page for divisions.

A species designated as C in a given habitat means it is *common* there; in a particular geographic area and habitat it can be expected to occur on most sizeable, rural tracts of land containing that habitat. A U, or *uncommon* species would occur on only a few such tracts of land. An R designation means a *rare* species, or one that infrequently occurs even on large tracts of land within a particular habitat.

| | Xeric Upland Communities | | | | | | Mesic Upland Communities | | | | Mesic Flatland Communities | | | | | | Wet Flatland Communities | | | | | |
| | Sandhill | | | Scrub | | | Mixed Hardwood Forest | | Pine Forest | | Prairie | | | Pine Flatwood | | | Wet Marl Prairie | | | Wet Prairie Hammock | | |
	P	N	S	P	N	S	P	N	P	N	P	N	S	P	N	S	P	N	S	P	N	S
1. Brahminy Blind Snake *Ramphotyphlops braminus*											U					U						
2. Southeastern Crowned Snake *Tantilla coronata*	C			C			R		U					R								
3. Peninsula Crowned Snake *Tantilla relicta relicta*	C	C		C	C										U	U				R	R	
4. Central Florida Crowned Snake *Tantilla relicta neilli*	R			R																		
5. Coastal Dunes Crowned Snake *Tantilla relicta pamlica*			U			U										U						

(see map on previous page)

	Xeric Upland Communities						Mesic Upland Communities				Mesic Flatland Communities						Wet Flatland Communities					
	Sandhill			Scrub			Mixed Hardwood Forest		Pine Forest		Prairie			Pine Flatwood			Wet Marl Prairie			Wet Prairie Hammock		
	P	N	S	P	N	S	P	N	P	N	P	N	S	P	N	S	P	N	S	P	N	S
6. Rim Rock Crowned Snake *Tantilla oolitica*																						
7. Marsh Brown Snake *Storeria dekayi limnetes*											U						C			C		
8. Florida Brown Snake *Storeria dekayi victa*							U				R	R		C	C		C	C		U	U	
9. Midland Brown Snake *Storeria dekayi wrightorum*							C		U					U						U		
10. Florida Redbelly Snake *Storeria occipitomaculata obscura*				R	R		C		R	R				R	R					U	U	
11. Rough Earth Snake *Virginia striatula*	R	R		R	R		R	R	R					U	U							
12. Eastern Earth Snake *Virginia valeriae valeriae*	R	R		R	R		R	R	U	U												
13. Pine Woods Snake *Rhadinaea flavilata*	R	R	R	R	R		R	R	R	R				R	U	R				R	R	
14. Southern Ringneck Snake *Diadophis punctatus punctatus*	R	R		R	R		C	C	U	U				C	C	C	U	U	U	C	C	C

Species	Sandhill P	Sandhill N	Sandhill S	Scrub P	Scrub N	Scrub S	Mixed Hardwood Forest P	Mixed Hardwood Forest N	Pine Forest P	Pine Forest N	Prairie P	Prairie N	Prairie S	Pine Flatwood P	Pine Flatwood N	Pine Flatwood S	Wet Marl Prairie P	Wet Marl Prairie N	Wet Marl Prairie S	Wet Prairie Hammock P	Wet Prairie Hammock N	Wet Prairie Hammock S
15. Key Ringneck *Diadophis punctatus acricus*																						
16. Eastern Garter Snake *Thamnophis sirtalis sirtalis*	R	R					C	C	C	C	U	U	U	C	C	C	C	C	C	C	C	C
17. Bluestripe Garter Snake *Thamnophis sirtalis similis*								C		C		U			C			C			C	
18. Eastern Ribbon Snake *Thamnophis sauritis sauritis*		R			R			U		U		C			C			C			C	
19. Peninsula Ribbon Snake *Thamnophis sauritis sackenii*	R	R		R	R			U		U	U	U		C	C		C	C		C	C	
20. Bluestripe Ribbon Snake *Thamnophis sauritis nitae*								U		U		U			C			C			C	
21. Redbelly Water Snake *Nerodia erythrogaster erythrogaster*							R	R												R	R	
22. Yellowbelly Water Snake *Nerodia erythrogaster flavigaster*								U													U	
23. Banded Water Snake *Nerodia fasciata fasciata*								R										C			C	

(table continued on next page)

	Xeric Upland Communities						Mesic Upland Communities				Mesic Flatland Communities						Wet Flatland Communities					
	Sandhill			Scrub			Mixed Hardwood Forest		Pine Forest		Prairie			Pine Flatwood			Wet Marl Prairie			Wet Prairie Hammock		
	P	N	S	P	N	S	P	N	P	N	P	N	S	P	N	S	P	N	S	P	N	S
24. Florida Water Snake *Nerodia fasciata pictiventris*									R					R	R		C	C		C	C	
25. Mississippi Green Water Snake *Nerodia cyclopion*																	U			U		
26. Florida Green Water Snake *Nerodia floridana*																	C	C	C	R	R	R
27. Brown Water Snake *Nerodia taxispilota*																	C	C	C	U	U	U
28. Midland Water Snake *Nerodia sipedon pleuralis*							U		R								U					
29. Gulf Salt Marsh Snake *Nerodia clarkii clarkii*																						
30. Atlantic Salt Marsh Snake *Nerodia clarkii taeniata*																						
31. Mangrove Salt Marsh Snake *Nerodia clarkii compressicauda*																						
32. Glossy Crayfish Snake *Regina rigida rigida*														R	R		U	U		R	R	

Species	Sandhill P	N	S	Scrub P	N	S	Mixed Hardwood Forest P	N	Pine Forest P	N	Prairie P	N	S	Pine Flatwood P	N	S	Wet Marl Prairie P	N	S	Wet Prairie Hammock P	N	S
Xeric Upland Communities																						
Mesic Upland Communities																						
Mesic Flatland Communities																						
Wet Flatland Communities																						
33. Gulf Crayfish Snake *Regina rigida sinicola*														R			U			R		
34. Striped Crayfish Snake *Regina alleni*																	C	C			U	U
35. Queen Snake *Regina septemvittata*																						
36. Eastern Mud Snake *Farancia abacura abacura*							R	R	R	R				R	R		C	C	C	U	U	U
37. Western Mud Snake *Farancia abacura reinwardtii*							R		R					R			C			U		
38. Rainbow Snake *Farancia erytrogramma erytrogramma*																				R	R	
39. South Florida Rainbow Snake *Farancia erytrogramma seminola*																						
40. North Florida Swamp Snake *Seminatrix pygaea pygaea*											C	C		R	R		C	C		U	U	

(table continued on next page)

19

Species	Xeric Upland Communities						Mesic Upland Communities				Mesic Flatland Communities						Wet Flatland Communities					
	Sandhill			Scrub			Mixed Hardwood Forest		Pine Forest		Prairie			Pine Flatwood			Wet Marl Prairie			Wet Prairie Hammock		
	P	N	S	P	N	S	P	N	P	N	P	N	S	P	N	S	P	N	S	P	N	S
41. South Florida Swamp Snake *Seminatrix pygaea cyclas*													C			R			C			U
42. Rough Green Snake *Opheodrys aestivus*	R	R		R	R	R	C	C	U	U				U	U	U				C	C	C
43. Eastern Coachwhip *Masticophis flagellum flagellum*	C	C	C	C	C	C	U	U	C	C	C	C	C	C	C	C	C	C	C			
44. Brownchin Racer *Coluber constrictor helvigularis*							C		C		C			C								
45. Southern Black Racer *Coluber constrictor priapus*	C	C	C	C	C	C	C	C	C	C	C	C	C	C	C	C	C	C	C	C	C	C
46. Everglades racer *Coluber constrictor paludicola*													C			C			C			C
47. Eastern Indigo Snake *Drymarchon corais couperi*	U	U	U	U	U		R	R	R		R	R		U	U	U	R	R		R	R	
48. Eastern Hognose Snake *Heterodon platirhinos*	C	C	U	C	C	U	C	C	C	C	U	U	U	U	U	R	R	R	R	U	U	U
49. Southern Hognose Snake *Heterodon simus*	U	C	R	U	C	R	R	R	R	R	R	R	R	R	R		R	R	R	U	U	U
50. Black Pine Snake *Pituophis melanoleucas lodingi*	R			R			R		R					R								

| | Xeric Upland Communities | | | | | | Mesic Upland Communities | | | | Mesic Flatland Communities | | | | | | Wet Flatland Communities | | | | | |
| | Sandhill | | | Scrub | | | Mixed Hardwood Forest | | Pine Forest | | Prairie | | | Pine Flatwood | | | Wet Marl Prairie | | | Wet Prairie Hammock | | |
	P	N	S	P	N	S	P	N	P	N	P	N	S	P	N	S	P	N	S	P	N	S
51. Florida Pine Snake *Pituophis melanoleucus mugitus*	U	U	R	C	C	R			U	U	R	R	R	U	R							
52. Corn Snake *Elaphe guttata guttata*	U	U	U	U	U	R	U	U	U	U				C	C	C				U	U	U
53. Grey Rat Snake *Elaphe obsoleta spiloides*	U	U		R	U		C	C	U	U				U	U		R	R		U	U	
54. Yellow Rat Snake *Elaphe obsoleta quadrivittata*	R	R		R	R		U		U		U			U	C		U	U		C	C	
55. Everglades Rat Snake *Elaphe obsoleta rossalleni*											U			U			U			U		
56. Short-tailed Snake *Stilosoma extenuatum*	R	R		R	R		R															
57. Mole Kingsnake *Lampropeltis calligaster rhombomaculata*	R			R			R		R					R								
58. South Florida Mole Kingsnake *Lampropeltis calligaster occipitolineata*											U						R					R

(table continued on next page)

	Xeric Upland Communities						Mesic Upland Communities				Mesic Flatland Communities						Wet Flatland Communities						
	Sandhill			Scrub			Mixed Hardwood Forest		Pine Forest		Prairie			Pine Flatwood			Wet Marl Prairie			Wet Prairie Hammock		
	P	N	S	P	N	S	P	N	P	N	P	N	S	P	N	S	P	N	S	P	N	S
59. Eastern Kingsnake *Lampropeltis getula getula*							R	R	U	U	U	U		U	U		U	U				
60. Florida Kingsnake *Lampropeltis getula floridana*								R	U		U	U		U	U		U	U		U	U	
61. Northern Scarlet Snake *Cemophora coccinea copei*	C	C		C	C		R	R	U	U	U	U		C	C		U	U		U	U	
62. Florida Scarlet Snake *Cemophora coccinea coccinea*	C	C		U	U			R	U		U	U		C	C		U	U		R	R	
63. Scarlet Kingsnake *Lampropeltis triangulum elapsoides*	U	U	U	U	U	U	U	U	U	U				C	C	C	R	R	R	C	C	C
64. Eastern Coral Snake *Micrurus fulvius fulvius*	C	C	C	C	C	C	C	C	U	U				U	U	U				U	U	
65. Southern Copperhead *Agkistrodon contortrix contortrix*	R			R			R		R													
66. Eastern Cottonmouth *Agkistrodon piscivorus piscivorus*							U			R	C			U			C				U	
67. Florida Cottonmouth *Agkistrodon piscivorus conanti*							U	U	U	U	C	C	C	U	U	U	C	C	C	U	U	U

	Xeric Upland Communities						Mesic Upland Communities				Mesic Flatland Communities						Wet Flatland Communities					
	Sandhill			Scrub			Mixed Hardwood Forest		Pine Forest		Prairie			Pine Flatwood			Wet Marl Prairie			Wet Prairie Hammock		
	P	N	S	P	N	S	P	N	P	N	P	N	S	P	N	S	P	N	S	P	N	S
68. Dusky Pigmy Rattlesnake *Sistrurus miliarius barbouri*	C	C	U	U	U	R	U	U	U	U	U	U	U	C	C	C	C	C	C	U	U	C
69. Timber Rattlesnake *Crotalus horridus*	R			R			R	U						U						U		
70. Eastern Diamondback Rattlesnake *Crotalus adamanteus*	C	C	U	C	C	U	R	R	C	C	U	U	U	C	C	C	R	R		R	R	

23

	Floodplain Wetland Communities							Southern Florida Limestone Rockland		Coastal Communities										
	Bottomland Forest			Floodplain Cypress Swamp			Everglades Swale	Pine Rockland	Rockland Hardwood Hammock	Coastal Strand			Maritime Hammock			Tidal Marsh			Tidal Mangrove Swamp	
	P	N	S	P	N	S	S	S	S	P	N	S	P	N	S	P	N	S	N	S
1. Brahminy Blind Snake *Ramphotyphlops braminus*								C	C				R							
2. Southeastern Crowned Snake *Tantilla coronata*												U								
3. Peninsula Crowned Snake *Tantilla relicta relicta*										R	R									
4. Central Florida Crowned Snake *Tantilla relicta neilli*																				
5. Coastal Dunes Crowned Snake *Tantilla relicta pamlica*										C			R							
6. Rim Rock Crowned Snake *Tantilla oolitica*								R	R											
7. Marsh Brown Snake *Storeria dekayi limnetes*												U	U							
8. Florida Brown Snake *Storeria dekayi victa*	U	U		U	U		C	U	U								R			
9. Midland Brown Snake *Storeria dekayi wrightorum*	R			C																
10. Florida Redbelly Snake *Storeria occipitomaculata obscura*	U	U		U	U															

	Floodplain Wetland Communities							Southern Florida Limestone Rockland		Coastal Communities										
	Bottomland Forest			Floodplain Cypress Swamp			Everglades Swale	Pine Rockland	Rockland Hardwood Hammock	Coastal Strand			Maritime Hammock			Tidal Marsh			Tidal Mangrove Swamp	
	P	N	S	P	N	S	S	S	S	P	N	S	P	N	S	P	N	S	N	S
11. Rough Earth Snake *Virginia striatula*																				
12. Eastern Earth Snake *Virginia valeriae valeriae*	U	R																		
13. Pine Woods Snake *Rhadinaea flavilata*																				
14. Southern Ringneck Snake *Diadophis punctatus punctatus*	U	U	U	U	U	U	R	U	C	C	C		C	C						
15. Key Ringneck Snake *Diadophis punctatus acricus*								R												
16. Eastern Garter Snake *Thamnophis sirtalis sirtalis*	C	C	C	U	U	U	C	C	U	R	R	R	U	U	U	R	R			
17. Bluestripe Garter Snake *Thamnophis sirtalis similis*	C			U						R			U			R				
18. Eastern Ribbon Snake *Thamnophis sauritis sauritis*	C			C						R			C			U				
19. Peninsula Ribbon Snake *Thamnophis sauritis sackenii*	C	C	C	C	C	C	C	U	C	R	R		C	C		U	U			R

(table continued on next page)

	Floodplain Wetland Communities							Southern Florida Limestone Rockland		Coastal Communities										
	Bottomland Forest			Floodplain Cypress Swamp			Everglades Swale	Pine Rockland	Rockland Hardwood Hammock	Coastal Strand			Maritime Hammock			Tidal Marsh			Tidal Mangrove Swamp	
	P	N	S	P	N	S	S	S	S	P	N	S	P	N	S	P	N	S	N	S
20. Bluestripe Ribbon Snake *Thamnophis sauritis nitae*		C			C															
21. Redbelly Water Snake *Nerodia erythrogaster erythrogaster*	C	C		C	C															
22. Yellowbelly Water Snake *Nerodia erythrogaster flavigaster*	C			C																
23. Banded Water Snake *Nerodia fasciata fasciata*	U			R									R							
24. Florida Water Snake *Nerodia fasciata pictiventris*	U	U		C	C		C		R				R	R					R	R
25. Mississippi Green Water Snake *Nerodia cyclopion*	U			C																
26. Florida Green Water Snake *Nerodia floridana*				C	C	C	C												R	R
27. Brown Water Snake *Nerodia taxispilota*	C	C	C	C	C	C	U									U	U	U		
28. Midland Water Snake *Nerodia sipedon pleuralis*	U																			
29. Gulf Salt Marsh Snake *Nerodia clarkii clarkii*																C	C			R

	Floodplain Wetland Communities							Southern Florida Limestone Rockland		Coastal Communities										
	Bottomland Forest			Floodplain Cypress Swamp			Everglades Swale	Pine Rockland	Rockland Hardwood Hammock	Coastal Strand			Maritime Hammock			Tidal Marsh			Tidal Mangrove Swamp	
	P	N	S	P	N	S	S	S	S	P	N	S	P	N	S	P	N	S	N	S
30. Atlantic Salt Marsh Snake *Nerodia clarkii taeniata*																R				
31. Mangrove Salt Marsh Snake *Nerodia clarkii compressicauda*																		C		C
32. Glossy Crayfish Snake *Regina rigida rigida*	U	U		C	C											R	R			
33. Gulf Crayfish Snake *Regina rigida sinicola*	U			C																
34. Striped Crayfish Snake *Regina alleni*	U	U	U	C	C	C	C									R	R		R	R
35. Queen Snake *Regina septemvittata*	R			U																
36. Eastern Mud Snake *Farancia abacura abacura*	R	R		C	C	C	U													
37. Western Mud Snake *Farancia abacura reinwardtii*	R			C																
38. Rainbow Snake *Farancia erytrogramma erytrogramma*				R	R											R	R			
39. South Florida Rainbow Snake *Farancia erytrogramma seminola*				R																

(table continued on next page)

	Floodplain Wetland Communities							Southern Florida Limestone Rockland		Coastal Communities										
	Bottomland Forest			Floodplain Cypress Swamp			Everglades Swale	Pine Rockland	Rockland Hardwood Hammock	Coastal Strand			Maritime Hammock			Tidal Marsh			Tidal Mangrove Swamp	
	P	N	S	P	N	S	S	S	S	P	N	S	P	N	S	P	N	S	N	S
40. North Florida Swamp Snake *Seminatrix pygaea pygaea*				C	C															
41. South Florida Swamp Snake *Seminatrix pygaea cyclas*						C	C		R											
42. Rough Green Snake *Opheodrys aestivus*	C	C	C	R	R	R			U	U				R	R						
43. Eastern Coachwhip *Masticophis flagellum flagellum*								R		U	U	U	U	U	U					
44. Brownchin Racer *Coluber constrictor helvigularis*	C			R						U			U			R				
45. Southern Black Racer *Coluber constrictor priapus*	C	C	C	U	U	U	C	C	C	U	U	U	C	C	C	R	R		U	U
46. Everglades Racer *Coluber constrictor paludicola*						U	C	C	C			U			C			R		U
47. Eastern Indigo Snake *Drymarchon corais couperi*	R	R		R	R			R	R				R	R		R	R			R
48. Eastern Hognose Snake *Heterodon platirhinos*	R	R						R	R											
49. Southern Hognose Snake *Heterodon simus*										U	U	U	R	R						

	Floodplain Wetland Communities							Southern Florida Limestone Rockland		Coastal Communities										
	Bottomland Forest			Floodplain Cypress Swamp			Everglades Swale	Pine Rockland	Rockland Hardwood Hammock	Coastal Strand			Maritime Hammock			Tidal Marsh			Tidal Mangrove Swamp	
	P	N	S	P	N	S	S	S	S	P	N	S	P	N	S	P	N	S	N	S
50. Black Pine Snake *Pituophis melanoleucas lodingi*																				
51. Florida Pine Snake *Pituophis melanoleucus mugitus*																				
52. Corn Snake *Elaphe guttata guttata*	U	U	U	R	R	R		C	C	R	R	R	C	C	C					R
53. Grey Rat Snake *Elaphe obsoleta spiloides*	C	C		U	U								U	U						
54. Yellow Rat Snake *Elaphe obsoleta quadrivittata*	R	R		C	C		U	C	C				C	C					U	U
55. Everglades Rat Snake *Elaphe obsoleta rossalleni*		R			U		U	U	U					U						U
56. Short-tailed Snake *Stilosome extenuatum*																				
57. Mole Kingsnake *Lampropeltis calligaster rhombomaculata*	R																			
58. South Florida Mole Kingsnake *Lampropeltis calligaster occipitolineata*																				
59. Eastern Kingsnake *Lampropeltis getula getula*	U	U		R	R								U	U		U	C		U	U

(table continued on next page)

	Floodplain Wetland Communities							Southern Florida Limestone Rockland		Coastal Communities										
	Bottomland Forest			Floodplain Cypress Swamp			Everglades Swale	Pine Rockland	Rockland Hardwood Hammock	Coastal Strand			Maritime Hammock			Tidal Marsh			Tidal Mangrove Swamp	
	P	N	S	P	N	S	S	S	S	P	N	S	P	N	S	P	N	S	N	S
60. Florida Kingsnake *Lampropeltis getula floridana*			U		R	R	U	U	U						U		U	U	U	U
61. Northern Scarlet Snake *Cemophora coccinea copei*	C	C								R	R									
62. Florida Scarlet Snake *Cemophora coccinea coccinea*	C	C						U	U	R	R		C	C						
63. Scarlet Kingsnake *Lampropeltis triangulum elapsoides*	U	U	U					R	R				U	U	U					
64. Eastern Coral Snake *Micrurus fulvius fulvius*	U	U	U					R	R											
65. Southern Copperhead *Agkistrodon contortrix contortrix*	U																			
66. Eastern Cottonmouth *Agkistrodon piscivorus piscivorus*	C			C									R				U			
67. Florida Cottonmouth *Agkistrodon piscivorus conanti*	C	C	C	C	C	C	C	U	U	U	U	U	U	U	U	U	U	U	U	U
68. Dusky Pigmy Rattlesnake *Sistrurus miliarius barbouri*	C	C	C	C	C	C	C	C	C	U	U	U	C	C	C					
69. Timber Rattlesnake *Crotalus horridus*	U	C			U															
70. Eastern Diamondback Rattlesnake *Crotalus adamanteus*	R	R						U	U	U	U	U	C	C	C	U	U	U		

Snakes and the Law[1]
State and Federal
Regulations

The eastern indigo (*Drymarchon corais couperi*) and Atlantic salt marsh (*Nerodia clarkii taeniata*) snakes are listed as threatened species by both the federal government and the state of Florida. Taking, possessing, transporting or selling either of these species is prohibited in Florida without permits from both the U.S. Fish and Wildlife Service and the Florida Game and Fresh Water Fish Commission.

State protection is also given to short-tailed (*Stilosoma extenuatum*), Key ringneck (*Diadophis punctatus acricus*), and rim rock crowned (*Tantilla oolitica*) snakes, along with the populations of corn (*Elaphe guttata guttata*), Florida brown (*Storeria dekayi victa*), and peninsula ribbon (*Thamnophis sauritus sackenii*) snakes living in the lower Florida Keys. None of these animals can be taken, possessed, transported, or sold in Florida without a permit from the Florida Game and Fresh Water Fish Commission. (State permits to hold these animals are issued only for scientific or

---

[1]Kevin M. Enge, Florida Game and Fresh Water Fish Commission

conservation purposes when the research activity is judged to have no negative impact on the survival potential of the species.)

The Florida pine snake (*Pituophis melanoleucas mugitus*) is a species of special concern and cannot legally be bought or sold in Florida, but a single animal may be possessed per person.

Anyone wishing to sell snakes in Florida must obtain an annual license for Commercialization of Wildlife from the Florida Game and Fresh Water Fish Commission. The cost for this license is $5 to sell up to 10 animals in a year and $25 to sell more than 10 animals in a year. Anyone selling or buying live native amphibians and reptiles for resale, as well as anyone buying wildlife carcasses or parts for resale, must report their transactions quarterly to the Commission.

Those who want to keep a venomous snake must have a venomous reptile permit, which costs $5 per year and requires a completed affidavit signed by a notary public.

In Florida it is illegal to hunt snakes in state parks, preserves, and recreation areas; national parks and monuments; bird sanctuaries, unless specifically authorized; and critical wildlife areas during designated periods of no disturbance.

It is illegal everywhere in the state to introduce gasoline into wildlife burrows or other retreats in an attempt to drive out reptiles.

It is legal to hunt snakes in the Apalachiacola, Osceola, and Ocala national forests, but it is illegal to sell snakes captured there. Individual State Wildlife Management Areas have differing regulations.

It is legal to collect snakes from Florida's roads. But (because of game poaching) it is illegal to use a light to do so at night while possessing a gun.

Venom Poisoning[1]

With bright, unblinking eyes, an ability to seemingly rejuvenate themselves by casting off their aged skins, and wonderful agility—"the way of the serpent upon the rock"—snakes are clearly different from other animals. For millennia, men have seen in them intimations of transcendence; the serpent that tempted Eve was part of a long historical line of omniscient reptiles. The essence of snakes' fascination, though, has always lain in their power. Early in the dynasties of Egypt, the serpent's ability to kill with a pinprick was taken as such a sign of potency that Naja haje, the Egyptian cobra, became the symbol of imperial authority. As the serpent-god Uraeus rose among the celestial pantheon to a position second only to that of Ra, the sun king, the jeweled face of a cobra came to glare from the brow of every royal headdress, whose flared neckpiece was itself designed to emulate the snake's spreading hood.

The priesthood believed that the lethal virulence of mortal cobras derived from Uraeus himself and, in the earliest version of modern fasciotomies, cut open the limbs of bitten individuals in hopes of releasing the supernatural vapors thought to have been implanted by the reptile's fangs.

---

[1]Approximately 6,000 snakebites occur annually in the United States, but the vast majority involve non-venomous serpents, and require nothing more than reassurance and a tetanus shot. Of the few true envenomations, most occur in the southwestern states, and less than a dozen a year are fatal. In Florida, approximately one fatality from envenomation occurs every year.

Successive versions of this interpretation held that the virulent symptoms of envenomation were caused by the *rage* of the serpent, somehow passed, like the "madness" of a rabid dog, into its victim by means of the otherwise innocuous saliva. This theory remained the norm until a more logical explanation for the mysteriously radical results of snakebite became a cause célèbre in seventeenth-century Florence. Here, in one of the lesser-known scientific confrontations of the Renaissance, Francesco Redi broke new intellectual ground by instead attributing the "direful effects" of snakebite to a merely poisonous fluid held in the reptile's "great glands."

Yet, with the advent of chemical analysis, researchers were surprised to find that reptile venom was not really a poison.[2] At least not like any known poison, for unlike other toxins, venom was entirely benign within the body of its host. Neither serpent venom's physical properties nor its chemical makeup approximated conventional caustic poisons like the toxic alkaloids. Venom, it turned out, was simply a protein, so nearly indistinguishable from egg white in structure that in 1874 the Commission on Indian and Australian Snake Poisoning reported:

> "It is quite impossible to draw any deductions as to the nature of the poison. It is merely a mixture of albuminous principles." (Wolfenden, 1886)

Six years later, with French physician John de Lacerda's conceptualization of the biological catalysts he termed enzymes, came the first real clue as to how a mixture of reptilian body fluids could bring about the immediate, catastrophic physical deterioration of another animal. As de Lacerda theorized, venom did this by digestion. Like stomach acid—harmless in the gut but able to break down devoured flesh into its constituent amino acids—most snake venom kills by enzymatically disintegrating its victim.

There's more to it than this, yet few but toxicologists have gotten substantially further in unraveling the complex biology of envenomation. And almost no practicing physicians have, for snake venom poisoning is such a rare injury that most clinicians (having generally gotten only an overview in medical school) still don't know exactly what envenomation entails. Therefore, people poisoned by snakes find it nearly impossible to comprehend the nature of the scary, painful process taking place within their bodies. It is less mysterious given some understanding of the physiological changes brought about by reptile venom, however, and what can and cannot be done about them.

Treatment and Toxicology

W. C. Fields liked to tell friends he always kept some whiskey handy in case he saw a snake—which he also kept handy. Only a few people still employ Fields' favorite remedy, but almost no one is aware that following conventionally espoused first-aid practices is often equally dangerous—far more

---

[2]No chemical poison known at the time could approach the toxic potency of snake venom.

so than doing nothing at all in the field. Without question, one shouldn't spend time trying to cut open a snakebite wound to suck out the venom, for even under the best of circumstances, this is of more harm than value. Fortunately, as a practical matter that destructive regimen is usually out of the question anyway, because being bitten by a venomous snake is such a terrifying experience that then being able to execute a precise, difficult, and frightening quasi-surgical procedure is simply impossible for most people. However, time is important, and it's better to spend it getting proper medical management than fumbling with field surgery. Immediate therapy should mean no more than: (a) Immobilizing the envenomated extremity, removing rings or shoes before swelling begins; (b) Firmly wrapping the limb in a splinted elastic bandage; and (c) Getting the victim to a good hospital as quickly as is safely possible.

Harm—sometimes permanent—comes from much of the traditional regimen of binding the limb with circulation-cutting cords, packing it in ice, or slicing open the punctures. These measures go awry because they are founded on a basic misunderstanding of the complex biological process that begins when a venomous snake injects its venom into another animal. The most widespread misconception is that a strike injects a dollop of lethal fluid that oozes inexorably toward the heart. If this were the case one would of course do whatever possible to arrest its progress. But that isn't what happens. Envenomation doesn't always accompany a bite, for one thing (even punctures by the hot-tempered pit vipers are free of toxins about a fifth of the time, while no more than 40 percent of coral snake bites result in poisoning); "dry," non-envenomating bites require nothing in the way of treatment but a tetanus shot. In 7 out of every 10 hospitalizations, moreover, only superficial envenomation has occurred, and unless heavy poisoning has been established, it is irresponsible to risk destroying nerve and muscle tissue by following incision/tourniquet measures whose objective is either to drain the venom or to prevent its transit through the circulatory system. Despite the fact that every county in Florida is inhabited by at least four species of venomous snakes, most of the state's 200 or so annual cases of snakebite are caused by non-venomous species. Of those that do involve venomous snakes (15 to 25 involve coral snakes, the rest pit vipers), only about half result in serious envenomation, and over 98% of the victims of venomous snakebites in the state survive.

Neither tourniquet nor incision is generally therapeutic, for pit viper venom doesn't ooze toward the heart after a bite. Its preliminary function is to immobilize small food animals so they can be captured, and most of venom's multitude of separate peptides and enzymes are simply devoted to digestion. These include hyaluronidase, collagenase, thrombinlike enzymes, L-amino oxidase (which gives venom its amber tint), phosphomonoesterase, phosphodiesterase, two kinds of kinases (both similar to pancreatic secretions and which prepare soft tissue for more extensive breakdown by analogous solutions in the reptile's stomach), nucleotidase, at least one phospholipase, arginine ester hydrolase, and various proteolytic enzymes. More than 30 such enzyme fractions have been identified, many of which seem to operate most powerfully in complementary combinations. Within the bodies of human beings bitten by rattlesnakes, cotton-mouths, and copperheads, just as occurs in the snakes' rodent prey, these enzymes actively disintegrate the living tissues.

Like all digestive processes, this one is complicated; each protease and kinase has a slightly separate metabolic function, often a different target organ, and sometimes a different route in getting there. Hyaluronidase, for example, breaks down connective fibers in the muscle matrix, allowing proteases and trypsinlike enzymes to penetrate the limbs directly. The deadliest venom fractions are the neurotoxically-active polypeptides, proteins that are present in varying proportions in all snake venom, even that of ostensibly haemotoxic species. Although slowly circulating lymphatic fluid is the major dispersive avenue of most venom components, the venom of elapid snakes tends to disperse almost instantly through the bloodstream; with these toxins it makes little difference whether the venom is injected deeply or infused just below the skin. For this reason, employing a *temporary* arterial tourniquet is appropriate in severe poisoning by the peptide-based venoms of elapids such as the coral snake.

Targeted toward the neural membranes branching from the upper spinal cord, most of these venom peptides eventually block acetylcholine receptor sites in the junctions between adjoining nuchal ganglia, progressively impairing neuromuscular transmission.[3] The victim therefore suffers progressive paralysis which, if not arrested, can stop contraction of the diaphragm and cause suffocation. Yet, if given respiratory maintenance until the venom's acetylcholine arrest is dispelled by the short effective life of its peptides, victims of coral snake envenomation eventually begin breathing on their own. Although symptoms such as muscle weakness may persist for up to a month, full neuromuscular control eventually returns, and the patient usually suffers no subsequent ill effects.

Pit viper toxins work differently. In concert with endothelial cell-specific thrombinlike enzymes, their peptide components perforate the vascular capillary walls, allowing a fine seepage of plasma thinned by the simultaneous assault of another set of venom enzymes. These include phospholi-

---

[3]Other components of elapid venom, including that of the coral snake, *Micrurus fulvius,* are haemolytic, or circulatory-system directed. While generally less potent than elapid venom's neurotoxic elements, in high doses its specifically cardiotoxic venom components can be lethal. Wyeth's equine-derived coral snake antivenin ("Antivenin, *Micrurus fulvius,*" Drug Circular, Wyeth, 1983) does not neutralize these haemolytic elements and is only effective against the neuroxtic elements in coral snake venom only in fairly high doses (median dose 6.5 vials; at which level 35% of patients experience side-effects; in 50% of those cases, side-effects are severe, resulting in anaphylactic shock or serum sickness). Another coral snake antivenin, with about the same dosage requirement, effectiveness, and problematic side effects, is manufactured by the Instituto Butantan in Sao Paulo, Brazil, from antibodies raised to a mixture of the venom of two South American coral snake species, *M. corallinus* and *M. frontalis frontalis.* Only the new, ovine-based *Micrurus* antivenin currently under development at St. Bartholomew's Hospital, Medical College, London, & the Liverpool School of Tropical Medicine, Liverpool, U.K., neutralizes both neurotoxic and cardiotoxic components of *Micrurus* venom. In preliminary trials during 1993, it has done so with a fourfold reduction in dosage. Because this antivenin is derived from sheep antibodies, the negative side-effects of prior sensitization to equine-based serums used in other, previous inoculations are absent.

pase A (which combines with lipids in the blood to inhibit their coagulatory function), toxic fibrinolytic and thrombinlike enzymes (which disintegrate the hematic fibrinogen also required for clotting), and a pair of related hemolysins, specifically keyed to the destruction of red blood cells. These hemolysins attack the erythrocytes directly, fraying their membranes and causing them to clump together in dysfunctional knots, useless for carrying oxygen.[4]

All this happens very fast. It has to, because a viper's predominantly rodent prey is so fleet that a snake whose venom doesn't disable its victim within yards stands a good chance of losing its meal altogether. And the only way a pit viper can cripple prey so rapidly is to deliver a large amount of venom relative to the size of food animal—venom that begins to disintegrate its vital organs within seconds. Structurally similar to the blood and tissues of its victim, venom enzymes immediately incorporate themselves into their host's cells, breaking down tissues into their component amino acids, so that what the viper swallows a few minutes later is a substantially predigested meal.

The same process occurs in humans bitten by rattlesnakes or moccasins. Rather than remaining intact—an isolated, removable foreign substance— reptilian venom proteins quickly bond to the cells, blood, and lymphatic fluid of its recipient, from which attempts to extract them are as hopeless as trying to retrieve ink dripped on a wet sponge.

Widely recognized among primitive peoples, the affinity of venom for protoplasm was the rationale for a widespread Native American snakebite antidote. This was to cut the flesh around the fang marks and press the freshly opened body of a bird or small mammal against the wound in the hope that some of the still unbonded serum might be drawn into the animal's unsaturated tissues. Venom was never actually withdrawn in this way, but the approach seemed promising enough for variations to have been recommended by frontier army medical officers looking for a better means of venom extraction than the traditional, but almost entirely ineffective, cut-and-suck technique. (As awareness of infective pathogens—and their prevalence in the mouth— became widespread, some military snakebite kits were equipped with small sheets of latex to place between one's mouth and the cut-open wound.)

At the time, there simply was no other option to suction, however. As late as the 1920s, physician Dudley Jackson managed only to take the conventional regimen a small step further by placing a series of heat-transfer suction cups over incisions both across the fang marks and around the perimeter of the

---

[4]The relative proportion of the constituent elements in the venom mix varies considerably. Each of more than a dozen secretory cells, located around the perimeter of the snake's storage bladder, or lumen (the big lateral bulge behind the corner of the jaw, which gives pit vipers their "triangular"-shaped heads), releases its particular toxin according to the rhythm of its individual output cycle. Because the day-to-day blend of these component serums is constantly in flux, venom is one of the most difficult biological substances to accurately describe. This also accounts for the disparity in venom potency so often observed between even similarly sized and sexed snakes of the same species. The different venom fractions' variable concentrations mean that their relative impact on each of the victim's organs may also be somewhat different from day to day. (Incidentally, outside the lumen, venom will even digest itself, for catalytic agents pumped into the serum from secondary glands located downstream from the primary storage bladder activate the enzyme fractions' metabolic assault.)

mound of edema that typically surrounds pit viper bites. Although the best of the old-line therapies, Jackson's approach still only extracted a minuscule amount of blood- and lymph-diluted venom—far too little to prevent the extensive tissue necrosis typical of severe rattlesnake bites. Jackson's heat-transfer cups were also entirely useless against the faster-spreading—if slower to manifest symptoms—peptide-based venom of the coral snake.

Finally, because conventional pharmacological treatment of snakebite was continuing to prove unfruitful, in response to the extensive tissue necrosis and resulting gangrenous toxemia that can accompany massive pit viper envenomation, a few doctors turned to surgery.

This approach was usually combined with steroid therapy. Due to their familiarity among the medical community, the same corticosteroids widely used to treat lesser inflammatory reactions are still administered to victims of snakebite, but opinion as to their desirability varies. Proponents of this sort of symptomatic management focus on steroids' relief of edema, allergic symptoms, and general discomfort. Yet corticosteroids are not only unable to inhibit the metabolic tissue dissolution of pit viper venom, they also increase arteriole and venule permeability, thereby exacerbating plasma leakage and falling blood pressure. Another drawback to steroids is that in cases of very severe venom poisoning they tend to mask the signs of deteriorating renal, vascular, and pulmonary function; for this reason, both Visser and Chapman (1978) and Russell (1980) feel that steroids should be avoided in the treatment of reptile envenomation except in response to a specific inflammatory condition like antivenin hypersensitivity.

Thomas G. Glass, professor of surgery at the University of Texas Medical School in San Antonio, eventually achieved considerable success with a primarily surgical approach. Glass's technique was particularly effective in severe cases where tissue death was already extensive. Although North American pit vipers tend to be shallow biters, with most of their toxins reaching only subcutaneous levels, a large rattlesnake occasionally penetrates much farther, sinking its fangs through skin, subcutaneous fatty layers, and the outer muscle fascia to deposit an infusion of venom in the the muscle. In this type of envenomation the toxins are encapsulated in the underlying layers of muscle where the venom's proteolytic enzymes work their digestive functions with fewer outward symptoms than most snakebites, in which the venom is dispersed within the subcutaneous tissues where it causes swelling, skin discoloration and severe pain. Because of its localization, in these very deep envenomations a considerable amount of the infusion can sometimes be removed by immediate incision and debridement, but only if the surgery is undertaken by one of the handful of those experienced in the delicate excision of this sort of embedded lacuna. The trick, of course, is being able to tell true subfascial poisoning from the far more common, but also largely symptomless, superficial snakebite in which little or no envenomation has occurred—and being able to do it fast.

Nevertheless, most of the time there is nothing to be gained from surgery. As far back as 1939, in experiments with western diamondback rattler and eastern cottonmouth venoms in cats and rabbits, F. M. Allen demonstrated that no benefit resulted from removing a large volume of tissue surrounding an injection of venom. Despite performing local excisions within five minutes of envenomation, during even this brief time the envenomated animals had already absorbed the toxins' most lethal peptide components, and any that had received a lethal dose ultimately succumbed. This led Allen to conclude that high dosages of crotalid venom disperse so quickly throughout a small mammal's body that even immediately removing a large amount of local tissue is useless, because the normal-looking tissue outside the excised area has still absorbed enough venom to cause a laboratory animal's death. Early-treatment excision has, therefore, long been discontinued in the practical treatment of snakebites.

Other properties of reptile venom also weigh heavily against "first aid" incision of fang marks. Reptilian toxins suppress the body's bactericidal and immune responses, particularly the action of its white blood cells. Without the leukocytes' prophylactic intervention, a receptive environment awaits the host of pathogens introduced by every deep field incision,[5] while their rapid dispersal is ensured by the seepage of contaminated plasma and lymphatic fluid suffused through tissues made more permeable by the fiber-dissolving properties of hyaluronidase. It is also generally painful to be touched in the area of a pit viper bite—even the touch of cloth may be abrasive—because the venom's proteolytic dissolution of blood releases bradykinin from the disintegrating plasma and serotonin from its serum platelets which, spread into the subcutaneous tissues, produces burning pain. Skin this sensitive makes the prospect of crude pocketknife surgery nearly unthinkable, especially when (as is fairly likely) the victim is simultaneously experiencing violent nausea and vomiting.

An even better reason to avoid incision is that the anticoagulant effect of pit viper venom on plasma fibrinogen so impairs the blood's ability to clot that opening an envenomated limb may produce much worse bleeding than would be expected. Risk of excessive blood loss is particularly high following severe envenomation because when people die of snakebite (which happens very rarely, in less than one percent of poisonings inflicted by North American species), loss of circulating blood volume is what kills them.[6] It takes hours to lose this much blood internally, though, because, except in the most severe envenomations, leakage through enzyme-perforated arterioles and venules is gradual, only very slowly allowing blood to pool in the interstitial spaces of the envenomated limb. Here it appears as edema, which in the heaviest poisonings can drop vascular pressure enough to put the patient into severe shock.[7] Therefore, as in every major trauma, maintaining suffi-

---

[5]Inflammation, discoloration, and edema produced by the almost inevitable infection of first-aid-generated wounds is one of snakebite's commonest complicating syndromes, and additional complications are the last thing one should add to the already complex choices of emergency room care.

[6]In *Crotalinae* poisoning the venom's ultimate target is not the heart—which almost invariably performs perfectly throughout the ordeal—but the lungs. But before congestive pooling of fluid in the lungs interferes with breathing, severe shock from loss of circulating blood volume has usually occurred. For this reason, deaths caused by crotalid venom are almost always due to depletion of vascular fluid volume rather than to respiratory failure, although among fatalities there is usually some degree of pulmonary thromboembolism.

cient circulating blood volume is crucial to initial management of critical snakebite poisoning. In the emergency room this is accomplished with the intravenous infusion of isotonic saline solution, although internal hemorrhage may require transfusion of whole blood—another reason for not cutting open a snakebite victim in the field, where such fluids are unavailable.

Ironically—horrible as it looks, and notwithstanding the vast amount of medical attention that has traditionally been focused upon it—edema itself seldom threatens the limb. Huge serosanguinous blisters sometimes bulge up around the bites of timber and eastern diamondback rattlers, yet both these distensions and the surrounding mound of swollen skin are typically soft, with swelling limited to the epidermal and outer cutaneous layers. Even severe edema of this type does not produce the limb-killing process that traditional medical texts depict as cutting off circulation like a hydraulic tourniquet. Only rarely does the deadly pressure occur that stops oxygen exchange and destroys tissue. Yet, under the misconception that leaving a limb opened for several days facilitates therapeutic drainage of its venom-saturated tissues, less sophisticated physicians still initiate fasciotomy.

Reptile toxins do not leave tissue to which they have metabolically bonded, however, and breaching the length of a limb risks infection, nerve damage, and the loss of flexion due to scarring. In treating some 200 venomous snakebites, Ken Mattox and his team at Houston's Ben Taub Hospital have used fasciotomy to relieve hydraulic tourniqueting less than a half-dozen times, while Findlay E. Russell, in treating more reptilian envenomations than anyone in North America, has never had to perform a fasciotomy due to excessive intracompartmental pressure.

Often equally damaging to local tissue is containment of the venom in the area of the bite. This is not due primarily to the toxins' enhanced destructiveness when kept concentrated, but because of the tissue death incurred by cutting off the flow of fluids into and out of the limb.[8] Nevertheless, for *short periods* a moderate level of limb cooling (an icepack on the forehead is also helpful) may offer a mild numbing of the pain as well as mitigate to some degree the intense nausea often associated with venom poisoning (because toxin-induced intestinal spasms are sometimes violent enough to provoke rupture and hemorrhage of the trachea, any reduction in their severity is of great importance).

---

[7]Findlay E. Russell, one of the country's leading authorities on snake venom poisoning, estimates that as little as a two-centimeter increase in the circumference of a thigh can account for the loss into the tissue spaces of nearly a third of the body's circulating blood volume. Yet, immediate shock is rare, ordinarily occurring only after the massive envenomation of a child or the chance injection of a large quantity of venom directly into a major blood vessel, when the hemolytic effect of so much toxic protein can bring about system-wide red blood cell clumping and the pooling of fluids even within the vascular system.

[8]The worst of the containment therapies was the ligature-cryotherapy regimen that was popular during the 1950s. It combined two of the most destructive things ever done to a human limb: putting a tourniquet around it, then radically chilling the constricted part by immersing it, sometimes for days, in ice. As might be expected, tissue deprived of the oxygen exchange and waste dispersal of normal blood flow, subjected to the cell membrane-cracking effect of lengthy chilling, and simultaneously attacked by corrosive digestive enzymes, died so frequently that amputations following ligature-cryotherapy became almost routine.

Other than the prevention of nausea, recent laboratory studies have shown that nothing is accomplished by cooling, for while the cell-disintegrating action of enzymes is slowed by extreme cold, it would take freezing—and hence killing a limb or digit—to achieve sufficient chilling to deactivate its infused venom enzymes.[9] The other major group of venom toxins, the rapidly-dispersing peptide fractions found in both elapid and pit viper venom, do not depend on warmth for their potency, and no mechanical constraint short of a total tourniquet impairs their dissemination along arterial pathways and through the tissue matrix. A total tourniquet will substantially contain both peptides and enzymes, of course, but cinched down for more than 40 minutes is almost sure to cause permanent injury, sometimes severe enough to require amputation. This is such a dangerous procedure that binding tourniquets around any pit viper envenomation (except that of a toddler deeply poisoned by a big rattler) is one of the few measures now decried by almost everyone involved in treating snakebites.

In contrast, most of a pit viper's toxins, namely its enzymatic venom fractions—by far the most numerous components of its venom—are dispersed primarily through the lymph system. These venom components may be restrained by firmly wrapping the bitten limb or digit in an elastic bandage, splinting it in place, then rewrapping the entire area. The objective is to allow essential oxygen exchange at the same time that the broad pressure of the elastic bandage compresses the lymph vessels and slows the largely muscular-contraction-pumped flow of venom-saturated lymphatic fluid. Sometimes referred to as the Australian method because it was developed as a field treatment for the bites of that continent's many neurotoxically-venomed elapids, this type of field therapy has also proven effective (Sutherland and Coulter, 1981) in the first-aid treatment of major envenomation by North American pit vipers.

This singularly safe field treatment also dovetails with the medical consensus that now prevails concerning hospital management of the most serious snakebite cases. Once admitted, with an unbreached limb, this approach relies almost entirely on the intravenous administration of antivenin, combined with antihistamines to stifle allergic reaction. Proponents of this method maintain that both the life-threatening systemic failures and local necrosis caused by pit viper toxins are best offset by antivenin antibodies.

Following the bites of pit vipers, the signs of extensive local tissue death that indicate antivenin therapy are almost always obvious: immediate pain, swelling, and discoloration in the vicinity of the bite, often accompanied by motor impairment, nausea, and tremor. In poisoning by elapids such as the coral snake, the first response is usually sharp pain, but initial symptoms of neurological distress may be as mild and ambiguously manifested as a tingling or numbness of the face, scalp, and fingers—an especially difficult set of indicators because anxiety over the bite can produce exactly the same

---

[9]"Local Heat and Cold Application After Eastern Cottonmouth Moccasin (*Agkistrodon piscivorus*) Envenomation in the Rat: Effect on Tissue Injury," Wayne R. Cohen, Warren Wetzel and Anna Kadish; *Toxicon*, Vol. 30, No. 11, pp. 1383–1386, 1992.

sensations. (Especially if the individual is familiar with what is supposed to happen: A companion of mine, bitten by a coral snake in West Texas, went through all the symptoms indicating the onset of neurological poisoning, only to have entirely "recovered" by the time San Antonio's medical facilities were reached.) Nevertheless, because the symptoms of *Micrurus* envenomation have been known to first appear as much as several hours after a bite, every coral snake bite that breaks the skin is potentially serious, and should probably be treated immediately with antivenin.

While primarily associated with elapid envenomation, neurological damage is also present to some degree in almost all rattlesnake and moccasin venom poisoning. As James L. Glenn, of the Western Institute for Biomedical Research has discovered, nervous system damage is often characteristic of envenomation by Florida's timber and eastern diamondback rattlesnakes, while it is well known from bites by the western rock and Mojave rattlesnakes. (Among the handful of fatal bites by the Mojave, failure of the central nervous system has been the principal cause of death, partly because the relatively mild immediate symptoms caused these poisonings to be initially diagnosed as minor and given insufficient attention until the most beneficial period for antivenin therapy had passed.)

Antivenins

Nearly as biologically complex as the venom it is cultured to neutralize, antivenin is still sometimes looked at askance by both doctors and laymen—with good reason, given the poor reputation of earlier serums. The old Institut Pasteur globulin, in particular, often caused adverse serum responses because so much was expected of it by European doctors using it under primitive conditions in the bush to treat the devastatingly toxic bites of South African cobras, mambas, and vipers. Because all antivenin sometimes triggers allergic histamine shock, or anaphylaxis—an intense allergic reaction—it should never be used outside a hospital. Like any other immunization, antivenin therapy depends on establishing a protective titer of antibodies in the entire bloodstream (this is why the serum should never be injected directly into an envenomated extremity: you can't build up immunity in a finger alone). Because rapid, massive infusion of antivenin's foreign proteins impacts the bodies' entire blood supply, serum anaphylaxis is therefore likely to be of far greater intensity than other allergic reactions, while the offending substance obviously cannot be removed. Unmoderated, enough swelling can occur to obstruct the respiratory passages, and even coronary attacks have occurred.

This sort of allergic reaction could probably be avoided altogether if animals other than horses were used to make antivenin, but historically only horses—the source animals for all other types of immunization vaccines—have been bled for the serum antibodies they produce ("raise" is the medical term) in response to small, periodic injections of snake venom. (These antibodies are so nearly the same for all North American pit vipers that Wyeth distributes a single antivenin, *Crotalinae,* for use against the bites of copperheads, cottonmouths, and all indigenous rattlesnake species; for coral snake envenomation,

Wyeth has a separate antivenin, *Micrurus*.) The problem is that horses have been used to produce so many unrelated but widespread antigen-bearing vaccines that many people prophylactically inoculated against typhoid, tetanus, and diphtheria bacilli have become sensitized to equine cellular matter and consequently experience allergic anaphylaxis when presented with the massive infusion of equine globulins required by antivenin therapy.

Other experimental animals have also been used to produce plasma antigens, but only on a small scale. Serum prepared from both sheep and goat's blood has produced milder reactions than the equine vaccines, probably because fewer people have been sensitized to sheep and goats than to horses. (The St. Bartholomew's Hospital Medical College/Liverpool School of Tropical Medicine group has used Welsh half-breed ewes to produce a very promising prototype elapid antivenin.) Antivenin has even been derived from western diamondback rattlesnake blood—to which, of course, no one is sensitized—and has afforded laboratory animals a high level of protection from the effects of pit viper envenomation, especially when combined with goat antibodies. Human beings could produce reaction-free antibodies as well, if anyone were willing to undergo the misery of periodic minimal poisoning. No commercial human-globulin antivenin has ever been produced, though William E. Haast, who for many years operated the Miami Serpentarium, has injected small, antigen-producing amounts of elapid venom into himself for decades, and as a probable result has survived a number of what in all likelihood would otherwise have been lethal cobra bites. (Haast is now in his eighties, and thoroughly vigorous.) By transfusing his own antigen-bearing blood into other victims of elapid poisoning, Haast has reportedly mitigated the effects of their envenomations.

Conventional antivenin therapy is quite different and, administered by an experienced physician with immediate access to intensive care facilities, both Wyeth's current North American elapid and crotalid antivenins are fairly safe. The most critical aspect of their use lies in the need for immediate intervention to offset the coronary or respiratory difficulties that even this antivenin may provoke. Those difficulties are especially pronounced because the need to immunize rapidly—crotalid toxins begin disintegrating tissues at once—entails challenging the body with a large quantity of foreign protein, a risk that should be taken only after severe envenomation and in a hospital equipped with critical care facilities. Before antivenin can be administered, however, each patient's sensitivity to equine proteins must be determined. This is done by means of a standard allergic-reaction skin test—a trial that, itself, can be undertaken with safety only in a medical facility where the adverse reaction that even this tiny amount of serum may (rarely) provoke can be alleviated with antihistamines.

Because anaphylaxis can be controlled by pharmacological means, however, even a positive skin test doesn't entirely preclude using antivenin, although careful monitoring of the early warnings of incipient anaphylaxis—hoarseness or stridor, a lump in the throat, flushing, or tightness in the chest—is essential in these cases. The serum initiates a major immunological response throughout the body, so, as infusion is begun, almost everyone receiving antivenin feels an unsettling combination of heart palpitations, shortness of breath, and tingling sensations. These reactions ordinarily go no further, for if they threaten to worsen into anaphylaxis, the antivenin's IV infusion can be shut off and a second intravenous drip of Benadryl or epinephrine begun, sometimes in combination with aminophylline for bronchial spasms.

Individuals vary so widely in their sensitivity to antivenin infusion that some people need nearly twice as long as others to build up the same blood level of antibodies, but if it can be tolerated, several vials of the vaccine may be given during the first hour. Infusion is then maintained at two or three vials per hour until an adequate plasma titer is established, after which a marked decrease in the discomfort of the poisoning is normally evident.

The reason for this dramatic improvement lies in the way in which antivenin acts to prevent the venom's proteolytic, fibrinolytic, and hemolytic action. Introduced into the bloodstream, its equine antibody clusters are drawn to the large, variably shaped toxic peptides and enzymes (enzymes are usually spherical, while peptides may be tubular, coiled, or globular in form), which the antibodies physically encrust so thickly that the toxins' keylike protuberances can no longer penetrate their target cells. Eventually, this protective frosting builds up enough layers to attract the body's particle-devouring macrophagocytes which, like giant amoebas, engulf and digest most of these conglomerate specks of alien protein. As the last of these deactivated antibody-antigen complexes precipitate out of the blood 6 to 10 days after treatment, they may lodge in vessel walls throughout the body, causing the skin rashes, hives, and temporary kidney impairment that collectively are known as serum sickness.

Long after recovery, however, a small cadre of the body's own antigens (spawned both by the venom and by the antivenin's equally foreign horse serum antibodies) still remains in the bloodstream, typically sensitizing the individual to any subsequently encountered equine globulins. This is usually not a problem unless the patient is poisoned by another venomous snake. In that case, as residual antigens remaining from the first antivenin treatment respond violently to a second influx of equine globulins, an intense histaminic/anaphylactic reaction is likely to occur.

Although both *Crotalinae* and *Micrurus* antivenin are kept by major hospitals, an emergency source is the producer, Wyeth Laboratories of Philadelphia (610-688-4400). Another option is to contact the Antivenin Index, compiled by the Arizona Poison Center, which offers a comprehensive array of data on venomous snakebite and a list of all the antivenins currently stored in the United States, including those for foreign species. Their 24-hour emergency number is 602-626-6016.

Finally, some authorities on envenomation by both native and exotic reptiles are:

L.H.S. Van Mierop, M.D.
Department of Pediatrics (Cardiology)
University of Florida Medical School
Gainesville, Florida 32611

David L. Hardy, M.D.
Arizona Poison Control System
Coagulation Research Laboratory
Department of Pediatrics,
University of Arizona Health Sciences
  Center
Tucson, Arizona

Sherman A. Minton, M.D.
Department of Biology,
Indiana University Medical Center
Bloomington, Indiana

James L. Glenn, M.D.
Western Institute for Biomedical
  Research
Salt Lake City, Utah

Damon C. Smith
Therapeutic Antibodies, Inc.
St. Bartholomew's Hospital Medical
  College
Charterhouse Square
London, EC1, U.K.
(New Coral Snake Antivenin)

Venom Potency

The following comparative values for the relative toxicity of the venoms of Florida's venomous snakes are based on an arbitrary, but widely accepted standard known as the LD50—for the Lethal Dosage, or amount of venom required to kill, within 24 hours, 50% of the laboratory mice injected with it. Used in slightly varying interpretations since the 1930s, a standard means of calculating a toxin's LD50 was set by the World Health Organization in 1981, using the Spearman-Karber method and employing genetically-uniform Swiss-Webster laboratory mice.

As a comparative measure of venom potency, the numbers used here are a compilation of 13 major studies of venom potency conducted over the last 63 years on snakes from several areas of the country. It is well known that the relative proportions of the various hemotoxic/neurotoxic components of ophidian venom, as well as the venom's overall potency, is slightly to highly variable both between local and regional snake populations as well as between individual specimens within these populations. Thus, the venom potency values cited here are an approximation of the relative toxicity of the venoms of these species. Included are the highest and lowest venom potency values (0 being the *most* toxic) recorded by the studies, as well as the mean.[10]

Venom Potency Table

Species	High	Low	Mean
Eastern coral snake, *Micrurus fulvius fulvius*	0.53	0.73	0.63
Eastern diamondback rattlesnake, *Crotalus adamanteus*	1.89	3.75	2.82
Timber rattlesnake, *Crotalus horridus horridus*	2.69	3.80	3.25
Florida cottonmouth, *Agkistrodon piscivorus conanti*	4.88	5.82	5.35
Dusky pigmy rattlesnake, *Sistrurus miliarius barbouri*	6.0	10.29	8.15
Southern copperhead, *Agkistrodon contortrix*	7.8	16.71	12.26

---

[10]Githens and Wolff (1939), Gingrich and Hohenadel (1956), Minton (1956), Russell and Emery (1959), Hall and Genarro (1961), Weinstein et al. (1962), Russel (1967), Cohen et al. (1971), Kocholaty (1971), Minton (1974), Glenn and Straight (1977), Glenn and Straight (1978), Russell (1980).

Scalation

Head Scales: Nonvenomous Snake

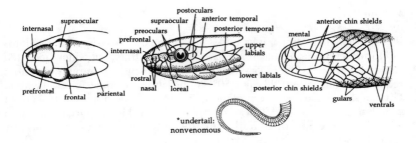

Head Scales: Pit Viper

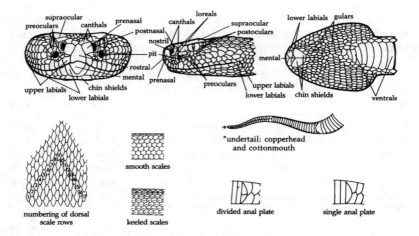

Typhlopidae

Blind Snakes

Blind Snakes

1 Brahminy Blind Snake
Ramphotyphlops braminus

Nonvenomous   The Brahminy blind snake is too small to bite humans.

Abundance   This primitive serpent, reminiscent of the sub-terranean late Cretaceous snakes from which all modern ser-pents are descended, is native to Southeast Asia. Yet, like many other exotic species, *R. braminus* has spread worldwide and established a large breeding population in southern Florida, where its progenitors first arrived in the soil of house plants imported by commercial Miami nurseries. In residential areas where there is well-watered sod and rich garden humus, the Brahminy blind snake is now common from Pinellas Co. and Lake Okeechobee south to the upper Keys.

Size   Even adult *Rampho typhlops braminus* are no more than 2.5 to 6.5 inches in length and not much thicker than coathanger wire.

Habitat   This little reptile is most often found in flower beds.

Prey   Primarily the eggs, larvae, and pupae of ants and termites.

Reproduction   Egg-laying **and** live-bearing. Also parthenogenic, for *R. braminus* is unisexual—an all-female species in which the ova begin cell division without spermatozoa, producing up to 8 genetically-identical offspring that may be either born alive or deposited as eggs between April and June.

Coloring/scale form   Brahminy blind snakes resemble shiny black earthworms (like worms, they are washed onto the pavement by heavy rains). The blunt head and tail seem nearly identical—there is no narrowing of the neck—for the vestigial eyes appear as no more than dots of black pig-ment and the few teeth are located in the barely visible lower jaw. The blind snake's non-tapering posterior end is tipped, however, by a tiny spur. Unlike the transversely widened ventral scutes of other serpents, the same size scales occur in 14 rows around the blind snake's entire body; there is no anal plate because the vent is surrounded by minuscule scales.

Similar snakes   None.

Behavior   The specialized spur on the Brahminy blind snake's tailtip is dug into the earth to obtain purchase for pressing its tiny body through soft soil. In the open (where these animals never cease wriggling in search of something to burrow in) the tail is brought forward, planted, and used to lever the body ahead.

Colubridae

Small Burrowing Snakes

2 Southeastern Crowned Snake
3 Peninsula Crowned Snake
4 Central Florida Crowned Snake
5 Coastal Dunes Crowned Snake
6 Rim Rock Crowned Snake
7 Marsh Brown Snake
8 Florida Brown Snake
9 Midland Brown Snake
10 Florida Redbelly Snake
11 Rough Earth Snake
12 Eastern Earth Snake
13 Pine Woods Snake
14 Southern Ringneck Snake
15 Key Ringneck Snake

Garter and Ribbon Snakes

16 Eastern Garter Snake
17 Bluestripe Garter Snake
18 Eastern Ribbon Snake
19 Peninsula Ribbon Snake
20 Bluestripe Ribbon Snake

Aquatic Snakes

21 Redbelly Water Snake
22 Yellowbelly Water Snake
23 Banded Water Snake
24 Florida Water Snake
25 Mississippi Green Water Snake
26 Florida Green Water Snake
27 Brown Water Snake
28 Midland Water Snake
29 Gulf Salt Marsh Snake
30 Atlantic Salt Marsh Snake
31 Mangrove Salt Marsh Snake
32 Glossy Crayfish Snake
33 Gulf Crayfish Snake
34 Striped Crayfish Snake

35 Queen Snake
36 Eastern Mud Snake
37 Western Mud Snake
38 Rainbow Snake
39 South Florida Rainbow Snake
40 North Florida Swamp Snake
41 South Florida Swamp Snake

Green Snakes

42 Rough Green Snake

Whipsnakes, Racers, and Indigo Snakes

43 Eastern Coachwhip
44 Brownchin Racer
45 Southern Black Racer
46 Everglades Racer
47 Eastern Indigo Snake

Brown-blotched Terrestrial Snakes

48 Eastern Hognose Snake
49 Southern Hognose Snake
50 Black Pine Snake
51 Florida Pine Snake
52 Corn Snake
53 Gray Rat Snake
54 Yellow Rat Snake
55 Everglades Rat Snake
56 Short-tailed Snake
57 Mole Kingsnake
58 South Florida Mole Kingsnake

Large Kingsnakes

59 Eastern Kingsnake
60 Florida Kingsnake

Red-and-black-banded Snakes

61 Northern Scarlet Snake
62 Florida Scarlet Snake
63 Scarlet Kingsnake

Southeastern Crowned Snake

Tantilla coronata

Nonvenomous   Although technically a rear-fanged serpent with salivary toxins that immobilize its diminutive prey (all *Tantilla* have enlarged, though still tiny, grooved teeth in the rear of their minuscule upper jaws), the crowned snake is unable to harm humans.

Abundance *Tantilla coronata* is uncommon in its Florida panhandle range where, like other small terrestrial reptiles, it has been negatively impacted by the recent invasion of South American fire ants.

Size   Adult *T. coronata* reach a maximum of 13 inches in length.

Habitat   Seldom found at the surface except beneath rocks, boards, or leaf litter, *T. coronata* is partial to dry microhabitats and prefers loose, silica-based soil in which to burrow. It occupies wooded and grass/brushland communities, occurring most often in pine or oak forest, though it has also been reported from mesic meadows, hardwood hammocks, and even swamps.

Prey   Primarily tenebrionid beetle larvae; also snails, centipedes, termites and their larvae, spiders, and cut- and wireworms. Vertebrates such as ground skinks are also reportedly taken.

Reproduction   Egg-laying. Reproduction in this species is complicated. First, for such a small reptile *T. coronata* requires a long period of maturation, with females reaching sexual maturity only in the spring of their third year at about 21 months of age, when they are still only about 7.5 inches long. Second, according to R. Aldridge and R. Semlitsch, who have analyzed the reproductive biology of this species, both male and female *T. coronata* store sperm. This is necessary because the two genders' procreative cycles differ markedly.[1] Males' spermatogenesis occurs in late summer while females ovulate during June and July, which means that for viable sperm to be present at the time of vernal copulation— April and May—it must remain active in the males' vas deferens throughout the winter. To fertilize the receptive eggs female *T. coronata* produce in midsummer, spermatozoa must continue to remain viable in seminal receptacles within the female's oviduct for 2 or 3 additional months. Compared to the short lifespan of avian and mammalian sperm this is an extraordinary period, but a necessary span given the gender difference in this snake's annual reproductive cycles.

---

[1]The eastern coral snake, *Micrurus fulvius fulvius,* although an entirely unrelated elapid, shares a similar, temporally dichotomous reproductive cycle, with female vitellogenesis taking place in late spring while male testicular enlargement and spermatogenesis occurs in autumn, well after the primary spring/summer breeding season. The same is true of many pit vipers.

Delayed fertilization is also reflected in the southeastern crowned snake's morphology. *T. coronata* is able to exist in its constricted subterranean environment in part because of its exceptionally slender body. This lets it slip though minuscule spaces in the soil—but the slimming process that made this possible meant foregoing an active left oviduct, which now serves as an auxiliary sperm storage receptacle.[2] The southeastern crowned snake's 2 to 5 oval, whitish eggs are laid in a cup-shaped cavity amid moist woodland debris, hatching into tiny neonates no more than 3 inches long.

Coloring/scale form   The southeastern crowned snake's back and sides are solid rusty-brown or tan. Its blackish head is crossed posteriorly by a cream-colored band that also occupies the nape; behind this pale collar is a broad black band, 3 to 5 scales in width, that extends well back onto the neck. There is no loreal scale. The venter is white to yellowish-pink, there are 15 rows of smooth dorsal scales, and the anal plate is divided.

Similar snakes   The **central Florida crowned snake (4)** has a faint or nonexistent light crossband between its crown and neck. Neither the **midland brown snake (9)** nor its relative the **Florida redbelly snake (10)** has a dark band behind its pale nape. Both brown and redbelly snakes have keeled dorsal scales while the Florida redbelly snake has a salmon pink to red to blue-black venter.

Behavior   Named *T. coronata* for its black-crowned head (to facilitate burrowing, the crowned snake's skull is no wider than its neck and is flattened from above and below into a penetrating wedge). This enables it to vanish in an instant among dense roots, or (as anyone knows who has taken one of these little reptiles inside, only to have it slip out of his fingers) magically disappear down through both the pile and woven backing of floor carpeting, searching for its subterranean home.

---

[2]Both ovaries are functional, with eggs from both sides descending through the solitary right oviduct (the left oviduct terminates just anterior to the cloaca). This places a greater burden on the right oviduct, through which all the eggs must pass, although by containing seminal storage receptacles the vestigial left oviduct contributes to the crowned snakes' crucial long-term storage of sperm. This adaptation is shared only with other small, fossorial serpents, primarily the entirely subterranean blind snakes of the family *Typhlopidae*.

3 Peninsula Crowned Snake

Tantilla relicta relicta

Nonvenomous   This little reptile does not bite larger animals.

Abundance   Perhaps most common of the state's endemic *T. relicta,* the peninsula crowned snake may be the most abundant serpent in Florida's xeric, sandy-soiled upland communities, although *T. r. relicta* is seldom noticed because its small size and cryptic microenvironment beneath vegetative ground cover enable it to escape human attention. It is found from Marion Co. in northern Florida, south to Highlands Co. in central Florida, while disjunct populations occur both on Cedar Key and in Sarasota, Charlotte, and Lee counties on the Gulf Coast.

Size   Adults are 7 to 8.5 inches long; the record is 9.5 inches.

Habitat   Within the xeric interior scrub of central Florida (as well as among a small strip of coastal dunes just north of Tampa), the peninsula crowned snake's sole microhabitat seems to be the thin subsurface layer where fallen vegetative litter meets the sand below. (In the sand pine scrub of the Ocala National Forest, peninsula crowned snakes were most abundant in re-growing burned or clearcut areas, but were also present in mature pine forests.)

Prey   According to C. R. Smith's study of food resource partitioning among fossorial reptiles, approximately 90% of this animal's prey is tenebrionid beetle larvae, with snails and centipedes making up the other 10%.

Reproduction   Egg-laying. Nothing is recorded, but reproduction is probably similar to that of the **southeastern crowned snake (2),** the only one of Florida's three *Tantilla* species for which data exist.

Coloring/scale form   Most individuals have a pale neck ring interrupted by a dark patch of pigment along the spine. To enable it to penetrate soil, *T. r. relicta* has evolved a pointed rostral scale, beneath which its lower jaw (unlike that of most snakes) is recessed within the overlap of its upper snout. One basal hook occurs on each hemipenis, the dorsal scales are smooth, arranged in 15 midbody rows, and the anal plate is divided.

Similar snakes   The **central Florida crowned snake (4)** has a black head and neck with a very dim nuchal crossband. The **Florida brown snake (8)** has a speckled dorsum and keeled scales, and the **southern ringneck snake (14)** has a black dorsum and a black-spotted, orange-to-red venter.

Behavior   Adept at prying its way through the tiniest soil crevice with its hard, flattened snout, *Tantilla relicta* has been observed burrowing or sand-swimming through loose grains of siliceous soil just below the surface.

Central Florida Crowned Snake

Tantilla relicta neilli

Nonvenomous   Rarely seen or photographed, the extremely secretive little central Florida crowned snake is unlikely to ever encounter a human being, much less bite one.

Abundance   Common. First described by Telford in 1966 and named for Florida herpetologist W. T. Neill, *T. r. neilli* occurs from Madison Co. south to Hillsborough and Polk counties in the central part of the state.

Size   *Tantilla relicta* is the tiniest of the state's three *Tantilla* species (themselves Florida's smallest native serpents): adults are no more than 7 to 9 inches in length.

Habitat   The Central Florida crowned snake's primary habitat is the well-drained sandhills of the state's north-central uplands, with most of the few individuals that have been found turning up on the eastern side of this region. Here, its microenvironment is relatively specific. According to state biologist Kevin Enge, "Central Florida crowned snakes apparently prefer areas with at least partial shade and a thin to moderate layer of leaves or pine needles in sandhills and xeric and mesic hammocks. Crowned snakes have also been found in pocket gopher and gopher tortoise mounds . . ."

Prey   See Peninsula Crowned Snake (3).

Reproduction   Egg-laying. See **Southeastern Crowned Snake (2)**.

Coloring/scale form   This glossy little brown snake has a mostly black head and neck whose pigment extends 3 to 8 scale rows behind its parietal plates. The only other marking is a pale blotch below the eye that shades into a light-hued lateral area on the neck; the venter is yellowish-white. There is no loreal scale, one basal hook occurs on each hemipenis, and the lower jaw is slightly less inset within the upper than is the case with Florida's other races of *T. relicta*. The 15 midbody rows of dorsal scales are smooth and the anal plate is divided.

Similar snakes   The **peninsula crowned snake (3)** has an interrupted, light-hued crossband between its head and neck.

Behavior   Behler and King report that when *T. relicta* occupies the mounds of sandy dirt piled around the mouths of pocket gopher burrows it sometimes basks beneath a layer of sun-warmed sand, extending only its head above the surface.

Small Burrowing Snakes

5 Coastal Dunes Crowned Snake
Tantilla relicta pamlica

Nonvenomous   Like other crowned snakes, *T. r. pamlica* is harmless.

Abundance   Rare.

Size   Adults are tiny: no more than 7 to 8.5 inches in length.

Habitat   A littoral reptile that makes its home in the east coast's grassy barrier dunes from northern Brevard Co. south to Palm Beach Co., *T. r. pamlica* is also reported from hardwood hammocks and pinelands.

Prey   Unknown in the wild, but like other races of *T. relicta,* the coastal dunes race probably preys on subterranean insects and their larvae. One study found that among the subspecies peninsula crowned snake, 90% of prey animals were tenebrionid beetle larvae, with snails and centipedes making up the other 10%. Arachnids, cut- and wireworms, and small vertebrates such as ground skinks, newborn snakes, and tiny frogs are found in the peninsula crowned snake's microhabitat and constitute the prey of other small, partially fossorial serpents, but it is not known if *T. relicta* feeds upon these animals.

Reproduction   Unknown, but probably much like that of the **southeastern crowned snake (2)** (the only member of Florida's three *Tantilla* species for which reproductive data are recorded).

Coloring/scale form   The shiny brown body—more reddish than that of other Florida *Tantilla*—is separated from the dark crown by a pale band across the rear of the skull followed by a broad black nuchal collar, 3 or 4 scale rows in width. The coastal dunes subspecies has more white on its head than other crowned snakes, with both a pale snout and labial scales; the venter is yellowish- to pinkish-white. Consistent with the coastal dunes crowned snake's sand-burrowing lifestyle, the grit it crawls through is excluded by its lower jaw being sunk well within the downturned overlap of its upper snout. There is no loreal scale, one basal hook occurs on each hemipenis, the smooth dorsal scales are arranged in 15 midbody rows, and the anal plate is divided.

Similar snakes   The **rim rock crowned snake (6)** has less light cephalic pigment than *T. r. pamlica*. It may have an interrupted pale collar, and male rim rock crowned snakes possess two basal hooks on each hemipenis. The **Florida brown snake (8)** has a speckled, grayish-brown dorsum and keeled scales. The young of **southern ringneck (14)** and **earth snakes (11,12)** appear similar to crowned snakes due to their more or less solid-colored dorsums and dim neck rings, but juvenile ringnecks are dark gray above and have black-speckled yellow to red venters, while both species of earth snakes lack a sharp delineation between their dark crowns and paler backs.

Behavior   Florida's *Tantilla* are the northeasternmost branch of a family of predominantly tropical serpents that range southward into western South America, for all three of the state's *Tantilla* species are former members of an ancient xeric-adapted fauna that once occupied a dry corridor that joined the desert Southwest to the Florida peninsula. After this community was split by the cooler, wetter Gulf Coast climate brought about by the northern advance of late Pleistocene glaciers, the crowned snakes survived as relict populations—the source of the coastal dunes crowned snake's species name, *relicta*—in Florida's central sandhills and coastal dunes.

Temperature and soil moisture are the major factors determining the presence of *T. relicta* at the surface. Dry summer heat induces a period of aestivation, while low winter temperatures often force these animals to withdraw several feet into the ground; warm midwinter spells usually bring crowned snakes to the surface again. The remarkable slenderness that allows crowned snakes to exist in their constricted subterranean environment has been achieved by evolving miniaturized skulls, teeth, and eyes, as well as by foregoing an active left oviduct—an adaptation this genus shares only with the even more thoroughly fossorial blind snakes of the family *Typhlopidae*.

Crowned snakes typically fare poorly in captivity, in part because their diminutive bodies, which are adapted to the more constant temperature of their subterranean microhabitat, have little resistance to the rapid fluctuations typical of atmospheric temperature. Unless captive *Tantilla* are given soil in which to burrow they will often die quickly from either overheating or chilling. In a natural terrarium matrix of sandy soil and vegetative litter these shy little burrowers will survive if given beetle and termite larvae, small brown centipedes, and small slugs as prey, but they invariably remain hidden from view.

Small Burrowing Snakes

6 Rim Rock Crowned Snake

Tantilla oolitica

Nonvenomous   Florida's crowned snakes do not bite humans.

Abundance   Extremely rare. Legally protected by the state of Florida, *T. oolitica* is one of the least known snakes in North America. Less than 10 individuals of this endemic species have been found, most associated with the low pine ridge called the Miami rim rock formation that parallels the tip of the state's southeastern coast. *T. oolitica* has also been found on Grassy Key and Upper Matecumbe Key, and a lone individual is reported from Key West. Because this limited range includes some of the nation's most valuable real estate, it has become a virtual ground zero for non-mobile wildlife. According to the U.S. Department of Fish and Wildlife, more than 99% of Dade County's natural upland areas have been destroyed, but the designation of upper Key Largo as federal and state refuges and parkland may provide *T. oolitica* a vestigial habitat.

Size   Adults are 6 to 9 inches; the record is 11.5 inches.

Habitat   Even before commercial development spread over its habitat of hardwood hammocks and pine rocklands (the type specimen is from a long-vanished Miami vacant lot), the rim rock crowned snake was probably a rare animal that seldom emerged from crevices within the porous oolitic limestone, overlain with a thin layer of pine needles, which makes up the subterranean rock formation for which *T. oolitica* is named.

Prey   Presumably, like other crowned snakes, tenebrionid beetle and termite larvae, snails, centipedes, spiders, and smaller snakes.

Reproduction   Probably similar to that of other crowned snakes.

Coloring/scale form   The dorsum is tan, with a creamy venter, a light-hued snout, and a blackish head and neck whose pigment extends below the rear corner of the mouth. There is no loreal scale, two basal hooks occur on each hemipenis, and the 15 midbody rows of dorsal scales are smooth. The anal plate is divided.

Similar snakes   The **coastal dunes crowned snake (5)** has a light-hued band between its head and neck, white pigment on its head, and only one basal hook on each hemipenis.

Behavior   Presumably much like that of other species of *Tantilla*.

Marsh Brown Snake

Storeria dekayi limnetes

Nonvenomous   The marsh brown snake does not bite humans.

Abundance   *Storeria dekayi limnetes* is an uncommon inhabitant of the northwestern Gulf Coast's marshy estuarine grasslands, where its range barely extends into the tip of the Florida panhandle.

Size   Adult size is 9 to 13 inches; the record is 16 inches.

Habitat   Marsh brown snakes live in the grass hummocks of wet, coastal prairie communities. They are also littoral reptiles, however, found among the high-tide flotsam of the Gulf's coastal islands; the type specimen from which this subspecies' description is drawn was collected under driftwood.

Prey   Mostly earthworms although, like other *Storeria dekayi,* slugs, arthropods, small salamanders, tiny fish, and newly metamorphosed frogs are also eaten.

Reproduction   Nothing is recorded, but reproduction is probably similar to that of other *S. dekayi,* with placental nourishment occurring during the latter stages of fetal development.

Coloring/scale form   Sometimes called DeKay's snakes, the marsh brown, midland brown, and Florida brown snakes were named by J. E. Holbrook in honor of 19th century naturalist James Ellsworth DeKay. The subspecies designation *limnetes* refers to the slim horizontal bar marking the temporal and postocular scales. The faintly dark-speckled back is brown, usually marked with a paler vertebral stripe; the dorsal scales are keeled and occur in 15 to 17 midbody rows, and the anal plate is divided.

Similar snakes   Its horizontally-lined temporal scale and unmarked upper and lower labial scales differentiate this race from its more inland subspecies, the **midland brown snake (9)**. Similarly pale-collared as newborns, **southern ringneck snakes (14)** have solid dark gray backs and black-spotted yellow to reddish-orange venters.

Behavior   Related to both garter and water snakes, *Storeria* exhibits the same defensive behavior as these larger reptiles. When disturbed, it musks from anal glands located within the cloaca, and despite its diminutive size, flattens its body and rolls over, mouth agape as if injured. Although not popular as captive animals, brown snakes thrive in terrariums—where they are almost never seen—living as long as 7 years.

Small Burrowing Snakes

8 Florida Brown Snake

Storeria dekayi victa

Nonvenomous   This little reptile does not bite human beings.

Abundance   The Florida brown snake is common throughout most of the state, although the population living in the lower Keys is considered to be threatened. Presently, *S. d. victa* is also under consideration for full-species status.

Size   Most adults measure 7 to 10 inches. In Florida *S. d. victa* probably does not get larger than 13 inches.

Habitat   Florida brown snakes are burrowers partial to the moist conditions often found beneath decaying logs and other woodland debris. Macrohabitat includes riparian bottomland, open deciduous woodland, and overgrown pastures, but not true swampland. Like most small burrowing snakes, *Storeria dekayi* is rare in the open sawgrass marshes of often-inundated areas like the Everglades, but it is common in the slightly elevated hardwood hammocks and pinelands than intersperse these wetlands.

Prey   Small terrestrial serpents such as brown, earth, and ringneck snakes are drawn to the planks and sheets of corrugated iron that litter abandoned rural outbuildings, for these sheltering planes provide optimal habitat for slugs and earthworms—the principal prey of *Storeria*—as well as for the arthropods, annelids, and larval insects that constitute their secondary prey.

Reproduction   Live-bearing. Most births occur from July to September, with litters consisting of 8 or 9 young, 3.5 to 4.5 inches in length, with unmarked gray-brown dorsums and a pale collar.

Coloring/scale form   Faintly speckled cinnamon to blue-gray above, Florida brown snakes have an indistinct light-colored vertebral stripe bordered by a row of dark spots or smudges. A wide pale band crosses the rear of the head, followed by a darker band across the nape. Directly below the eye is a pronounced brown spot. The tan or pinkish venter is unmarked except for black dots along its outer edges. There are 15 midbody rows of strongly keeled dorsal scales, no loreal scale, and a divided anal plate.

Similar snakes   The subspecies **midland brown snake (9)** has 17 midbody rows of dorsal scales, while the paired dark spots flanking its vertebral stripe are sometimes linked by dark pigment across the spine. **Florida redbelly snakes (10)** are orange-brown above with a pale collar across the nape instead of the rear of the skull, a light spot on the upper labials, and a red venter.

Behavior   See **Midland Brown Snake (9)**.

9 Midland Brown Snake

Storeria dekayi wrightorum

Nonvenomous This is a tiny and entirely harmless snake which, if confronted, may bravely pull its neck into the same threatening, pre-strike S-curve as larger serpents. When grasped, it often squirms about, smearing the contents of its cloaca over the source of its distress.

Abundance Well-studied over most of its broad eastern distribution (where *S. d. wrightorum* is often a suburban, backyard snake), within its restricted Florida range the midland brown snake's habits are not well documented. According to R. H. Mount, it is numerous in the Alabama highlands just to the north of Florida's coastal plain, but it is far less common from Jackson to Taylor counties in the eastern panhandle. This area has recently been overrun by two species of South American fire ants—voracious predators on small terrestrial herpetofauna—whose infestations constitute a threat to entire populations of little fossorial snakes, including *Storeria*.

Size Although most Florida specimens are much smaller, measuring 7 to 9 inches in length, the record midland brown snake is 20.75 inches.

Habitat A resident of damp fields and open woodlands, this secretive little snake is associated with moist microhabitats. Yet, though it is often found along the edges of ponds, marshes, and canals, it does not inhabit truly wet areas, and is, instead, found on higher ground beneath both natural and manmade debris—fallen logs (especially pines), newspapers, tarpaper, and discarded lumber.

Prey The primary prey of *Storeria dekayi* is slugs, but earthworms are a secondary food source. Arthropods, salamanders, tiny fish, and newly metamorphosed frogs are also occasionally taken.

Reproduction Live-bearing. Breeding takes place both spring and fall, with spermatozoa from autumn pairings being retained in the female's oviducts until her late spring ovulation. Born in mid- to late summer, most litters vary between 5 and 20, although one Alabama female observed by G. Folkerts deposited 31 young. F. W. King notes that large litters such as this would be likely to consist of smaller neonates (often no more than 3 inches in length) than average-sized litters, for among *Storeria dekayi* there appears to be a "clear trade-off between offspring number and offspring size." Not only large litters but those born earlier in the year have been found to contain slightly smaller-sized young. This disparity is probably due to brown snakes' evolutionary position as a lecithotrophic species in which the embryo's egg yolk provides the primary source of its nutrition, although during the later stages of pregnancy the placenta delivers a share of developmental nutrients. Brown snake litters born later in the year thus benefit from the more generous placental nourishment available from females that have had more foraging time to build their reserves of body fat.

Coloring/scale form   First described by H. Trapido in 1944, the midland brown snake is similar in coloration to other *S. dekayi,* varying from tan through light brown to olive or reddish-brown above. A dorsolateral row of darker spots is present, and though most descriptions stipulate that these dark spots are connected by dark lines across the spine, this is not always the case: in actuality the various races of brown snakes are difficult to identify and their differentiating characteristics may overlap.

Among *S. d. wrightorum,* the crown of the head is less narrow than that of other small serpents found in woodland leaf litter, and is normally darker than the body. A light vertebral line may be present between the sometimes-linked dark dorsolateral spots, and the venter is cream to pinkish-white. A dark subocular blotch on the pale cheeks makes the eye appear quite large, while larger dark temporal and nuchal spots are the midland brown snake's most distinctive marking. The scales are keeled (although it may take a hand lens to ascertain this), and arranged in 17 midbody dorsal rows. The anal plate is divided.

Similar snakes   The **Florida redbelly snake (10)** has a *pale* spot beneath its eye, 15 midbody dorsal scale rows, and a red to black venter. **Pine woods snakes (13)** have smooth scales and a white-bordered black line through the eye. The **southeastern crowned snake (2)** has smooth scales, a narrow black head, and a whitish collar. **Earth snakes (11, 12)** have unmarked backs, narrow heads without a dark subocular blotch, and a horizontal loreal scale.

Behavior   Because midland brown snakes find favorable conditions in the soft soil of well-watered suburban yards, they are sometimes found beneath leaf litter while gardening. During cool, damp weather they may move about in the open, even in daylight, but in the hottest months brown snakes are nocturnal.

Florida Redbelly Snake

Storeria occipitomaculata obscura

Nonvenomous   This shy little animal does not bite humans.

Abundance   Uncommon. Throughout much of the southeastern U.S. *S. occipitomaculata* is common in damp woodland, but in Florida the subspecies *S. o. obscura* is far less abundant.

Size   Adults are 8 to 10 inches, reaching a maximum of 16 inches.

Habitat   In northern peninsular Florida and the panhandle *S. o. obscura* occurs sporadically in moist, heavily-vegetated hardwood forest; it is less often found in upland and flatwood pine forest, bottomland forest, and wet prairie hammocks. Microhabitat includes leaf litter and the underside of decaying logs.

Prey   Slugs and snails are this reptile's primary prey, but earthworms are also taken. As the soil dries during summer, both mollusks and annelids are followed deeper into the earth along a soil-moisture gradient.

Reproduction   Live-bearing. Small serpents are so short-lived that they must reproduce rapidly. Litters of *S. o. obscura* total up to 23—a large brood for such a small snake—with the 2.5- to 4-inch-long young being born between April and August. Of 61 marked specimens, only 4 were recaptured, an unusually low percentage for such a sedentary reptile. This suggests a rapid population turnover—in response to which the largest females invest proportionately more of their available energy in reproduction than smaller females, allocating their resources to larger litters rather than to larger offspring.

Coloring/scale form   The three big pale spots behind the head often form a light-hued collar, while a double row of dark flecks runs along both sides of the speckled back which, in Florida, is usually cinnamon or blue-gray. A prominent white spot, bordered by black, is visible beneath the eye, and the venter is red. Grayer than adults and lacking dorsal spots, neonates are marked with a pale band across the nape. There are 15 midbody rows of keeled dorsal scales, no loreal (a postnasal scale touches the preocular), and the anal plate is divided.

Similar snakes   Florida and **midland brown snakes (8, 9)** have a *dark* subocular spot, pale cheeks, bellies, and 17 midbody scale rows.

Behavior   Unable to defend itself, *S. o. obscura* employs a death-feigning display: After rolling over, mouth agape, it may flatten its body in several places as though partially crushed.

Small Burrowing Snakes

11 Rough Earth Snake
Virginia striatula

Nonvenomous   This little snake is not big enough to bite humans.

Abundance   Rough earth snakes are common in both the western panhandle and northern Florida.

Size   *V. striatula* may reach 12.5 inches in length, but is no thicker in diameter than a pencil.

Habitat   Macrohabitat is primarily wet pine flatwoods, where rough earth snakes are largely fossorial, generally emerging onto the surface only when the soil is moist from recent rains. Microhabitat is the semi-subterranean world found beneath fallen leaves, pine needles, and the rusting roofing metal that litters abandoned farms.

Prey   The stomachs of 45 *V. striatula* contained only earthworms.

Reproduction   Live-bearing. According to J. K. Stewart "*Virginia striatula* represents a stage in . . . evolution in which placental nourishment supplements yolk nutrition (with a consequent) enhancement of newborn quality." Sixteen litters ranged in number from 3 to 8 young, measuring 3 to 4.5 inches in length.

Coloring/scale form   Rough earth snakes are unmarked grayish brown above (newborns have a pale collar) with slightly darker pigmentation around the eyes and on the upper labial scales; the belly is creamy white. There are 17 midbody rows of dorsal scales—several of the vertebral rows are lightly keeled, which gives them the slightly "rough" texture of the common name. A horizontally-elongate loreal touches the front of the eye, there are 2 small postocular scales, typically 5 upper labials, and usually a divided anal plate.

Similar snakes   Most similar is the **eastern earth snake (12),** which has a more brownish back and rusty lower sides, 6 upper labial scales, and entirely smooth dorsal scales. **Southeastern** and **central Florida crowned snakes (2, 4)** have tan dorsums, dark-crowned heads with no loreal scale, a single postocular, and smooth dorsal scales.

Behavior   The rough earth snake's lightly-shielded head is less effective in rooting through rocky ground than the hooked or armored rostral scutes of larger burrowing serpents, but its pointed snout allows it to penetrate the moist loam where its annelid prey is most plentiful. This substrate is typical of residential lawns where, because there are few natural predators, *V. striatula* is often seen by gardeners. These little reptiles tend to be shallow burrowers, so that even a few warm midwinter days bring them to the surface.

¹² Eastern Earth Snake

Virginia valeria valeria

Nonvenomous   Eastern earth snakes are too small to bite humans.

Abundance   Rare. *Virginia v. valeria* is only occasionally found in peninsular Florida: 4 specimens have come from scrub habitat in the Lake Wales Ridge area, but aside from that disjunct population, according to Paul E. Moler of the Florida Wildlife Research Laboratory, there are only 5 records south of the Suwannee River. In the northern part of the state this snake is more abundant, and is occasionally found in the Tallahassee area by homeowners raking leaves. Elsewhere in the panhandle these little snakes have been captured during drift-fence surveys of upland hardwood forest, sandhills, and pine flatwoods.

Size   Adults measure 7 to 13 inches in length.

Habitat   Primarily pine woodland, although this species also occurs in scrub habitat in the Lake Placid area of Highlands County. Microhabitat is most often the damp soil beneath tree litter as well as the underside of logs and abandoned debris.

Prey   Eastern earth snakes feed mainly on earthworms, but small snails and insects also sometimes constitute prey.

Reproduction   Live-bearing. One 11.5-inch-long female *V. valeria* deposited seven 4-inch-long charcoal-gray neonates on August 20.

Coloring/scale form   The dorsum is unmarked rusty-brown, more reddish laterally, while the venter is white, sometimes with a yellowish wash. The either 15 or 17 midbody rows of dorsal scales are generally smooth, although faint keels may appear along the posterior spine, and hairline seams that resemble keels mark the centers of adjacent scales. The forward edge of the eye is touched by a horizontally-lengthened loreal scale, there is a pair of small postoculars, 6 supralabial scales, and the anal plate is divided.

Similar snakes   The **rough earth snake (11)** is grayer, without a russet lateral cast. It has 5 supralabials and several vertebral rows of lightly-keeled dorsal scales. **Southeastern** and **peninsula crowned snakes (2, 3)** have chocolate-capped heads, pinkish bellies, no loreal scale, a single postocular, and 15 midbody rows of entirely smooth dorsal scales.

Behavior   Eastern earth snakes are burrowers, appearing at the surface only when conditions are optimal. During hot weather the lack of moisture in surface soil brings about subterreanen aestivation, and in Florida *V. v. valeria* is more likely to emerge onto the surface during the cooler months.

Small Burrowing Snakes

13 Pine Woods Snake
Rhadinaea flavilata

Nonvenomous   Technically, weakly venomous. Pine woods snakes are entirely harmless to humans, however, and virtually never bite when picked up, although *Rhadinaea flavilata* has, on a very miniature scale, progressively longer posterior teeth.[1] The most rearward pair of these is separated from the anterior dentition to allow the teeth to puncture the minuscule lizards, frogs, and salamanders on which pine woods snakes feed. This introduces a few droplets of the salivary toxins produced in the well-developed Duvernoy's glands. Although these toxins eventually render prey sufficiently inactive to be swallowed, this saliva is so minimally paralytic that it can take more than two hours to overcome even very small food animals.

Abundance   *Rhadinaea flavilata* is secretive, and generally uncommon. In an unusual distribution pattern, it seems to occupy two disjunct areas. The much larger range encompasses peninsular Florida (including the Gulf barrier islands) from Lake Okeechobee northward past the Georgia state line. A smaller range occurs in the north-central panhandle. Only a handful of pine woods snakes have been found there, however: one collected in Okaloosa Co. by J. T. Collins and a couple in Gulf Co. by K. Enge of the Florida Game and Fresh Water Fish Commission.

A great deal of seemingly ideal habitat occurs between these widely separated areas, and both Enge and R. D. Bartlett attribute this apparent distributional hiatus to a lack of herpetological scrutiny. Few drift-fence studies have been done in the western panhandle and the only people really looking for snakes there are commercial collectors with no interest in small woodland serpents devoid of market value.

Size   Most specimens found are between 10 and 12 inches in length; the record is 15.75 inches.

Habitat   As its name would indicate, pine woods snakes' principal environment is the heavily shaded, damp ground litter of lowland pine flatwoods, where its favored microhabitat is rotting pine logs and the shelter found beneath loosened pine bark. Unless periodically burned, these pinelands follow normal vegetational succession, eventually becoming brushily-understoried deciduous forest uninhabitable by *R. flavilata*. Slash and longleaf pine woodland are also occupied, and *R. flavilata* is even rarely seen in the wetter parts of mixed hardwood hammocks and in scrub.

---

[1]The teeth of most non-venomous snakes are all approximately the same size, but both *Diadophis* and *Rhadinaea flavilata* are members of the mostly neo-tropical subfamily *Xenodontinae*, which means uneven-toothed; other members of this subfamily are the hognose snakes of the genus *Heterodon*, meaning "different-toothed," which also have uneven tooth lengths.

Prey   Pine woods snakes feed on salamanders, small frogs (especially hylids), small lizards (especially ground skinks), and possibly small snakes, often, but not invariably, immobilized by its weak venom before being swallowed. The pine woods snake's salivary toxins are no defense against the ophiophagus eastern and scarlet kingsnakes, though, which frequent the same rotting pine stumps as *R. flavilata,* feeding on it along with other small serpents.

Reproduction   Egg-laying. No natural nests are known, but this species reportedly produces 2- to 4-inch-long eggs between May and August; very few of the 5-inch-long hatchlings have been observed.

Coloring/scale form   This satiny little reptile's yellowish- to reddish-brown dorsum has a polished appearance. The lower sides are considerably lighter, and on some individuals the upper back darkens into a blackish vertebral stripe. The crown is also darker than the back, while the distinct black eyestripe, which broadens behind the eye, is thinly bordered above by a pale yellow or white line and below by the prominent yellowish-white labial scales—scales from which this animal's other common name, "yellow-lipped snake," is drawn.

The venter is unmarked whitish-yellow or yellow-green. Like that of the related mud and rainbow snakes, the tailtip ends in a small spine, thought perhaps to aid in burrowing through soft soil. The 17 midbody rows of dorsal scales are smooth and lack apical pits. The anal plate is divided.

Similar snakes   Numerous other small, brownish woodland snakes occur within the range of the pine woods snake, but neither the **brown** or **redbelly snakes (7—10)**, the **earth snakes (11, 12)**, nor the **crowned snakes (2—5)**, have a dark eye-stripe bordered above with a pale line and below with yellowish labial scales.

Behavior   *R. flavilata* is most active at the surface during its March to early May breeding season; at other times, after warm rain or during temporary flooding it may briefly emerge from below ground, but only as far as the underside of natural debris like decomposing logs or moisture-retaining human detritus like newspaper, plastic, boards, and tin. Like most small serpents, pine woods snakes are not long-lived: just over 3 years is the longest recorded captive lifespan.

Small Burrowing Snakes

14 Southern Ringneck Snake

Diadophis punctatus punctatus

Nonvenomous Ringneck snakes are members of the uneven-toothed subfamily *Xenodontinae,* and both Florida's races of *Diadophis* have minuscule, but slightly longer, posterior teeth. Their salivary glands secrete enzymes that slowly immobilize their tiny prey, but ringnecks are not dangerous and almost never bite when handled, although an occasional individual may nip with determination.

Abundance The southern ringneck is common throughout Florida and the upper Keys. Several individuals may share the lower layers of a rotting log or live beneath the same piece of discarded roofing material. Currently, however, these microhabitats are becoming infested with South American fire ants—exotic predators that threaten to extirpate much of the state's small herpetofauna.

Size Adults average 6 inches, with a maximum size of 10 inches.

Habitat *Diadophis punctatus punctatus* is abundant in damp meadows and woodlands, but it is not a wetland animal and is rare in swamps. Hardwood hammocks, pinelands, melaleuca stands, and residential areas are also occupied: individuals are sometimes found in swimming pools.

Prey Ringnecks take mainly earthworms and slugs as prey, as well as small vertebrates. Ground skinks and other terrestrial lizards, salamanders, newborn snakes, and tiny frogs are located by scent beneath woodland ground cover, then pinned down with a body coil.

Reproduction Egg-laying; 2 to 8 elongate, 0.75-inch-long eggs are laid during the summer in moist soil or within rotting logs, sometimes in a communal nest site used by several females. The 3- to 4-inch-long young can emerge in as little as 5 weeks.

Coloring/scale form The ringneck's gray-black dorsum is punctuated by a yellow nuchal ring; darker pigment occurs on its crown and supralabials. The golden venter, which is marked with a double row of tiny black spots, usually becomes orange-red under the tail. The 15 (sometimes 17) forebody rows of dorsal scales are smooth, a loreal scale is present, and the anal plate is divided.

Similar snakes The **Key ringneck snake (15)** lacks a distinct neck ring; **brown** and **redbelly (7, 8, 9, 10) snakes** have keeled scales.

Behavior Like other *Diadophis,* the southern ringneck employs a defensive combination of color and posture that includes hiding its head under a body coil, twisting its tail over to expose its bright orange-red underside, and voiding musk and feces.

15 Key Ringneck Snake

Diadophis punctatus acricus

Nonvenomous   *Diadophis punctatus* is tiny and does not bite humans.

Abundance   Rare. Legally protected by the state of Florida, *D. p. acricus* is threatened, like many of the state's other small island-living animals, by human encroachment into its range. Small serpents are often able to adapt to residential areas, but the Keys are now so thoroughly developed that on most of the islands the Key ringneck has lost most of its limited natural environment.

Size   The few observed adults have been about 6 inches in length.

Habitat   The primary habitat is the sparse hardwood hammocks and pinelands of the lower Keys, particularly Big Pine and the Torch Keys.

Prey   Herpetologist John Decker, who has thoroughly studied these reptiles in the wild, found the Key ringneck's favored prey to be the tiny Cuban greenhouse frogs now established on the Keys. Other small frogs and their tadpoles (taken from rain-filled limestone solution depressions), earthworms, anoles, and geckos are also prey species.

Reproduction   Egg-laying. A single clutch of 3 minuscule white eggs has been reported. After incubation in moistened vermiculite the eggs hatched into very small newborns (which were fed mouse tails) and after a few weeks were released. Perhaps due to the pale limestone substrate on which *D. p. acricus* lives, several very light-hued individuals are known from even the few recorded Key ringnecks, and one of these newborns was mostly off-white.

Coloring/scale form   The Key ringneck's dorsum is slate gray, with slightly darker pigment occurring on its crown and labial scales; the yellow collar of the mainland and upper Keys-living southern ringneck snake is absent or indistinct. The venter is yellow, shading to orange-red beneath the tail. There are 15 forebody rows of smooth dorsal scales and the anal plate is divided.

Similar snakes   The **southern ringneck snake (14)** has a darker back, a bright yellow neck ring, and darker pigment on its supralabial scales; the **midland brown snake (9)** has keeled dorsal scales.

Behavior   Like other ringnecks, *D. p. acricus* is a burrower found under leaf litter and rocks. Yet in many places the small, low-lying offshore keys where this snake is endemic are devoid of ground cover. Here, Decker reports that *D. p. acricus* lives in a largely saline, mangrove, and bare limestone habitat.

Small Burrowing Snakes

Eastern Garter Snake

Thamnophis sirtalis sirtalis

Nonvenomous   Wild-caught individuals may emit musk, flatten their necks and feign strikes, sometimes bumping one's hands with their snouts, but the few that choose to bite can hang on tenaciously.

Abundance   Eastern garter snakes are abundant throughout Florida, often occurring along heavily-vegetated waterways such as canals through wet prairie and marshlands.

Size   Average adult length is 20 to 28 inches, although the largest recorded eastern garter snake measured 49 inches.

Habitat   Primarily open or semi-open lowland including marl prairie, canal and stream banks, ditches containing water, and Everglades swale. Pinelands, hardwood hammocks, bottomland forest and stands of cypress and melaleuca are also inhabited.

Prey   *Thamnophis sirtalis sirtalis* will prey on almost any smaller creature, but most of its diet consists of aquatic or semi-aquatic life: small fish, frogs, and salamanders. Terrestrial food animals such as toads and earthworms are sought by scent and seized with the aid of sight, but aquatic prey is often taken without using either of these senses. For example, eastern garter snakes often move along the margins of shallow ponds, periodically thrusting their foreparts below the dark surface, then wagging their open mouths from side to side randomly groping for fish or tadpoles.

Reproduction   Live-bearing. Most eastern garter snake litters are born during May, June, and July,[1] and number from 6 to nearly 60 offspring. This great range in litter size closely reflects the size of the mother, with large females giving birth to many more young.[2]

Coloring/scale form   Garter snakes are named for men's old striped leg garters, and although *T. s. sirtalis* is somewhat variable in both color and pattern (individuals found along the panhandle's Gulf Coast sometimes have red markings amid the dark pigment separating their straw-colored ver-

[1]At this time of year reptile dealers sell hundreds of baby garter snakes obtained from wild-caught gravid females they have held in confinement in anticipation of their approaching parturition.

[2]Among garter snakes, the size of each individual offspring is mainly determined by the minimal size it needs to survive. All *T. s. sirtalis* newborns are therefore between 5 and 9 inches in length, the only size discrepancy being that females tend to have slightly larger heads. The eastern garter snake's embryological position midway between lecithotrophic species (in which the embryo's egg yolk provides most of its nutrition) and predominantly placentotrophic species (in which the placenta is the major source of developmental nutrients) places these reptiles at an evolutionary turning point where both placental fetal nourishment and the more primitive method of feeding the fetus with its own egg yolk exist simultaneously.

Garter and Ribbon Snakes

tebral and lateral stripes), a distinct light brown to yellowish-green vertebral stripe is always evident. A similarly-colored lateral stripe occupies the 2nd and 3rd scale rows above the pale venter. The 19 midbody rows of dorsal scales are keeled; the anal plate is undivided.

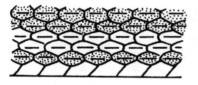

Lateral stripe marking: Garter snake

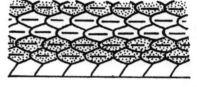

Lateral stripe marking: Ribbon snake

Similar snakes   In a little-understood anomaly of coloration, along Florida's upper Gulf Coast the eastern garter is replaced by the **bluestripe garter snake (17)**, a race distinguished by its blackish-brown dorsum and pale blue lateral stripe. **Ribbon snakes (18—20)** are slimmer, with longer tails and a distinct white spot in front of the eye. Their pale side stripe occupies the 3rd and 4th scale rows above the belly.

Strangely enough, a blue side-striped color morph occurs among ribbon snakes in the same part of the state, with the **peninsula ribbon snake (19)** being replaced by the **bluestripe ribbon snake (20)**. Ribbon snakes are garter snakes' most similar-appearing relatives, and bluestripe garters and bluestripe ribbon snakes look so much alike that distinguishing between them means checking for the white spot in front of the ribbon snake's eye or picking the animal up to check the position of its pale lateral stripe (one row higher in the ribbon snake). Yet, on the basis of the molecular similarities of their body proteins, garter and ribbon snakes are no more closely related to each other than to the much larger and very different-appearing water snakes of the genus *Nerodia*. (Despite the fact that *Nerodia* do not resemble the slender, vertebrally pale-striped garter and ribbon snakes, water snakes are now regarded as a comparatively recent Pliocene aquatic specialization on the part of some members of the much older, terrestrially-generalized Miocene genus, *Thamnophis*.)

Behavior   On land, *T. s. sirtalis* is a deliberate, scent-trail forager. Individual ranges are generally restricted to about 2 acres, with the average activity area measured in one 3-year study being about 600 by 150 feet; the greatest distance traveled by any of the project's subject snakes was less than ⅙ mile. Few snakes reach old age in the wild but, as the most-studied serpent in confinement, a few captive *T. s. sirtalis* have lived for as long as 14 years.

Garter and Ribbon Snakes

69

17 Bluestripe Garter Snake
Thamnophis sirtalis similis

Nonvenomous   Some individuals do no more than flatten the head and body, feign strikes, and emit musk when cornered, but when picked up, other garter snakes may bite sharply.

Abundance   Common along the Gulf Coast from eastern Wakulla Co. in the panhandle to Hernando Co. in central Florida.

Size   Adults are the same size as the eastern garter snake.

Habitat   See **Eastern Garter Snake (16)**.

Prey   Bluestripe garters prey on earthworms, small fish, frogs, and toads.[1] Vision is used for capturing prey, but sight is less important in garter snake predation than scent, and the instinctually-recognized smell of appropriate prey species such as earthworms, anurans, and fish is what elicits predatory attacks.

Reproduction   See **Eastern Garter Snake (16)**.

Coloring/scale form   Except for its pale blue vertebral stripe and uniformly blackish-brown dorsum, *T. s. similis* is identical to the eastern garter snake.

Similar snakes   The similarly-colored **bluestripe ribbon snake (20)** is slimmer, has a distinct white spot in front of its eye and a pale lateral stripe on the 3rd and 4th scale rows above its belly. It also lacks black labial scale sutures. See **Eastern Garter Snake (16)**.

Behavior   Garter snakes are active all day during even the hottest summer months, almost always in some sort of watery habitat such as wet prairie hammocks and tall-grass marshes. Confronted with danger, *T. sirtalis* can partially alter its normally dark appearance by inflating its lungs to spread its ribs, splaying its dorsal scales to reveal previously unseen patches of light-hued skin along its sides that make it look larger and more formidable.

---

[1]All predators incur costs during hunting: search-energy, exposure-to-danger, and difficulty-of-capture costs, with natural selection favoring animals that make the most efficient choices. It seems strange to think of garter snakes (which sometimes forage for tadpoles by groping open-mouthed in muddy ponds or puddles) as making efficient choices. Yet, when *T. s. similis* were presented with different-sized bodies of water containing smaller and larger fish, they actively chose the optimal hunting conditions of larger fish in smaller areas, thereby maximizing their chance of making contact with fast-swimming prey under turbid conditions.

18 Eastern Ribbon Snake

Thamnophis sauritus sauritus

Nonvenomous   Ribbon snakes are gracile, small-headed serpents that do not bite humans unless they are seized, but they can nip firmly.

Abundance   Common in Florida's panhandle.

Size   *Thamnophis sauritus sauritus* averages 20 to 34 inches (as with all *Thamnophis*, females are the larger gender) with a body so slender that adults generally weigh less than 6 oz. The record length is 38 inches.

Habitat   Throughout the eastern ribbon snake's range—4 races occur from the Great Lakes to the Florida Keys—*T. s. sauritus* is found, though seldom far from water, in pinelands, cypress groves, hardwood hammocks (both inland and coastal), prairies, brushy fields, and stands of melaleuca.

Prey   Most often a creature of creek, lake, and pond margins, *T. s. sauritus* typically ranges along marshy shorelines taking whatever small prey—insects, crustaceans, or small vertebrates—it encounters; only when movement on the surface attracts its attention does it make forays into the water. On land, *T. sauritus* uses scent-tracking to locate fossorial food species such as earthworms, as well as to ferret small toads and frogs from beneath grass and leaf litter. Ribbon snakes are able to prey on toads because enlarged adrenal glands allow them to partially neutralize toads' epidermal gland-generated digitaloid toxins—exudate that causes dogs that have bitten a toad to gag and froth at the mouth—which can slow or even stop the heartbeat of other small predators.

Reproduction   Gravid individuals appear as early as April; by July most female *T. s. sauritus* are pregnant.

Coloring/scale form   The extremely slender body and tail are black or dark olive above, with a pale yellow, orange, or greenish-tan vertebral stripe. Two tiny white dashes often punctuate the rear of the dark crown, a prominent, vertical white spot is visible in front of the eye, and the pale upper labial scales are unmarked. A light tan lateral stripe occupies the 3rd and 4th scale rows above the yellowish-green belly. The strongly keeled dorsal scales are arranged in 19 rows at midbody and the anal plate is undivided.

Similar snakes   For similar snakes, see **Bluestripe Ribbon Snake (20).**

Behavior   See **Peninsula** and **Bluestripe Ribbon Snakes (19, 20).**

Garter and Ribbon Snakes

19 Peninsula Ribbon Snake

Thamnophis sauritus sackenii

Nonvenomous   See **Eastern Ribbon Snake (18)**.

Abundance   This snake is common throughout Florida south to the lower Keys (where it is threatened by commercial development). On the mainland, in areas of good habitat, peninsula ribbon snakes can be extremely abundant, but when these areas are disturbed by plowing or clearing for subdivisions, newly exposed *T. sauritus* suffer heavy predation by cattle egrets and other herons.

Size   Adult *T. s. sackenii* are 20 to 28 in.; the record is 40 in.

Habitat   See **Eastern Ribbon Snake (18)**.

Prey   See **Eastern Ribbon Snake (18)**.

Reproduction   Live-bearing. Breeding takes place from April through June. Litters of up to 20 are deposited between July and September.

Coloring/scale form   The dorsum is dark brown to tan, with both a pale vertebral stripe and a pale lateral stripe on the 3rd and 4th scale rows above the yellowish venter. The lips, light lateral stripes, and bellies of individuals living along the lower Gulf Coast have a bluish cast. The 19 midbody rows of dorsal scales are keeled and the anal plate is undivided.

Similar snakes   In a little-understood anomaly of coloration, along Florida's upper Gulf Coast, the peninsula ribbon snake is replaced by the **bluestripe ribbon snake (20)**, a race identical except for its black dorsum and striking blue lateral stripe. (In the same area the eastern garter snake is also replaced by a bluish race.)

Behavior   In most of Florida, *T. s. sackenii* is active year-round, occupying a home territory of several acres—much of which is at least seasonally flooded. Although ribbon snakes forage throughout their territories they seem to prefer canal banks to almost any other microenvironment. Here, these reptiles can be ubiquitous immediately after warm summer rains when frogs and toads are most active, and are easily observed because (although ribbon snakes also forage at dusk and during the night) they are often diurnally active. *T. sauritus* is also fond of basking on bankside elevations such as logs and fallen fence posts, where these animals sometimes remain motionless until approached very closely or even touched, when they streak away across the surface to hide beneath overhanging vegetation further down the bank. During late August and September newborn ribbon snakes can frequently be found sheltering under creekside brush and planks.

20 Bluestripe Ribbon Snake

Thamnophis sauritus nitae

Nonvenomous   Like most *Thamnophis,* a large individual can deliver a sharp nip, but only if picked up roughly.

Abundance   Common from eastern Wakulla Co. in the Panhandle down the Gulf Coast to Hernando Co. in central Florida. (One subspecies of ribbon snake or another is likely to be found near any rural body of fresh water throughout the state.)

Size   Small even for a ribbon snake, most adult *T. s. nitae* measure less than 23 inches in length; the record is less than 30 inches.

Habitat   This coastal plain serpent is seen most frequently in open marshes, prairies, and prairie hammocks; pine flatwoods and bottomland forest are also commonly occupied.

Prey   Ribbon snakes' prey is seasonally variable. During late spring, tadpoles constitute much of the diet; at other times, adult frogs and toads, lizards, and fish are principal food animals.

Reproduction   Live-bearing. Recorded broods range from 5 to 27.

Coloring/scale form   The bluestripe ribbon snake is identical to the subspecies peninsula ribbon snake except for its sooty black dorsum and striking, bright to pale blue lateral stripe.

Similar snakes   Bluestripe garter snakes (17) are slightly heavier-bodied and proportionately shorter-tailed. They lack the paired white spots on the ribbon snakes' posterior crown and the vertical white spot in front of its eye, while their pale lateral stripe is located on the 2nd and 3rd scale rows above the belly. Inland from Florida's upper Gulf Coast the bluestripe ribbon snake is replaced by the **peninsula ribbon snake (19),** whose dorsum is dark brown to tan rather than black, and whose pale lateral stripe is yellow.

Behavior   Young ribbon snakes living in well-vegetated areas are often partially arboreal and given to basking in low branches above water. *T. s. nitae* is preyed upon by larger serpents such as racers, kingsnakes, and coachwhips, as well as by mammals and carnivorous birds. Its conspicuous vertebral stripe may help it evade some predators, however, for in a sort of optical illusion this pale vertebral line, seen through gaps in vegetation, appears to remain static as the snake slides away. So many predators, in fact, manage to grab only ribbon snakes' fragile tailtip—which is easily broken off, thus perhaps satisfying a small carnivore—that it is not unusual to capture otherwise healthy *T. sauritus* that lack complete tails.

Garter and Ribbon Snakes

21 Redbelly Water Snake

Nerodia erythrogaster erythrogaster

Nonvenomous   In self-defense, redbelly water snakes will flatten their necks and bodies and make false strikes. If pressed further they will bite, and large *Nerodia* are strong enough to do so with vigor.

Abundance   Redbelly water snakes are common in portions of both the eastern panhandle and northern peninsular Florida.

Size   Adults are between 28 and 48 inches in length. The record size is 62 inches—almost certainly a female because males do not reach more than three-quarters the length of the largest females, nor attain their thickness of girth.

Habitat   *Nerodia erythrogaster erythrogaster* spends most of its life in and around rivers, lakes, and ponds, most often those occurring in bottomland forest. Cypress swamps are another prime habitat. These aquatic environments are preferred as habitat because they are rich in both food sources and shelter (murky water is a good place to hide), although there is nothing in the biology of water snakes to limit them to a wet environment. If food is available and predators are not present—captives often ignore their pools except just before shedding— these animals are able to thrive far from aquatic habitats. Adults may be found in wet prairies more than a mile from open water, but because juveniles are both less mobile and more vulnerable to predation, they tend to keep to the comparative safety of aquatic environments.

Prey   Most reptiles partition habitat; snakes usually partition prey. The diverse population of sympatric water snake species occupying the same waterways in the southeastern United States tend to partition their food resources, and for both Florida's races of *N. erythrogaster,* their share of aquatic prey consists mostly of fish and frogs.

Reproduction   Live-bearing. Like their relatives the garter snakes, water snakes are characterized by large numbers of offspring. *N. e. erythrogaster* fits this pattern, depositing, after a 3½-month gestation period, litters containing from 11 to over 30 young. These range from 9 to 11.5 inches in length and, after their birth in late summer, the young are often numerous in farm ponds and other shallow bodies of water. Here their mortality to wetland-foraging predators such as raccoons and herons is extremely high.

Coloring/scale form   Redbelly water snakes are stout-bodied, short-tailed serpents with comparatively narrow necks and distinctly-wider heads, which, when flattened in threat, heighten their resemblance to pit vipers. Their back and sides are reddish brown to dark chocolate (some specimens are grayish green laterally). As with other large water snakes, a film of water-deposited sediment and algae often makes the true dorsolateral coloring of these animals difficult to determine. The venter of adults, if not always red is at least bright orange. Juvenile *N. e. erythrogaster* are quite different in appearance: their faintly pinkish ground color is conspicuously patterned over the forebody with dark dorsal bands which break up posteriorly into dark saddles alternating with vertical lateral bars. The belly of juveniles is pale yellow, with dark pigment lining the forward edges of the midbody ventral scutes. The keeled dorsal scales occur in 23 rows at midbody and the anal plate is usually divided.

(In the Florida panhandle *N. e. erythrogaster* intergrades with its olive-backed subspecies, the yellowbelly water snake, *N. e. flavigaster*. Intermediately-colored individuals with pale yellow bellies occur throughout the panhandle, but those more characteristic of the western race prevail to the west of Panama City.)

Similar snakes Water snakes' similar albumin proteins indicate that they are the garter and ribbon snakes' closest relatives,[1] yet water snakes' heavy bodies and dark coloring most often cause them to be mistaken for the **cottonmouth (66, 67)**. Water snakes have rounded heads and circular pupils however, and lack a sunken heat-sensing pit between eye and nostril. Water snakes also swim more vigorously than cottonmouths, their bodies drooping below the surface when they stop (the cottonmouth's entire body is buoyantly suspended on the surface). Cornered water snakes may strike, but they do not gape motionless in threat as the cottonmouth commonly does. Both **Mississippi** and **Florida green water snakes (25, 26)** have a row of subocular scales between the eye and the upper labial scales.

Behavior When restrained, like other reptiles attempting to discourage a predator by making themselves as unappetizing as possible, *N. e. erythrogaster* forcibly discharges the contents of its cloaca. This substance is more than just feces, for its foul smell is amplified by musk discharged from glands located within the cloacal cavity.

During temperate weather, redbelly water snakes are daytime foragers, but during the hottest months they are active mainly in the early morning, evening, and at night.

---

[1]Water snakes of the genus *Nerodia* are now widely regarded as a Pliocene evolutionary departure toward aquatic specialization on the part of some members of the much older, terrestrially-generalized genus, *Thamnophis*.

22 Yellowbelly Water Snake

Nerodia erythrogaster flavigaster

Nonvenomous   Yellowbelly water snakes will bite in self-defense.

Abundance   This subspecies is among the most abundant of aquatic snakes in the western panhandle.

Size   Most adults are 30 to 48 inches in length. The record is just over 59 inches, and because large *N. erythrogaster* are very heavy-bodied, an individual this massive would be almost certain to be misidentified as a cottonmouth.

Habitat   Yellowbelly water snakes are found in most rural wetland environments, more often in wooded than in open areas. See **Redbelly Water Snake (21)**.

Prey   Juvenile *N. e. flavigaster* eat small fish, tadpoles, and aquatic insects; adults feed primarily on fish, frogs, and other amphibians. One instance of predation was noted by Bill Marvell:

> At 2 p.m. on March 16 I was standing beside a roadside ditch, when a 36-inch yellowbelly water snake backed out of the water with a 10-inch lesser siren grasped about mid-body. The snake crawled up the embankment, where it began "walking" its jaws along the siren's body toward the head. The siren attempted to escape by burrowing among the grass roots and by twisting movements that forced the snake to turn on its back. The siren also uttered several shrill distress cries. Although the snake crawled across my boots during this struggle, it did not seem to notice my presence. After it had swallowed the siren it raised its head, flicked its tongue, then crawled back into the ditch and swam away under water. The whole operation took about 45 minutes.

Reproduction   Live-bearing. See **Redbelly Water Snake (21)**.

Coloring/scale form   *Flavi,* which is Latin for "yellow", combined with *gaster,* Greek for "belly," describes this subspecies as the yellow-bellied western race of the eastern redbelly water snake, *N. e. erythrogaster* (*erythro* means "red"). The venter of more easterly individuals—genetically-influenced by the redbelly races of *N. erythrogaster*—is orange, while the dark gray-green back is usually unpatterned, though the sides may have faint vertical bars. The lips are yellow, with dark labial sutures, there are 23 midbody rows of keeled dorsal scales, and the anal plate is usually divided.

Similar snakes   See **Redbelly Water Snake (21)**.

Behavior   See **Redbelly Water Snake (21)**.

23 Banded Water Snake

Nerodia fasciata fasciata

Nonvenomous   If cornered, *N. f. fasciata* may discharge an odorous musk from its cloaca, flatten its forebody, and strike repeatedly in self-defense; but, like other large, dark-bodied water snakes that resemble the cottonmouth, it is harmless to humans unless it is harassed.

Abundance   Common in northwestern Florida, particularly in aquatic environments within wet marl prairie and prairie hammock.

Size   Adult length is 22 to 40 inches; the record is 60 inches.

Habitat   Banded water snakes occur in and around permanent bodies of slow-moving or currentless water—forest-bordered ponds, lakes, and small streams—as well as in wet prairie, hydric hardwood hammocks, and coastal wetlands.

Prey   *Nerodia fasciata fasciata* preys primarily on cold-blooded vertebrates—fish, frogs, toads, salamanders, and crayfish—taken on both diurnal and nocturnal forays. Typically swimming parallel to the shore, banded water snakes seize the frogs that, flushed from bankside resting places, fling themselves into the water directly in their path. At other times, these reptiles may also be seen slowly searching the bottoms of shallow ponds.

Reproduction   Live-bearing. Mating has been reported to occur in April followed, after 70 to 80 days of gestation, by litters of up to 50 young. Only the largest females, however, deliver this many offspring, and most broods are closer in number to the 15 young—all 5 to 7 inches in length and about ⅛ ounce in weight—deposited on July 20 by one 32-inch-long captive female.

Coloring/scale form   The ground color of *N. f. fasciata* can be yellowish- to reddish-gray, while the dark-edged dorsolateral crossbands vary from reddish-brown to black. Juveniles are paler and more boldly patterned with dark crossbands, while very old individuals are often nearly solid dark brown above, with lighter scales on their lower sides. A prominent blackish stripe extends from the eye through the last supralabial scale. The yellow venter is ordinarily marked with squarish brown blotches, but herpetologist W. Lamar reports that some individuals have bright red ventral blotches and even crossbars (See Photo 23B). Arranged in 21 to 25 rows at midbody, the dorsal scales are keeled and the anal plate is divided.

Similar snakes   Water snakes' oval heads and snouts, round pupils, and lack of a sunken heat-sensing pit between eye and nostril set them off from the **cottonmouth (66, 67),** as does their more gradually-tapered tail, whose undersurface bears a double row of scales. The subspecies **Florida water snake (24)** has a dark lateral blotch between each of its dorsal crossbands and dark brown to red posterior borders on its ventral scutes.

Aquatic Snakes

The relationship of the banded water snake to other water snake species is problematical. In 1963, a group of six races, termed *Nerodia fasciata*, was taxonomically separated from the northern water snake complex, *Nerodia sipedon*, by Roger Conant. This was based on both the morphological and habitat disparities he observed between populations of northern water snakes that in the Carolinas inhabited adjacent but distinctly different habitats and seemed not to interbreed. During the 1980s, because of the same evident lack of genetic intermingling between differing groups within this newly split-off population, the banded water snakes were themselves separated to form a new, salt marsh snake species, *N. clarkii*.

Yet, interbreeding has since been reported between banded water snakes and several races of the northern water snake, as well between the banded water snake and the salt marsh snakes. For example, one of the original northern water snake races, the **midland water snake (28)** is an inland, freshwater stream-living snake that has crossbands on the anterior portion of its trunk and lateral bars on its posterior body, while the **Gulf salt marsh snake (29)** is a longitudinally light-and-dark striped serpent that occurs in the Gulf Coast's brackish marshes. Yet, in the western Florida panhandle (where the ranges of both these animals overlap that of the banded water snake) individuals exhibiting various combinations of the laterally dark-barred midland water snake, the longitudinally-striped salt marsh snake, and the entirely dorsolaterally-crossbanded banded water snake are not uncommon.

Whether all three animals are actually: (a) a single species that should never have been divided, or (b) three valid, separate species that live in the same area but yet are closely related enough to sometimes interbreed, is a complex taxonomic issue—an issue that brings into question the basic concept of what constitutes a species.

One explanation for this interbreeding, offered by P. E. Moler, is that this sort of limited interspecies genetic exchange occurs only within ecotonal areas on the periphery of the primary species' range, and because no genetic introgression into the core of either of the parent populations occurs, it is still correct to designate them as separate species.

But if adjacently ranging species regularly hybridize—even if only along the intersecting edges of their respective ranges—what genetic barriers are there to separate, and therefore distinguish, those core species from each other? And if only geographical distance keeps these core populations from interbreeding, what then constitutes a species?

Behavior   On sunny days banded water snakes spend hours basking on partially submerged logs or on overhanging tree limbs (like most water snakes, *N. fasciata* is a good climber), but in wintry weather banded water snakes retire to bankside dens or burrow beneath vegetative debris.

Florida Water Snake

Nerodia fasciata pictiventris

Nonvenomous Florida water snakes will bite only if molested. Because this animal has a stout body that becomes even more heavily proportioned with age (and because individuals often flatten their heads and strike repeatedly in self-defense), large *N. fasciata* are frequently mistaken for the venomous cottonmouth.

Abundance The most common water snake in peninsular Florida, *N. f. pictiventris* is found from the northeastern border of the state to the tip of peninsular Florida. Habitats in which the Florida water snake is most abundant include wet marl prairie and its incorporated hardwood hammocks, cypress swamps, and the sawgrass swale of the Everglades.

Size Most adults measure between 22 and 40 inches. The record length is much larger, however: 62.5 inches.

Habitat Aquatic microhabitats include the margins of lakes, ponds, rivers and streams, as well as within all types of floating vegetation: lily pads, hyacinths, and other aquatic plants. During hunting forays, Florida water snakes are also found in mesic terrestrial prairies, in flooded stands of melaleuca, and even in saline estuarine wetlands.

Prey *Nerodia fasciata* take a variety of aquatic life, including crayfish, salamanders, frogs, and fish.

Reproduction Live-bearing. Following a midwinter breeding season, females from southern Florida give birth as early as late spring to litters of 20 to 30 young (as many as 57 can be carried by very large females), 5 to 9 inches long; by June, baby Florida water snakes are often abundant in bankside vegetation. In the northern part of the state breeding occurs from April to June, with the young being born between July and September.

Coloring/scale form The Florida water snake's grayish cheeks (labial scales) are paler than its dark crown and are marked, behind the eye, with a chocolate-colored stripe that extends posteriorly through the last supralabial scale. Otherwise, this animal's dorsolateral coloring is variable: ground color ranges from tan to dark brown, with reddish-brown to black crossbands and dark intervening lateral blotches. Other individuals may be so heavily pigmented as to appear entirely black. This variant is especially likely to be mistaken for the cottonmouth.

If its back is both variable and nondescript, the Florida water snake's belly is its signature. Named for its painted (*pictum*, in Latin) venter, *N. f. pictiventris* is distinguished by the bold, wavy markings (from red to dark brown to black) that border its yellowish ventral scales. The young have a

Aquatic Snakes

light beige ground color, with distinct dark dorsolateral crossbands. There are 23 to 27 rows of keeled dorsal scales at midbody and the anal plate is generally divided.

Similar snakes Unlike any water snake, the **cottonmouth (66, 67)** has a triangular, slab-sided head, a dark pit midway between its nostril and its vertically-slit pupil, and a single row of scales beneath its tail (water snakes have a double row). The Florida water snake's subspecies **banded water snake (23)** has a more blotched or even checkered venter and lacks lateral blotches between its dorsolateral crossbands; the **Florida green water snake (26)** has a speckled back, possesses subocular scales, and has an unpatterned venter.

Behavior For the most part, *Nerodia* (the present genus for many North American water snakes previously classified as *Natrix*) have not made a radical physical accommodation to aquatic life. Instead, they are able to take advantage of the rich food supply and ubiquitous hiding places provided by murky lakes and rivers primarily by behavioral adaptations. Most important of these is their ability to offset the heat-draining property of water—some 40 percent greater than that of air—by basking on logs and floating aquatic vegetation. Frequently seen draped along tree limbs overhanging water, *N. f. pictiventris* is also encountered crossing roads in the evening, especially following heavy rainstorms that bring out feeding frogs. During the anurans' breeding season, drawn by the annual congregations of frogs and toads that gather to deposit their eggs in ditches and temporary puddles, Florida water snakes may venture a mile or more from their home lakes and rivers.

25 Mississippi Green Water Snake

Nerodia cyclopion

Nonvenomous   The Mississippi green water snake is often confused with the venomous cottonmouth, especially because, as a dark, thick-bodied aquatic serpent, *N. cyclopion* may flatten its head and body, and strike if molested. When handled, many individuals discharge an odorus musk from the cloaca.

Abundance   To the west of its limited northwestern Florida range, where there are only a few records of its occurrence, the Mississippi green water snake is sometimes common in cypress swamps, and it appears sporadically in other aquatic habitats.

Size   Most adults measure between 30 and 45 inches in length; the record is 50 inches.

Habitat   The Mississippi green water snake inhabits inundated wooded land and tree-lined sloughs; unlike the Florida green water snake, which is an open-marsh species, *N. cyclopion* is scarce in the brackish coastal estuaries favored by its more easterly relative, and is common only in cypress swamps.

Prey   R. H. Mount reports that in Alabama "fish appear to be by far the most important food. Amphibians are eaten infrequently."

Reproduction   Live-bearing. Reproduction is much the same as that of the **Florida green water snake (26)**; unlike the adults, the 6- to 8-inch-long newborns (litters average 15 to 25) are distinctly spotted and crossbarred.

Coloring/scale form   The dorsum is dark olive green, both dark- and pale-speckled among younger animals. The definitive characteristic of *N. cyclopion*, however, is the row of small subocular scales that separates the lower half of its eye from the supralabial scales. (See illustration.) The venter

Green Water Snake

Mississippi Green and Florida Green Water Snake: Row of subocular scales

Other Water Snakes

All other water snakes: No row of subocular scales

is also distinctive, with the pale forebelly darkening posteriorly to gray, heavily infused with yellow half moons. The keeled dorsal scales occur in 27 to 29 rows at midbody; the anal plate is divided.

Similar snakes   The **Florida green water snake (26)** has an unpatterned yellow belly except for dark marks and smudges beneath its tail. All of **Florida's other water snakes (21−24, 27−30)** lack subocular scales.

Behavior   Mississippi green water snakes are occasionally seen during the day basking at the water's edge, but this species is a largely nocturnal forager most often observed moving about—both in the water and on shore—by spotlighting after dark.

Sandhills

Pine Flatwoods

A. Tennant

Everglades Swale with Rockland Hardwood Hammock

Scrub with Ground Lichens

R. D. Bartlett

Hydric Hammock

Rockland Hardwood Hammock

85

W. B. Montgomery

Mixed Hardwood Forest

Bottomland Forest

A. Tennant

Tidal Marsh

Upland Pine Forest

A. Tennant

Foodplain Cypress
Swamp

Mangrove/Buttonwood Swamp

R. D. Bartlett

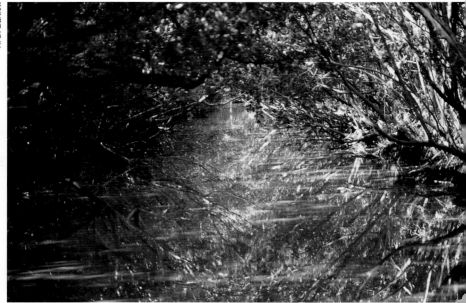

1   Brahminy Blind Snake, *Ramphotyphlops braminus*

2   Southeastern Crowned Snake, *Tantilla coronata*

3   Peninsula Crowned Snake, *Tantilla relicta relicta*

4   Central Florida Crowned Snake, *Tantilla relicta neilli*

R. D. Bartlett

5   Coastal Dunes Crowned Snake, *Tantilla relicta pamlica*

6   Rim Rock Crowned Snake, *Tantilla oolitica*

B. Mansell

7   **Marsh Brown Snake,** *Storeria dekayi limnetes*

8   **Florida Brown Snake,** *Storeria dekayi victa*

9   Midland Brown Snake, *Storeria dekayi wrightorum*

10   Florida Redbelly Snake, *Storeria occipitomaculata obscura*

11   Rough Earth Snake, *Virginia striatula*

12   Eastern Earth Snake, *Virginia valeriae valeriae*

R. D. Bartlett

13   Pine Woods Snake, *Rhadinaea flavilata*

14   Southern Ringneck Snake, *Diadophis punctatus punctatus*

K. L. Krysko

95

15 Key Ringneck Snake, *Diadophis punctatus acricus*

16 Eastern Garter Snake, *Thamnophis sirtalis sirtalis*

17   Bluestripe Garter Snake, *Thamnophis sirtalis similis*

18a Eastern Ribbon Snake, *Thamnophis sauritus sauritus*

97

18b Eastern Ribbon Snake, *Thamnophis sauritus sauritus*

19　Peninsula Ribbon Snake, *Thamnophis sauritus sackenii*

20 Bluestripe Ribbon Snake, *Thamnophis sauritus nitae*

21a Redbelly Water Snake, *Nerodia erythrogaster erythrogaster*

21b Redbelly Water Snake, *Nerodia erythrogaster erythrogaster* (juvenile)

22 Yellowbelly Water Snake, *Nerodia erythrogaster flavigaster*

23a Banded Water Snake, *Nerodia fasciata fasciata*

23b Banded Water Snake, *Nerodia fasciata fasciata* (juvenile)

24a Florida Water Snake, *Nerodia fasciata pictiventris*

24b Florida
Water Snake,
*Nerodia fasciata
pictiventris*

102

25 Mississippi Green Water Snake, *Nerodia cyclopion*

26 Florida Green Water Snake, *Nerodia floridana*

27 **Brown Water Snake,** *Nerodia taxispilota*

28 **Midland Water Snake,** *Nerodia sipedon pleuralis*

104

29 Gulf Salt Marsh Snake, *Nerodia clarkii clarkii*

30 Atlantic Salt Marsh Snake, *Nerodia clarkii taeniata*

31a Mangrove Salt Marsh Snake, *Nerodia clarkii compressicauda*
(red color phase)

31b Mangrove Salt Marsh Snake, *Nerodia clarkii compressicauda*
(gray color phase)

106

31c **Mangrove Salt Marsh Snake,** *Nerodia clarkii compressicauda*
(juvenile)

32 **Glossy Crayfish Snake,** *Regina rigida rigida* (gravid female)

33   Gulf Crayfish Snake, *Regina rigida sinicola*

34   Striped Crayfish Snake, *Regina alleni*

35 **Queen Snake,** *Regina septemvittata*

36a **Eastern Mud Snake,** *Franancia abacura abacura*

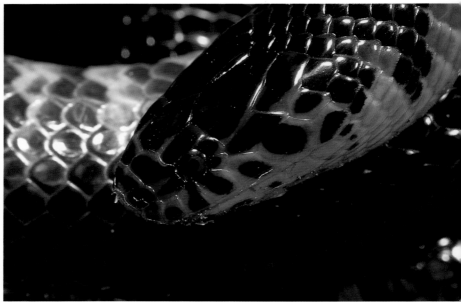

36b Eastern Mud Snake, *Farancia abacura abacura*

37   Western Mud Snake, *Farancia abacura reinwardtii*

110

38 Rainbow Snake, *Farancia erytrogramma erytrogramma*

39 South Florida Rainbow Snake, *Farancia erytrogramma seminola*

111

40   North Florida Swamp Snake, *Seminatrix pygaea pygaea*

41a South Florida Swamp Snake, *Seminatrix pygaea cyclas*

W. B. Love

41b South Florida Swamp Snake, *Seminatrix pygaea cyclas*

42 Rough Green Snake, *Opheodrys aestivus*

M. J. Bowerman

43a Eastern Coachwhip, *Masticophis flagellum flagellum* (adult)

43b Eastern Coachwhip, *Masticophis flagellum flagellum* (juvenile)

114

44 Brown Chin Racer, *Coluber constrictor helvigularis*

45a Southern Black Racer, *Coluber constrictor priapus* (adult)

45b Southern Black Racer, *Coluber constrictor priapus* (juvenile)

46   Everglades Racer, *Coluber constrictor paludicola*

116

47a Eastern Indigo Snake, *Drymarchon corais couperi*

47b Eastern Indigo Snake, *Drymarchon corais couperi*

47c **Eastern Indigo Snake,** *Drymarchon corais couperi* (hatching from egg)

48a **Eastern Hognose Snake,** *Heterodon platirhinos*

48b Eastern Hognose Snake, *Heterodon platirhinos* (black color phase)

48c Eastern Hognose Snake, *Heterodon platirhinos* (defensive tail coiling and neck swelling)

49   Southern Hognose Snake, *Heterodon simus*

50a **Black Pine Snake,** *Pituophis melanoleucas lodingi* (intergrade with Florida pine snake)

R. D. Bartlett

50b Black Pine Snake, *Pituophis melanoleucas lodingi* (intergrade with Florida pine snake)

51a Florida Pine Snake, *Pituophis melanoleucas mugitus*

B. Mansell

121

51b Florida Pine Snake, *Pituophis melanoleucas mugitus*

51c Florida Pine Snake, *Pituophis melanoleucas mugitus*

122

52a **Corn Snake,** *Elaphe guttata guttata*

52b **Corn Snake,** *Elaphe guttata guttata*

123

52c **Corn Snake,** *Elaphe guttata guttata* (hatching from egg)

52d **Corn Snake,** *Elaphe guttata guttata* (anerytheristic color phase)

52e Corn Snake, *Elaphe guttata guttata* ("Miami" color phase)

52f Corn Snake, *Elaphe guttata guttata* (amelanistic color phase)

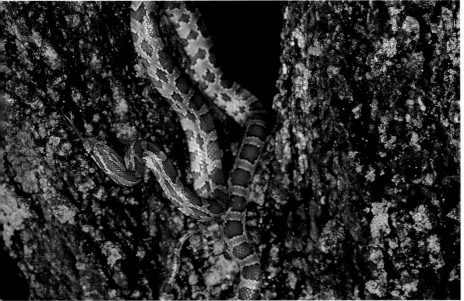

52g Corn Snake, *Elaphe guttata guttata* ("butter corn" captive-bred color phase)

53a Grey Rat Snake, *Elaphe obsoleta spiloides*

126

53b Grey Rat Snake, *Elaphe obsoleta spiloides* ("white oak" color phase)

54a Yellow Rat Snake, *Elaphe obsoleta quadrivittata*

54b Yellow Rat Snake, *Elaphe obsoleta quadrivittata*

54c Yellow Rat Snake, *Elaphe obsoleta quadrivittata*
    (Gulf hammock variant)

128

55a Everglades Rat Snake, *Elaphe obsoleta rossalleni*

55b Everglades Rat Snake, *Elaphe obsoleta rossalleni*

55c Everglades Rat Snake, *Elaphe obsoleta rossalleni*
(Upper Keys Deckert variant)

56 Short-tailed Snake, *Stilosoma extenuatum*

57a Mole Kingsnake, *Lampropeltis calligaster rhombomaculata* (juvenile)

57b Mole Kingsnake, *Lampropeltis calligaster rhombomaculata* (adult)

131

57c **Mole Kingsnake,** *Lampropeltis calligaster rhombomaculata*
(older animal)

58a **South Florida Mole Kingsnake,** *Lampropeltis calligaster occipitolineata*
(juvenile)

58b South Florida Mole Kingsnake, *Lampropeltis calligaster occipitolineata*

59a Eastern Kingsnake, *Lampropeltis getula getula*

59b Eastern Kingsnake, *Lampropeltis getula getula* (pale color phase)

59c Eastern Kingsnake, *Lampropeltis getula getula* (intergrade with Florida kingsnake)

62b Florida Scarlet Snake, *Cemophora coccinea coccinea* (aberrant
color phase)

63a Scarlet Kingsnake, *Lampropeltis triangulum elapsoides*

63b Scarlet Kingsnake, *Lampropeltis triangulum elapsoides*
(two color phases)

64a Eastern Coral Snake, *Micrurus fulvius fulvius*

140

64b Eastern Coral Snake, *Micrurus fulvius fulvius*

65   Southern Copperhead, *Agkistrodon contortrix contortrix*

66a **Eastern Cottonmouth,** *Agkistrodon piscivorus piscivorus*

66b **Eastern Cottonmouth,** *Agkistrodon piscivorus piscivorus*

142

K. Love

67a Florida Cottonmouth, *Agkistrodon piscivorus conanti*

67b Florida Cottonmouth, *Agkistrodon piscivorus conanti*

R. D. Bartlett

143

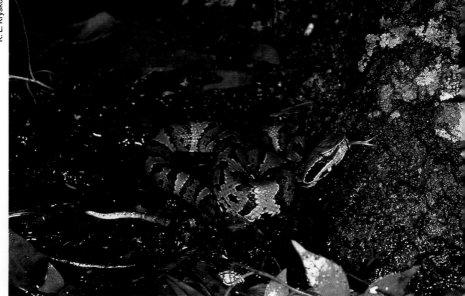

67c **Florida Cottonmouth,** *Agkistrodon piscivorus conanti* (juvenile)

68 **Dusky Pigmy Rattlesnake,** *Sistrurus miliarius barbouri*

69   Timber Rattlesnake, *Crotalus horridus*

70a Eastern Diamondback Rattlesnake, *Crotalus adamanteus*

R. D. Bartlett

70b Eastern Diamondback Rattlesnake, *Crotalus adamanteus*

70c Eastern Diamondback Rattlesnake, *Crotalus adamanteus* (albino)

W. B. Love

146

Florida Green Water Snake

Nerodia floridana

Nonvenomous   See **Mississippi Green Water Snake (25)**.

Abundance   Widespread throughout the state. In flooded marl prairie and Everglades sawgrass swale, *Nerodia floridana* may be the most abundant aquatic snake.

Size   *Nerodia floridana* is usually 30 to 55 inches; the record is 74 in.

Habitat   The snake's optimal habitat is open wetland filled with herbaceous vegetation. This includes reed- and cattail-marshes, hyacinth-choked waterways, wet sawgrass prairies and brackish estuarine environments. It is abundant in the Payne's Prairie Preserve, the Everglades, and the marshes along the St. Johns River.

Prey   Unlike the Mississippi green water snake, which feeds mostly on fish, *N. floridana* may prey more heavily on frogs; an examination of 75 stomachs revealed 10 frogs, 4 fish, and a single large salamander in one individual; the young take tadpoles and small fish.

Reproduction   Live-bearing. Breeding occurs from March to June, with litters deposited between June and September. Litters average 20 to 30, although the largest females sometimes give birth to extraordinary numbers of young: up to 100 have been reported. See **Brown Water Snake (27), Prey.**

Coloring/scale form   Dorsolateral coloring and scutellation are like that of the **Mississippi green water snake (25)**, as is the distinctive row of subocular scales between the eye and the supralabial scale. But unlike the Mississippi green, the venter is unpatterned except for faint smudges beneath the tail.

Similar snakes   Similar in dorsolateral coloring, the **Mississippi green water snake (25)** has a patterned venter: yellowish white on the forequarters, darkening posteriorly to gray and becoming heavily infused with yellowish half moons. All other water snakes lack these two species' distinctive row of subocular scales.

Behavior   *Nerodia floridana* is sometimes encountered crossing roads in the evening, especially after rain.

Aquatic Snakes

27 Brown Water Snake

Nerodia taxispilota

Nonvenomous   As a dark, heavy-bodied aquatic serpent, *N. taxispilota* is often confused with the venomous cotton-mouth, especially because if harassed it may flatten its head in threat, and strike and bite vigorously in defense.

Abundance   Common throughout Florida, and so locally abundant that in favorable habitats a dozen or more may be seen in the same area.

Size   Most adults are 30 to 55 inches long, with the record being 69.5 inches. Any brown water snake this big would almost certainly be a female, for males do not reach the size of the largest females. In one Virginia sample of 55 males and 87 females, males averaged 23.7 inches in length while females averaged nearly 32 inches. In weight the difference was even more pronounced: males averaged 6.5 oz., non-pregnant females were nearly twice as heavy, at almost 11 oz., and gravid females, at an average of over 35 oz., were more than 5 times as heavy as males.

Habitat   Most aquatic environments in Florida can support brown water snakes if they contain fallen trees, or even bushes suitable for basking, for *N. taxispilota* is not an animal of entirely open marshes. It is most common around the hardwood hammocks of wet marl and sawgrass prairies and in cypress swamps and waterways through bottomland forest, although these animals are also found in canals, ponds, swamps, flooded stands of melaleuca, and near the tree-bordered margins of brackish tidal marshes.

Prey   Brown water snakes prey primarily on frogs and fish, but they also regularly take carrion. In one study, much of the food obtained by pre-gravid *N. taxispilota* was scavenged fish, for giving birth to as many as 60 offspring places a great burden on the female's ability to meet her embryo's nutritional needs. Because fetal reptiles are nourished primarily by the fat yolks deposited within their membranous egg shrouds, female *N. taxispilota* must acquire these lipid reserves well in advance of their pregnancies. Building up this much fat is a major metabolic labor that occupies the winter prior to ovulation, when female *N. taxispilota* increase their bodies' store of lipids by some 50% (only females that acquire this amount of body fat have sufficiently high blood lipid levels to ovulate and become pregnant). Slowed by the weight of their burgeoning fat reserves, female *N. taxispilota* are thus limited in their hunting strategies, and during this period may come to rely on scavenging, for among reptiles, sit-and-wait ambush predation seldom allows the rapid acquisition of prey-calories.

Reproduction   Brown water snakes breed in most of Florida between late February and early May, with the 7- to 11- inch-long neonates appearing over a long period from June to October. Snakes do not have the set gestation periods of mammals because pregnancy is initiated by the female's ovulation, not by the deposition of semen, and viable sperm may be stored for months or even years within the cloaca of inseminated but not-yet-fertilized females.

Coloring/scale form The brown water snake's most distinctive marking is the separation between its big brown (usually light-edged), squarish vertebral blotches and the similarly-colored lateral blotches that occur along the length of its body. The dorsolateral ground color is light brown and the pale yellow venter is heavily pigmented with both dark blotches and black crescents. The brown water snake's strongly keeled dorsal scales are highly variable in the number of midbody rows: from 25 to 33, and its anal plate is divided.

Similar snakes The **cottonmouth (66, 67)** has a triangular, slab-sided head with a dark pit midway between its nostril and its slit-pupilled eye. Unlike any water snake, there is a single row of scales under its tail. Five species of *Nerodia* occur within the pan-Florida range of *N. taxispilota,* all with the same general shape, and often, coloration. (Any large water snake may appear uniformly dark-backed due to both the dimming of their patterning with age and the wet algae and sediment that frequently coats their dorsums.) But there are distinct differences: **redbelly** and **yellowbelly water snakes (21, 22)** have solid reddish-brown to dark-olive dorsums and unmarked venters; the **midland water snake (28)** has dark brown crossbands on its neck, forebody, and tail, and squarish brown bars along its sides; except for all-dark specimens, **banded** and **Florida water snakes (23, 24)** have dark crossbands across their entire bodies and a distinct dark postocular stripe that extends from the eye through the posterior supralabial scale; **Mississippi green** and **Florida green water snakes (25, 26)** have grayish to olive-brown speckled dorsums and a unique row of subocular scales between the eye and the supralabial scales. The Florida green water snake also has an unmarked venter.

Behavior Like most other water snakes *N. taxispilota* is a good swimmer and climber. In early spring it can be seen basking either along the water's edge or on overhanging tree limbs, but during the hottest part of the summer it turns to primarily nocturnal activity.

28 Midland Water Snake

Nerodia sipedon pleuralis

Nonvenomous   When cornered, *N. s. pleuralis* may flatten its head and body, void musk from its cloaca, vibrate its tail, and strike repeatedly in self-defense. In Alabama, herpetologist R. H. Mount found that this reptile ". . . is considered venomous and killed on sight by a large segment of the populace, who designate it 'water moccasin.' [Yet] in spite of relentless persecution, the midland water snake persists in considerable numbers throughout nearly all its range."

Abundance   Uncommon within its limited Florida range except in cool, clear, sand-bottomed steephead streams along the northern border of the panhandle, where *N. s. pleuralis* can be more numerous than any other aquatic snake.

Size   Adults are 24 to 48 inches long; the record is 59 inches.

Habitat   As the only race of the northern water snake to reach the Gulf Coast, *N. s. pleuralis* is found most often in waterways such as the Choctawhatchee, Yellow, and Escambria Rivers, which originate in the Alabama uplands. Below these rivers' rapidly-flowing headwaters, the midland water snake is much less numerous than the redbelly and banded water snakes typical of the Gulf's coastal lowlands.

Prey   Midland water snakes prey mostly on small fish, but frogs, tadpoles, and salamanders are also taken.

Reproduction   Live-bearing. Newborn *N. s. pleuralis,* litters of which number from 12 to 30, appear from July to early September.

Coloring/scale form   The rusty-brown dorsum is marked with dark-edged brown anterior crossbands, which from midbody to tail are replaced with dark vertebral blotches. (Crossbands and vertebral blotches total less than 30.) Squarish lateral bars extend upwards from the belly line. The yellow venter has a double row of rearward-facing brown crescents, the 21 to 25 midbody rows of dorsal scales are keeled, and the anal plate is divided.

Similar snakes   The **cottonmouth (66, 67)** has a dark pit between its vertically-slit pupil and its nostril and a single row of subcaudal scales. The **banded water snake's (23)** dorsal bands occur all the way to its tail, its yellow belly has squarish markings, and a dark stripe extends from its eye to the last supralabial.

Behavior   A mostly nocturnal forager, the midland water snake searches stream bottoms for the small fish it captures in their nighttime shelters beneath overhanging banks and submerged logs.

29 Gulf Salt Marsh Snake

Nerodia clarkii clarkii

Nonvenomous   *Nerodia clarkii clarkii* bites only if harassed.

Abundance   Common on the Gulf Coast from central Florida north to the western tip of the panhandle.

Size   Adults are 15 to 30 inches long; the record is 36 inches.

Habitat   Salt marsh snakes live in brackish and salt water tidal estuaries and salt grass meadows (*N. c. clarkii* is seldom found in freshwater); microhabitat includes crayfish and fiddler crab burrows in tidal mud flats.

Prey   Primarily fish, especially shallows-living species such as killifish and small mullet (which are often taken when they become trapped by the falling tide), as well as crayfish and shrimp.

Reproduction   Live-bearing. Little else is known, but the 9- to 10.5-inch-long young weigh only .25 to .33 oz. at birth and, except for slightly bolder dorsolateral striping, resemble the adults.

Coloring/scale form   A pair of dark brown dorsolateral stripes stands out against the grayish ground color. The belly is reddish-brown, with a central row of cream-colored oval blotches often flanked by a row of pale spots. The keeled dorsal scales occur in either 21 or 23 rows at midbody, there is a double row of subcaudal scales, and the anal plate is divided.

Similar snakes   The **Atlantic salt marsh snake's (30)** back is only striped anteriorly; posteriorly it is blotched. The **mangrove salt marsh snake (31)** largely lacks dorsolateral stripes (there is often a short, dark nuchal line); its back ranges from black, to gray-green with dark crossbands, to unmarked orange. The **striped crayfish snake (34)** has a uniformly colored venter, and the **queen snake (35)** has fewer than 19 dorsal scale rows at midbody.

Behavior   The fluid conservation difficulties faced by marine reptiles are as severe as those confronting desert-dwellers. Not only is freshwater absent from their environment but seawater—which is saltier than their body fluids—exerts a continual osmotic draw on their tissues' electrolyte balance. Scaly reptilian skin is a good barrier against external dehydration but, because intestinal membranes are salt-permeable, if seawater is ingested it draws the less-salty fluid from blood and tissues into the stomach. Only *N. clarkii* has established itself in an entirely saline niche; salt marsh snakes apparently manage this metabolic feat by drinking rainwater when it is available, and at other times by swallowing nothing but prey animals—whose body fluids are as dilute as their own.

Aquatic Snakes

Atlantic Salt
Marsh Snake
Nerodia clarkii taeniata

Nonvenomous The Atlantic salt marsh snake bites only in
self-defense.

Abundance Threatened. Protected by both the federal government and the state of Florida, *N. c. taeniata* is a rare reptile
found only along a narrow strip of the Atlantic coast—primarily in
Volusia Co.—where much of its habitat has been lost to commercial development of the area's limited ocean frontage. See **Snakes and the Law.**

Size *N. c. taeniata* is the smallest of the state's water snakes: most adults
are less than 20 inches long. The record is just under 24 inches.

Habitat All three of Florida's salt marsh snakes were formerly classified
as subspecies of the freshwater-living banded water snake, *Nerodia fasciata*.
Because salt marsh snakes have morphological differences from *N. fasciata*
and rarely enter freshwater, they are presently recognized as the separate,
saline-environment salt marsh snake, *Nerodia clarkii*. See **Banded Water
Snake (23), Similar snakes.**

Prey See **Gulf Salt Marsh Snake (29).**

Reproduction Live-bearing. See **Gulf Salt Marsh Snake (29).**

Coloring/scale form Against a light grayish-tan ground color, the
Atlantic salt marsh snake's anterior back and sides are dark-striped; posteriorly, the stripes become dark blotches or even crossbands. The venter, like that
of other salt marsh snakes, is reddish brown with a central row of large yellowish blotches. The 21 (sometimes 23) midbody rows of dorsal scales are
keeled, there is a double row of subcaudal scales, and the anal plate is divided.

Similar snakes The **cottonmouth (66, 67)** has a much stouter body, an
unstriped back, a flat-sided head with vertically-slit pupils, and a single row
of subcaudal scales. The subspecies **mangrove salt marsh snake (31)** largely
lacks dorsolateral stripes (there is often a dark nuchal bar, however); its dorsum ranges from dark greenish gray, sometimes with black crossbands, to
unmarked orange. The **striped crayfish snake (34)** has stripes running the
length of its dorsum and a uniformly-colored venter.

Behavior Like other water snakes, *N. c. taeniata* may flatten its head and
body when cornered, and when handled often discharges an odorous musk
from its cloaca.

31 Mangrove Salt Marsh Snake

Nerodia clarkii compressicauda

Nonvenomous   Mangrove salt marsh snakes bite only in self-defense.

Abundance   Common, although infrequently seen, along both Gulf and Atlantic coastlines from north-central Florida to Key West.

Size   Adults are 14 to 28 inches. The record is 36.75 inches.

Habitat   *N. c. compressicauda* primarily inhabits inundated estuarine forests of buttonwood and red mangroves. In this brackish-to-saline environment, competition with Florida's numerous freshwater *natricines* (whose more-inland habitat intersects the inshore margins of the mangrove salt marsh snake's narrow strip of coastal wetland) is minimized. Roadside canals in the boundary zone between inshore marsh and coastal mangroves are usually inhabited by both types of water snakes. *Nerodia clarkii compressicauda* is also found on entirely saline offshore islands along both coasts as well as in the Florida Keys.

Prey   In their study of the predatory behavior of mangrove salt marsh snakes, S. Mullin and H. Mushinsky found that sheepshead minnows were the most abundant of the small estuarine fish preyed upon by *N. c. compressicauda*. Because of the small number of prey species selected from the great variety of appropriately sized prey animals present in the mangrove water snake's biotically-rich marine/estuarine community, *N. c. compressicauda* was judged to be a foraging specialist. Its foraging techniques in capturing fish were studied by simulating a field of mangrove prop roots projecting above the leutic surface. Prop roots in mangrove forest have a six-fold variation in density, and as expected, *N. c. compressicauda* captured the most fish when the root density level in the laboratory setting equalled that of the site at Placido Bay, near Tampa, where the tested snakes were captured.

Under these conditions mangrove water snakes turned out to be quite sedentary predators. More time was spent in the water than atop the artificial prop roots with which the snakes were provided, but by far the largest amount of time was devoted to resting. Only when the density of sheepshead minnows in their pool was raised to more than six times that of the fishes' naturally-occurring population level was the mangrove snakes' foraging stimulated. At that time, these animals seemed ". . . to respond most to tactile cues, as they often remained motionless until ripples in the water, generated by fish swimming within a few inches of their bodies triggered predatory behavior. Following an unsuccessful capture attempt, individuals sometimes submerged and touched their snouts to or tongue-flicked along the sand, perhaps in an attempt to capture prey hidden in the upper layers."

Aquatic Snakes

This tendency toward minimal foraging except under the optimal conditions of maximum prey density and/or proximity is confirmed by the field observations of herpetologist John Decker, who reports feeding behavior among free-ranging *N. c. compressicauda* that actively sought small fish and crayfish only when they were concentrated in shallow water by the falling tide.

Reproduction   Live-bearing. Little is known of courtship or breeding, but 22 young were recorded in one litter.

Coloring/scale form   Mangrove salt marsh snakes are strikingly patterned and variably colored reptiles. They vary from tan to almost black, but there are 2 primary color phases. The gray-green color morph has a dark-crossbanded olive gray dorsum (some individuals have partial lateral striping on the forebody) with a clouded, gray-green venter. The other color variant is orange—its striking hue perhaps an adaptation to its home among the reddish-orange arching prop roots of the red mangrove. Adults of this phase have an unmarked orangish back and sides; juveniles are orange with dark dorsal crossbands. The venter of both adults and juveniles is pale yellow. The dorsal scales are keeled and arranged in 21 to 23 rows at midbody; both the subcaudal scales and the anal plate are divided.

Similar snakes   The subspecies **Gulf salt marsh snake (29)** has full-length dark brown dorsolateral stripes on a grayish-tan ground color and a pale-spotted reddish-brown venter. The **Atlantic salt marsh snake (30)**, also a subspecies, is dorsally striped on its forebody; posteriorly it is blotched. The **striped crayfish snake (34)** has stripes running the length of its dorsum and a uniformly-colored belly. The **cottonmouth (66, 67)** has a stouter body, an unstriped back, a flat-sided head with vertically-slit pupils, and a single row of subcaudal scales.

Behavior   Sometimes seen crossing canal-side roads at night, *N. c. compressicauda* is also fond of basking on mangrove limbs during the day. When approached, instead of plopping noisily headfirst into the water like other *natricines*, mangrove salt marsh snakes typically slip gently backward off the limb, silently disappearing tail first into the water or wet mangrove litter below.

32 Glossy Crayfish Snake
Regina rigida rigida

Nonvenomous   *Regina rigida rigida* does not bite humans.

Abundance   Uncommon. Although not generally distributed, the glossy crayfish snake is found from the eastern panhandle through northern Florida south into the central part of the state. Reportedly abundant in some areas, long days may nevertheless be spent in the glossy crayfish snake's woodland swamp habitat without seeing one.

Size   Most adults measure 14 to 23 inches; maximum is 31 inches.

Habitat   The glossy crayfish snake is both aquatic and fossorial, inhabiting cypress ponds and sloughs in flatwoods, where its primary microhabitat is the burrows of the crayfish on which it feeds. *Regina r. rigida* may also burrow deep into the earth beneath rotting stumps, logs, or planks at the water's edge. Perhaps because neither this semi-subterranean lifestyle nor predation on slow-moving crayfish calls for agility, crayfish snakes are decidedly stiff-bodied—feeling taut to the touch—an attribute from which their species name, *rigida,* is derived.

Prey   The stomachs of a number of these snakes have contained only freshly-molted crayfish, but dragonfly nymphs may also be taken.

Reproduction   Live-bearing. Although it is not known if all members of the genus *Regina* engage in this behavior, some species are reported to breed in the water at night, with several pheromone-drawn males entwining themselves around a single female, forming a mass within which only a single copulation probably occurs. More often, solitary breeding pairs float wrapped together with their tails hanging downward.

Coloring/scale form   This slim water snake's back and upper sides are shiny chocolate brown, usually dimly dark-striped. Along the belly line, the 2 lowest rows of dorsal scales are yellowish, split by a dark seam, while the pale sides of the throat are streaked with brown. On most of the dark yellow venter, a double row of big brown half-moons is distinct. There are 54 or fewer subcaudal scales in females, 62 or fewer in males; the keeled dorsal scales are arranged in 19 rows at midbody, and the anal plate is divided.

Similar snakes   The subspecies **Gulf crayfish snake (33)** has more numerous subcaudal scales (55 or more in females, 63 or more in males), as well as a laterally patterned throat.

Behavior   Although amphiumas constitute the prey of most adult *natricine* water snakes, these giant salamanders can also be snake predators: A 40-inch-long, two-toed amphiuma trapped by K. Enge disgorged a somewhat shorter glossy crayfish snake.

Aquatic Snakes

155

33 Gulf Crayfish Snake
Regina rigida sinicola

Nonvenomous   Like all crayfish snakes, this shy little reptile does not bite human beings even if it is handled.

Abundance   Uncommon.

Size   Adults average around 20 inches in length. The maximum recorded size for *R. rigida* is 31.5 inches.

Habitat   In the western Florida Panhandle the Gulf crayfish snake inhabits cypress sloughs and bottomland forest waterways, as well as (in places where crayfish are common) irrigation ditches, wet marl prairies, and muddy pastures.

Prey   Primarily crayfish, lesser sirens, small fish, frogs, and aquatic insects such as dragonfly nymphs.

Reproduction   Live-bearing. Eleven newborns measured between 7 and 8.5 inches in length.

Coloring/scale form   The back is shiny chocolate brown, sometimes with dimly darker-striped sides above a yellowish-tan lateral stripe (split by a thin black seam) that occupies the first and second scale rows above the belly line. The labial scales, as well as the unpatterned sides of the throat, are yellowish, and the pale venter is marked with a double row of rearward-arced black crescents that form a single line beneath chin and tail. The keeled dorsal scales are arranged in 19 rows at midbody and the anal plate is divided.

Similar snakes   The subspecies **glossy crayfish snake (32)** is distinguished by its fewer subcaudal scales: 54 or fewer in females and 62 or fewer in males, as well as by the lateral brown striping along its throat. The **queen snake (35)** has a dull brown dorsum, a much more prominent yellowish lateral band, and (except for its lower back) smooth scales. **Florida** and **Mississippi green water snakes (24, 25)** are much more heavily proportioned, with dark-speckled backs and a unique row of subocular scales; all other **water snakes (21–23, 26–28, 35)** living within the range of *R. r. sinicola* lack its pale lateral color demarcation.

Behavior   Crayfish snakes are probably predominantly nocturnal, although P. E. Moler has observed diurnal foraging in this subspecies. Because of its semi-subterranean lifestyle, *R. r. sinicola*—active mainly between March and early November—is sometimes able to subsist in city park ponds and suburban creeks where larger, more visible water snakes would quickly be killed, for it is almost never observed except during drainage or roadway excavation, or at night after heavy rain.

³⁴ Striped Crayfish Snake

Regina alleni

Nonvenomous   Crayfish snakes do not bite humans.

Abundance   Common from the eastern panhandle south throughout the state.

Size   Adults are 14 to 20 inches; the record is just under 26 in.

Habitat   *Regina alleni* occupies heavily vegetated aquatic environments, especially hyacinth-filled canals, in which the microenvironment differs from open water in having a higher level of dissolved oxygen and lessened temperature extremes. Among its emergent leaves and submerged roots, *R. alleni* and its crayfish prey find refuge. This snake is also common in wet sawgrass prairies and cypress sloughs, while sphagnum bogs and inundated melaleuca stands are also inhabited.

Prey   Like other *Regina*, prey is almost entirely crayfish—a food animal unavailable to other small serpents due to its hard, spiny carapace. *Regina alleni* sidesteps this armor, however, by swallowing crayfish tail first, while some *Regina*, such as the queen snake, preferentially prey on freshly molted, soft-bodied crayfish. Small fish and dragonfly naiads, or nymphs, are taken as well.

Reproduction   Live-bearing. See **Glossy Crayfish Snake (32)**.

Coloring/scale form   The dark brown dorsum is marked with a single black vertebral stripe and a dark upper lateral stripe; a pale yellow or rusty-brown stripe occupies the lower sides. The yellow belly is unpatterned or midventrally marked with spots. Cephalic scutellation is unique: *R. alleni* has only one internasal scale, while—also unusual in a genus whose other member-species are entirely keel-scaled—the 19 midbody rows of dorsal scales are smooth except above the cloaca. The anal plate is divided.

Similar snakes   Glossy crayfish snakes (32) are not distinctly striped, and their bellies are marked with a double row of brown crescents. All other dark-backed **water snakes (21–24, 26, 27)** living in the range of *R. alleni* lack a pale lateral color demarcation.

Behavior   This muscular, stiff-bodied little reptile forages at night during the summer, but is more crepuscular in spring and fall, when it is sometimes seen crossing low-lying dirt roads.

Aquatic Snakes

35 Queen Snake
Regina septemvittata

Nonvenomous Like many snakes attempting to discourage a predator, *R. septemvittata* may void the odorous
contents of its cloaca, but it seldom bites even when first handled in the field. Once past their initial fear of being handled,
queen snakes adapt well to confinement, living as long as
19 years in captivity if their specialized diet of crayfish can be
provided.

Abundance Uncommon in its northwestern Florida Panhandle range.

Size A moderately slender reptile with a slim head no wider than its body,
R. septemvittata averages 14 to 23 inches in length as an adult, reaching a
maximum length of just over 36 inches.

Habitat The queen snake is a woodland stream, or cypress dome
dweller, preferring forested aquatic habitats with sandy or hard-substrate
bottoms to the open marshes favored by its *Regina* relatives.

Prey Newly molted, soft-bodied crayfish are by far the most common—
and often almost the only—prey.

Reproduction Live bearing. The young, numbering 10 to 12 per litter,
are born in mid-summer.

Coloring/scale form The queen snake's slender body varies from grayish-brown to black. On lighter-hued individuals 3 dark dorsolateral stripes
are dimly defined above a prominent yellowish-tan lateral stripe. Florida
specimens tend to be darker, and their stripes are hard to see except on the
sides of the neck. The reddish venter is marked with a double row of dark
spots that converge to form a single line beneath the chin and tail, but very
old individuals may have predominantly dark bellies. The dorsal scales are
keeled, and arranged in 19 rows at midbody; the anal plate is divided.

Similar snakes The **Florida green water snake (26)** has an unstriped
dark-speckled gray-green dorsum, while all other **water snakes (21, 23, 24,
26, 27, 30–33)** living within the range of *R. alleni* have patterned backs and
lack the queen snake's pale lateral color.

Behavior Both a diurnal and a nocturnal forager, the queen snake does
not occur in the coastal estuarine marshes where larger *Nerodia* water
snakes are numerous. In its more inland, streamside environment, *R.
septemvittata* is often found among or on top of bankside bushes or overhanging limbs from which, when approached, it drops into the water and
swims away rapidly.

36 Eastern Mud Snake

Farancia abacura abacura

Nonvenomous *Farancia abacura abacura* does not bite humans. See **Rainbow Snake (38)**.

Abundance Common throughout Florida. Despite mud snakes' secretive, aquatic/burrowing habits, they can be among the most numerous serpents found on roads through wetland areas: in a 4-year-long survey of Payne's Prairie near Gainesville, R. Franz of the Florida Museum of Natural History found *F. a. abacura* to be one of the five nocturnal snake species that most often appeared after dark on the section of US 441 that crosses the prairie.

Size Although the record *F. a. abacura* measured 81.5 inches, few adults are more than 50 inches long.

Habitat Eastern mud snakes may be found in and around most freshwater environments, but especially favor turbid bodies of water with swampy margins and profuse aquatic vegetation, marshes of all kinds, wet marl, sawgrass prairies, irrigation canals, cypress stands, and flooded stands of melaleuca.

Prey Identical to that of the **Western Mud Snake (37)**.

Reproduction Egg-laying. Mud snakes deposit their eggs during July and August, and do so prolifically—one clutch numbered 60, another 104. The eggs are parchment-like in texture, and adherent, forming a glued-together mass. They are typically laid in a moist substrate such as a bankside cavity, inside which the female often remains coiled about her clutch throughout its 8- to 12-week incubation period.[1] The 7- to 9.5-inch-long young hatch in early autumn but, particularly in northern parts of the range, may remain in the nest for extended periods. This probably significantly enhances their chances for survival because the aquatic habitat of *Farancia* is at its driest during autumn, when the neonates' amphibian prey is both scarce and simultaneously being sought by large numbers of newborn natricine water snakes.

Aquatic Snakes

---

[1]At least 5 nests, one in northern Florida and 4 in Louisiana, have been located (some of them with the mothers in attendance) within the nests of American alligators. The huge piles of vegetative material that alligators amass so that the warmth generated by the composting plant matter will incubate their eggs also benefits the eggs of *F. abacura,* whose incubation period closely matches the 9-week incubation period of alligator eggs. Additional benefits of commensal nesting in alligator mounds—behavior also reported for several turtle species—are the increased humidity provided by the decaying plant debris and the fact that female alligators actively defend their nests from predation by raccoons and other carnivores that also take mud snake eggs. The elevated location of these alligator-mound nest cavities also minimizes the mortality of *F. abacura* eggs caused by the frequent flooding of low-lying shoreline nest hollows.

Coloring/scale form   The bluish-black dorsum is laterally marked with 53 or more carmine-colored bars. Among juveniles, these pink lateral bars extend well up the sides; adults are entirely black above, although red lateral markings are still prominent along the belly line. Black rectangles checker the pinkish-red venter; subcaudally this rectangular pattern becomes black crossbands.[2] There is no preocular scale and, like all *Farancia,* the terminal caudal scale is enlarged and stiffened into a point. Mud and rainbow snakes share this attribute with both the pine woods and the burrowing blind snakes. The 19 midbody rows of dorsal scales are smooth, except for keeled scales on the lower back above the anal plate, and the anal plate is usually divided.

Similar snakes   The **western mud snake (37)** has fewer (52 or less) red lateral bars, which do not extend as far up the sides as those of the eastern mud snake. Both the subspecies **rainbow snake (38)** and the **Florida swamp snakes (40, 41)** lack pink lateral blotches as well as the mud snake's checkered belly. The **cottonmouth (66, 67)** has a triangular head with a dark pit between its nostril and its slit-pupilled eye. The **redbelly water snake (21)** has a reddish-brown to dark olive back and sides and an unmarked venter; except for all-dark specimens, **banded** and **Florida water snakes (23, 24)** have both dark dorsolateral crossbands and a distinct dark postocular stripe across the cheek. The **Florida green water snake (26)** has a speckled grayish to olive-brown dorsum and an unmarked belly.

Behavior   *Farancia abacura abacura* typically responds to restraint by curling the rear of its body around one's hands and wrists, pressing its hardened, hornlike tailtip inward so firmly that it was once believed that this spur could deliver a mortal sting. When mud snakes' habit of lying in a circular coil was factored into the story, the legend arose of the horn-tailed hoop snake that could take its tail in its mouth, roll down a fleeing man, and tail-sting him to death with venom "powerful enough to kill a tree." See **Western Mud Snake (37), Behavior.**

---

[2]According to P. E. Moler of the Florida Game and Fresh Water Fish Commission's Wildlife Research Laboratory, all-black anerythrystic mud snakes occasionally turn up.

37 Western Mud Snake

Farancia abacura reinwardtii

Nonvenomous   This big, docile serpent is generally unwilling to bite, even when first handled in the field. See **Rainbow Snake (38), Nonvenomous.**

Abundance   The western mud snake occurs in Florida only as an intergrade with the eastern mud snake, *F. a. abacura,* in the western end of the Panhandle. Here it is common but seldom seen.

Size   Adult western mud snakes reach 74 inches in length, but most adults measure 36 to 52 inches. Hatchling *F. a. reinwardtii* may be as small as 6.25 inches, however.

Habitat   Identical to that of the **Eastern Mud Snake (36).**

Prey   A relatively prey-specific predator, *F. a. reinwardtii* has a heavily muscled neck, jaws, and body adapted to overpowering the giant salamanders—sirens and amphiumas—that are its principal prey species. Frogs and fish are also taken.

Reproduction   Egg-laying. See **Eastern Mud Snake (36).**

Coloring/scale form   Western mud snakes live in wet soil, but they are anything but muddy in coloration. Their glossy blue-black dorsums are laterally marked with fewer than 52 round-topped reddish-pink lateral blotches; among juveniles, these red blotches extend up the sides as far as the lower back. The venter has a bright, red-and-black checkerboard pattern that beneath the tail becomes a series of crossbands. The 19 midbody rows of dorsal scales are smooth, except for the vertebral rows directly above the cloaca, where they may be keeled. There is no preocular scale, the terminal caudal scale is enlarged and hardened into a point, and the anal plate is usually divided.

Similar snakes   The **eastern mud snake (36)** has more numerous (53 or more) reddish lateral bars, which are taller than those of the western mud snake and have sharply pointed tops. The subspecies **rainbow snake (38)** has a colorfully striped dorsum, and it and the **Florida swamp snakes (40, 41)** lack both pink lateral blotches and the mud snake's checkered belly.

Behavior   Western mud snakes are aquatic, nocturnal burrowers. Unlike the related rainbow snakes, which regularly ascend cypress knees, mud snakes do not climb. The horny tailtip, which captured *F. a. reinwardtii* typically press against one's hands, may have evolved to help these snakes grasp or immobilize their large, slippery prey. Alternatively, the pointed tailtip may have developed primarily to obtain purchase in pressing through tractionless muddy soil. See **Eastern Mud Snake (36), Behavior.**

Aquatic Snakes

38 Rainbow Snake
Farancia erytrogramma erytrogramma

Nonvenomous   Like other members of the genus *Farancia*, rainbow snakes have a Duvernoy's gland—a mucous-secreting organ frequently associated with some degree of toxicity. Rainbow snakes also have enlarged posterior maxillary teeth, perhaps an adaptation to help hold their very slippery prey. However, there are few snakes more unwilling to bite their captors than the *Farancia,* and even newly captured adults can be handled with impunity.

Abundance   Uncommon to rare. Even in its optimal habitat in the spring-runs, streams and river-swamps of northern Florida, *F. e. erytrogramma* often goes unnoticed. Because of its secretive behavior and largely subterranean lifestyle, it is generally extremely difficult to find, yet, when conditions are right, these animals are regularly encountered. Apparently isolated populations also occur in Pinellas and southern Pasco counties.

Size   Although most rainbow snakes are considerably smaller—between 40 and 54 inches in length—the record is a heavy-bodied 66 inches. Hatchlings vary from 7 to 10 inches in length.

Habitat   The rainbow snake is a fossorial and aquatic species principally associated with clear, unpolluted moving water. It also occurs in lakes, cypress swamps, and marshes of the southeastern coastal plain (in both freshwater and brackish tidal environments), where its microhabitat is often floating vegetation. Rainbow snakes also shelter beneath shoreline debris such as mats of Spanish moss, the trunks of fallen trees, and manmade detritus like newspapers and plywood. *Farancia e. erytrogramma* is also found beneath logs and planks washed into tidal mudflats.

Out of several hundred South Carolina, Georgia, and Florida individuals observed by W. T. Neill (who first described the rainbow snake's southern race), . . . "only one was not in the water or immediately beside it . . . In the southern part of its range, this species is among the most aquatic of snakes."

Prey   Of the rainbow snake's predation in the wild, Neill wrote: "Among rural residents it is well known that the rainbow snake eats *Anguilla*. The snake is, therefore, vernacularly known as 'eel moccasin' because 'Ever time you see one, he got a eel tail hangin' out his mouth.' The rainbow snake, upon catching an eel, climbs out of the water, usually into the exposed roots of a bald-cypress tree, but sometimes into stream-side shrubs. The prey is swallowed head first [after which] the snake often rests with the eel's tail dangling from its jaws."

In captivity, juvenile rainbow snakes' preferred prey is tadpoles and larval and adult salamanders. Young rainbow snakes will thrive for a year or more on tadpoles and an occasional small fish or frog, but as they grow they gradually become more reluctant to accept tadpoles. Somehow these reptiles know instinctively what an eel is, and even when their tadpole prey is scented with eel, maturing juveniles eventually hold out for a real *Anguilla*. Adults cannot be induced to accept any other prey.

Reproduction   Egg-laying. Although little is known about the courtship or reproductive biology of the rainbow snake, from the many nests that have been found it is evident that clutch size may be as small as 10 or as large as 52. During the years when itinerant sawmills were commonplace, R. D. Bartlett recalls finding rainbow snake eggs, as well as the snakes themselves, concealed in piles of sawdust on the edge of ponds and swamps. Nests are usually placed in moist, sandy soils, and it is likely that in at least some instances the female remains with her clutch during incubation, as is the case with rainbow snakes' *Farancia* relatives, the mud snakes.

Coloring/scale form   As multi-hued as its namesake, the rainbow snake is one of North America's most beautiful serpents. The back is olive-brown to black or purplish black, its bright dorsolateral pigments separated by dark areas that set off isolated spots of color. Prior to ecdysis, however, the rainbow snake's entire body becomes overlain with a bluish sheen that obscures its normally brilliant coloring. There is a red vertebral stripe, while another pinkish stripe occupies each of the dark (often darker than the dorsum, especially among juveniles) upper sides. Below these lateral stripes, the lower sides are yellow, with each scale containing a red dot. According to Neill, males tend to be more heavily marked than females, while the large scales of the head are often edged with red. A pair of black spots flank each yellowish-pink ventral scute, between which the mid-belly is brighter red; posterior to the yellow chin a row of smaller black midventral dots, which terminates several scutes anterior to the anal opening, may also be present. The 19 midbody rows of dorsal scales are smooth (except on the lower back and sides, where they may be weakly keeled); the tail is tipped with an enlarged, pointed terminal scute and the anal plate is usually divided.

Similar snakes   As members of the primarily neo-tropical colubrine subfamily *Lycodontinae*, Florida's rainbow and mud snake races are the only North American serpents possessing their unusual dental morphology and unique suite of dorsolateral colors. The one or two preserved specimens of the extremely rare (perhaps even extinct) **South Florida rainbow snake (39)** have almost entirely black venters and lower sides. The **eastern** and **western mud snakes (36, 37)** lack dorsal striping, as does the much smaller **North Florida swamp snake (40)**.

Behavior   Rainbow snakes usually emerge from their often fully submerged daytime retreats only well after sundown, then seek seclusion again around midnight. On warm, rainy days, especially during the low barometric pressure associated with a passing frontal system, rainbow snakes may be

Aquatic Snakes

active both earlier and later in the day than usual, however, and flooding rains can bring rainbow snakes in terrestrial microhabitats to the surface at any time of day. This is probably more in response to increased foraging opportunities flooding provides than to being flushed out like other serpents, for *F. e. erytrogramma* is so well adapted to aquatic conditions that it thrives in the sudden inundations that displace many terrestrial serpents.

Rainbow snakes can sometimes be found by quietly canoeing after dark among the inundated trees of shallow swamplands, or by scrutinizing cypress boles along the edges of rivers or creeks, where *F. e. erytrogramma* often lie with only their heads protruding from submerged crevices. Success in capturing a rainbow snake is often followed by the snake curling its muscular tail around one's hand or arm, harmlessly thrusting inward with its hardened, hornlike tailtip—behavior thought by some researchers to reflect the rainbow snake's natural predatory manipulation of its slippery eel and amphibian prey into a better swallowing position. (The other theory for this behavior is that, like the soft-soil-living blind snakes, *Farancia* use their pointed tailtips as anchors to obtain burrowing purchase against the viscous underwater substrate in which they burrow.) This defensive maneuver has, among the more numerous eastern and western mud snakes, given rise to the myth that the caudal spur of these aquatic species can deliver a mortal sting. See **Eastern Mud Snake (36), Behavior.**

39 South Florida Rainbow Snake

Farancia erytrogramma seminola

Nonvenomous   The only specimens collected were taken at night, and according to their captor, W. T. Neill, they "made no attempt to bite."

Abundance   Extremely rare or possibly extinct. *F. e. seminola* is the rarest snake in North America, for only 3 specimens have been recorded. It was first described in 1952 by Neill, who termed it *seminola* for the Seminole tribe that once inhabited the vicinity of Lake Okeechobee, where he captured the holotype specimen. Since the discovery of this adult female only 2 other South Florida rainbow snakes—both female—have been reported; no males have been found. The size of the population remains unknown, if indeed *F. e. erytrogramma* still exists. Though the race may still be present, several specific searches for it have failed.

Size   The largest of the three recorded specimens was 51.5 inches in length and quite heavily-bodied.

Habitat   Neill's 2 specimens were taken, at night, "in the water of a sizeable stream" named Fisheating Creek, which flows into the west side of Lake Okeechobee. The third female, now in the collection of the late reptile showman E. Ross Allen, was taken from the same area.

Prey   Like its northern subspecies *F. e. erytrogramma,* the South Florida rainbow snake probably feeds on freshwater eels and sirens.

Reproduction   Egg-laying. See **Rainbow Snake (38)**.

Coloring/scale form   Neill's type specimen (now preserved in the Florida Museum of Natural History in Gainesville) resembles a partially melanistic rainbow snake. Dark pigment obscures most of the red-spotted yellow scales of this individual's lower sides and occupies most of its venter, where both a well-defined black patch posterior to the throat and the black spots beneath the tail are narrowly ringed with red. Scutellation is the same as that of the rainbow snake: 19 midbody rows of smooth dorsal scales (except for very weak posterior carination on both the vertebral row and adjacent rows 6 through 9). The tail is tipped with a pointed terminal scute and the anal plate is divided.

Similar snakes   The **rainbow snake (38)** has less dark pigment on both its sides and its predominantly pinkish-red belly. The **eastern mud snake (36)** lacks dorsolateral stripes and has a red- and black-checkered venter.

Behavior   Everything about this animal is enigmatic, but its life history is probably similar to that of *F. e. erytrogramma.*

Aquatic Snakes

40 North Florida Swamp Snake

Seminatrix pygaea pygaea

Nonvenomous   *Seminatrix pygaea pygaea* does not bite humans.

Abundance   Locally abundant from the panhandle to central Florida.

Size   Most adults measure 10 to 15 inches; the record is 18.5 inches.

Habitat   North Florida swamp snakes inhabit both fresh and saline wetlands: bayheads, hyacinth-filled canals, sphagnum bogs, sawgrass prairies, cypress stands, marshes, and temporary ponds and sloughs.

Prey   Foraging is mostly nocturnal. See **South Florida Swamp Snake (41)**.

Reproduction   Live-bearing. See **South Florida Swamp Snake (41)**.

Coloring/scale form   The dorsum is shiny black, its pigment extending onto the outer sutures of the more than 117 red ventral scales. The 17 midbody rows of dorsal scales are smooth (although streaks on the lateral scales resemble keels) and the anal plate is divided.

Similar snakes   The **South Florida swamp snake (41)** has fewer than 117 ventral scales.

Behavior   It is often assumed that reptiles with clearly defined habitats—such as water snakes inhabiting small ponds—simply "live" there. Yet these bodies of water regularly dry up, forcing even partially fossorial serpents like *S. p. pygaea*—which can retreat from drought by burrowing into wet mud—to find their way to more permanent aquatic environments. Travel over land exposes swamp snakes to physiological stress, increased predation, and the uncertainty of finding prey in a new locale. Yet success in making these journeys is crucial to their survival, and studies have shown that they do not undertake these odysseys at random.

During the severe drought of the late 1980s, *S. p. pygaea* regularly moved between a small Putnam County pond and a pair of nearby lakes. Because 9 out of 10 of these travelers were juveniles, and because the only adults captured at the pond were gravid females, such outlying ponds are now thought to serve as developmental-habitat for juveniles (being free of predatory fish, temporary pools typically harbor numerous frogs, tadpoles, and the small aquatic invertebrates on which young swamp snakes feed).

Occasionally, conservation decisions are based on such observations: if, for example, temporary ponds are cut off by human development from the more permanent bodies of water that have historically recolonized them after droughts, then their natural cycles of drying and refilling could also depauperize neighboring bodies of water that depend on these little ponds as developmental habitat for juvenile herpetofauna.

41 South Florida Swamp Snake

Seminatrix pygaea cyclas

Nonvenomous   South Florida swamp snakes do not bite humans.

Abundance   Locally abundant from central Florida south to the tip of the peninsula.

Size   See **North Florida Swamp Snake (40).**

Habitat   Swamp snakes' primary habitat is heavily-vegetated wetlands, hyacinth-filled canals and ponds, as well as inundated stands of cypress. *Seminatrix pygaea cyclas* inhabits wet marl, sawgrass prairies habitats, brackish estuaries, and it is common in the Everglades in hardwood hammocks, willow heads, and canals.

Prey   In brackish tidal bays *S. p. cyclas* feeds mainly on small fish, including mosquitofish and sailfin mollies. Worms, leeches, and other aquatic invertebrates, along with frogs and tadpoles, salamanders, sirens, and amphiumas are taken in freshwater environments.

Reproduction   Live-bearing. Like most water snakes, female *S. pygaea* are longer and weigh more than males, but they are still so small that litter size ranges from only 2 to 11. On August 1 a 15-inch-long captive female gave birth to 7 offspring that averaged 5.3 inches in length.

Coloring/scale form   Except for having fewer ventral scales, the South Florida swamp snake is almost identical to the northern subspecies, *S. p. pygaea*. Its back and upper sides are shiny black (pale lateral streaks occur on the lower lateral scale rows), and its venter is red, with black pigment edging the distal margins of the fewer than 117 ventral scutes. There are 17 midbody rows of smooth dorsal scales and the anal plate is divided.

Similar snakes   The **North Florida swamp snake (40)** has 118 or more ventral scales.

Behavior   Swamp snakes are adapted to enduring periods of sparse rainfall by burrowing (often by descending into crayfish burrows) deeply within the mud beneath drying ponds. In this respect *S. p. cyclas* is a specialist in dealing with a low-energy environment, for in these damp subterranean refugia it can survive prolonged shortages of water, food, and oxygen that would kill birds, mammals, and most fish. In fact, if the subsurface soil retains sufficient moisture, swamp snakes may remain underground for months, emerging unharmed when the wetland above them refills.

Aquatic Snakes

Rough Green Snake

Opheodrys aestivus

Nonvenomous   Also known as the vine snake, *Opheodrys aestivus* (unlike the true neo-tropical vine snakes) is unlikely to bite humans.

Abundance   Abundant in mixed hardwood and bottomland forest throughout Florida, rough green snakes are also found in the hardwood hammocks that occur in wet prairies and sawgrass marshes.

Size   Most adults measure 22 to 32 inches; the record is 45.5 inches.

Habitat   The arboreal rough green snake prefers thickly-foliaged trees and shrubs whose closely spaced stems allow it to move about easily.[1] This leafy microhabitat occurs most often on the sunlit edges of fields, woodland ponds, and along thicket-bordered roads. Here, rough green snakes can be so abundant that thousands of these little reptiles—almost all of which soon die—are taken for the pet trade.

Prey   Plucked from leaves and stems, most of the rough green snake's prey is insects. In one study 85% of the diet consisted of caterpillars, spiders, grasshoppers, crickets, and odonates.

Reproduction   Egg-laying. Spring and summer rainfall strongly affects the well-being of rough green snakes. The abundant insects available in rainy years means higher fat levels among *O. aestivus*—which in turn affects green snakes' winter survival and determines females' egg-laying capacity. Rainfall also influences the survival of green snakes' 3 to 12 eggs (which are laid in grass roots or vegetative litter between April and July) because they are highly vulnerable to desiccation. Hatchlings are grayish and 6 to 8.5 inches in length; they can reach adult size in a year but seldom breed until their second spring.

Coloring/scale form   Often called "grass snake," emerald-backed *O. aestivus* is color-adapted, instead, to the verdant hue of tree leaves; its lips, chin, and belly are pale yellow. (After death these reptiles turn blue-gray.) The 17 midbody rows of dorsal scales are keeled; the anal plate is divided.

Similar snakes   No other bright green snake occurs in Florida.

Behavior   Slow-moving and unwary, *O. aestivus* depends solely on camouflage for protection; when approached it responds by freezing, sometimes swaying to match the movement of surrounding foliage.

---

[1]This sometimes takes *Opheodrys aestivus* into the tops of large live oak trees, from which, on two occasions, K. Enge has seen individuals seized by swallow-tailed kites.

Green Snakes

Eastern Coachwhip
Masticophis flagellum flagellum

Nonvenomous If cornered, this long, wiry serpent rapidly vibrates its tail and doesn't hesitate to strike and bite—often several times in succession. Rather than hanging on to an aggressor, however, coachwhips quickly grab and pull away, leaving long, shallow scratches.

Abundance Found throughout Florida except for the Keys, *M. f. flagellum* is locally common, but it is generally less abundant than its smaller relative the racer, *C. constrictor*.

Size The record eastern coachwhip measured 102 inches in length, but an individual this size would be very unusual. Most adult *M. f. flagellum* reach somewhere between 50 and 72 inches.

Habitat Commonly found in hardwood hammocks, pine forest, sandhills, scrub, flatwoods, and prairie, coachwhips occupy a majority of rural communities. Coastal strand and maritime hammock are also good habitat for coachwhips, while *M. flagellum* seems to be particularly abundant around abandoned farms.

Prey Coachwhips' prey can include almost any smaller vertebrate. Lizards, other snakes, mammals, birds and their eggs, frogs, and small turtles are recorded; insects may also be taken by juveniles. Both coachwhips and racers are serpentine greyhounds adapted for sight-hunting—evolutionary specializations whipsnakes have achieved only with specific physiological costs. J. A. Ruben's research suggests that adaptations favoring the coachwhip's speed and agility, such as lengthening the segmentation spacing of three major epaxial muscles, may limit its use of the constrictive tactics employed by other large terrestrial snakes. Rather than suffocating their prey by constriction, whipsnakes overpower sizeable food animals by pinning them against the ground, then disabling them with bites from their strong jaws.

Here, as with most other snakes, the coachwhip's primary instinctive feeding response is determined by vomerolfaction. Cooper, Buth, and Vitt found that hatchling coachwhips with no prior exposure to natural prey nevertheless "detected integumentary chemicals from potential prey species (the strongest responses were to cotton swabs rolled over the skin of lizards and snakes abundant within the young coachwhips' range) and discriminated them from stimuli from other animals." (Thus, if a highly visually-oriented, pursuit-hunting species such as *M. flagellum* is primarily responsive to chemical cues from prey, it seems likely that this sort of reliance on vomeronasal cues as attack triggers is universal, or nearly so, among snakes.)

Whipsnakes, Racers, and Indigo Snakes

Reproduction   Egg-laying. Little is known about courtship and nesting among free-ranging *M. f. flagellum*. The 10- to 15-inch-long hatchlings, which emerge in July and August, have brown anterior dorsal crossbars on their tan backs, and whitish, anteriorly spotted venters. This patterning is so different from the adults that in spite of the large eyes, pronounced supraocular scales, slender bodies, and crosshatched tails they share with their parents, the young are frequently assumed to belong to another species.

Coloring/scale form   Most adult *M. f. flagellum* exhibit unique two-toned coloring: the unmarked dark forebody fades posteriorly to lighter shades of brown and tan, and even the occasional black specimen usually has a reddish tail. Yet some local populations, such as that living in the Trail Ridge area east of Gainesville, have members that are uniformly light-colored, while other individuals have narrow brownish crossbands. (On the Atlantic coastal ridge, some eastern coachwhips resemble *Masticophis* from the western U.S. in being more or less uniformly reddish in color.)

The coachwhip's ventral color matches that of its dorsum, while on the posterior trunk the smooth scales' slightly darker borders create a cross-hatched, braided whip-like pattern from which the common name is derived. The head is angular and elongate, yet wider than the wiry neck, with large eyes shielded by projecting supraocular scales and anteriorly bordered by a pair of small preoculars. The dorsal scales are arranged in 17 rows at midbody (13 just ahead of the vent) and the anal plate is divided.

Similar snakes   Adult **brownchin, southern black,** and **Everglades racers (44, 45, 46)** lack a two-toned, dark forebody-lighter posterior trunk, as well as caudal cross-hatching. Racers also have 15 rows of dorsal scales just anterior to the vent.

Behavior   Like other racers and whipsnakes, *M. f. flagellum* is exceptionally alert and even curious—I have often been observed by coachwhips that had raised their heads above tall grass for a long look. Because *M. flagellum* can traverse open ground more swiftly than any other North American serpent, coachwhips are able to evade predators well enough to forage in more open environments than less mobile serpents. Nevertheless, even with their great speed and agility (when pursued coachwhips can streak up into low trees), diurnal travel across open terrain leaves them vulnerable to predation by hawks: long *Masticophis* bodies are often seen dangling from the talons of raptors perched on power line poles. The high metabolism and nervous energy that fuels this vigorous lifestyle generates a constant need to move about, moreover, and without being able to do so, most coachwhips are clearly miserable in confinement—although they are such resilient animals that individuals have lived for nearly 17 years in captivity.

44 Brownchin Racer
Coluber constrictor helvigularis

Nonvenomous *Coluber constrictor. c. helvigularis* does not hesitate to coil, strike, and bite when cornered.

Abundance Brownchin racers are common within their very restricted range, which principally involves the Apalachicola River drainage of the Florida panhandle.

Size Adult *C. c. helvigularis* are 26 to 62 inches long.

Habitat Racers can be found in nearly all terrestrial habitats, both rural and urban, but the brownchin subspecies is most often seen crossing the sandy lumbering roads that traverse the pine flatwoods of the Apalachicola National Forest.

Prey Despite the name *C. constrictor,* racers are not in fact constrictors. Small prey such as insects is snapped up and quickly swallowed, but when feeding on larger vertebrates—birds, frogs, lizards, snakes, and rodents—rather than suffocating their prey by constriction, racers overpower it by using a coil of their muscular bodies to press their prey against the ground while they disable it by biting.

Reproduction Identical to that of the **Southern Black Racer (45).**

Coloring/scale form Coloring is similar to that of the subspecies southern black racer except for the brownish hue mottling the lips, chin, and throat of *C. c. helvigularis.*

Similar snakes The **southern black racer (45),** whose range entirely surrounds that of the brownchin racer, has whitish lips, chin, and throat. Based on blood allozyme and albumin genetic typing (which can establish fine degrees of relatedness between animal groups), the fundamental biological concept of subspecies—particularly subspecies based on local differences in coloration—is presently under intense biological scrutiny. In the future, many color-based nomenclature differentiations like the distinction between the currently recognized separate races of brownchin, southern black, and everglades racers may be retermed as localized color variants rather than different subspecies. For other **Similar snakes** See **Southern Black Racer (45).**

Behavior By engaging in robust predatory activity, racers take the physiological risk that their increased energy expenditures may not bring in enough additional prey-calories to offset the metabolic and exposure-risk costs this activity incurs.[1] Because this balancing act is rather different from

---

[1]Warm-blooded, endothermic species use a significant portion of their total available energy just to maintain a constant body temperature, and by living vigorous lives, active warm-blooded animals add proportionately less to their total energy expenditure than do intermittently active reptiles like racers, whose at-rest energy consumption is extremely low.

Whipsnakes, Racers, and Indigo Snakes

that of other snakes, the activity profile of *C. constrictor* is an especially significant part of its ecology—a part recently chronicled by M. Plummer and J. Congdon with the aid of radio-telemetry.

Their subjects were active on 3 out of 4 days during the summer, with their inactive periods generally being devoted to ecdysis, or shedding—during which time most of the snakes hid in rodent burrows. Warm weather home ranges were usually several square acres in extent, and while many of these ranges overlapped, big racers had no larger ranges than did small ones. Males had larger daily cruising radii,[2] and females seeking egg-laying sites also traveled farther than other racers. In autumn all the snakes' activity areas decreased significantly, but in all other seasons shrub thickets remained the racers' preferred habitat, where they often climbed into the branches to escape danger.

Despite its place at the most-active end of the terrestrial reptilian spectrum and its name "racer," Plummer and Congdon found that *C. constrictor* is incapable of achieving the higher levels of avian/mammalian energy output. Maximum burst speed was no more than 12 mph, and even at a much slower pace maximum to-exhaustion time was less than 20 minutes. This is still great stamina for a terrestrial ectotherm because, compared to that of other reptiles, racers' physiology is well advanced. Measurements have shown that within 30 seconds of seizing a mouse a racer's heart rate increases to 3 times its resting level while its arterial blood pressure increases nearly fourfold. This large-scale cardiovascular acceleration is necessary to generate the increased blood flow that enables *C. constrictor* to respond almost as rapidly from a resting state as a bird or mammal. This sort of sophisticated defense/attack system has always been attributed solely to ectotherms, but now—as field experience has long suggested—it is evident that a reptile need not be a warm-blooded dinosaur to enjoy the benefits of a quick-reacting neuromuscular system, nor to sustain that system with considerable cardiovascular stamina.

---

[2] Its home range is usually defined as an animal's entire area of activity, which contains all its essential needs for food, water, and cover. An animal's territory, in contrast, is the defended part of its home range; although home ranges of different individuals may overlap, territories generally do not. The cruising radius is the usual scope of an animal's daily movement within its home range.

45 Southern Black Racer

Coluber constrictor priapus

Nonvenomous   *Coluber constrictor* is a high-strung species that will bite in self-defense. See **Everglades Racer (46).**

Abundance   Racers occur throughout Florida: One of the state's three subspecies (the brownchin in the central panhandle, the Everglades from the Tamiami Trail south to Key Largo, and the southern black throughout peninsular Florida and the lower Keys) is present everywhere in the state.

Size   Adults are 20 to 56 inches in length; 72 inches is the recorded maximum.

Habitat   *Coluber constrictor* is a habitat generalist which thrives in a multitude of both rural and even suburban areas. Common in all terrestrial habitats and many semi-aquatic ones, racers are among the few sizeable snakes seen by city dwellers.

Prey   Southern black racers prey on a variety of small animals, from insects and their larvae to vertebrates such as frogs, toads, lizards, snakes, birds and their eggs, and rodents.

Reproduction   Egg-laying. The 6 to 20 (most often 7 or 8) elongate, 1 by 1.75-inch rough-textured eggs have characteristic star-like markings on the ends of their shells. They are laid in humid subsurface cavities or within rotting logs, some of which are used communally, year after year, by several females. The 6- to 9-inch-long hatchlings emerge in July and August and may display death-feigning when handled. Very different in coloring from the adults (juveniles do not turn uniformly dark above until reaching about 22 inches in length), young racers are conspicuously patterned with chestnut-brown vertebral saddles that merge into a solid-colored tail. They have pale, often posteriorly pinkish venters.

Coloring/scale form   The slender body is glossy black above, with a bit of white on the chin and throat; the rest of the venter may be pale gray to nearly black. The iris is dark reddish-orange. There are 17 rows of smooth dorsal scales at midbody (15 just anterior to the vent) and the anal plate is divided.

Similar snakes   All color phases of the **eastern coachwhip (43)** have a somewhat lighter-hued tail and posterior belly, a darker forebelly, and 13 rows of dorsal scales just ahead of the vent.

Behavior   In Florida, southern black racers have been observed more than 10 feet up in trees, where they often seek refuge after having eluded a pursuer on the ground.

Whipsnakes, Racers, and Indigo Snakes

173

46 Everglades Racer
Coluber constrictor paludicola

Nonvenomous   Like other racers, *C. c. paludicola* is quick-tempered and likely to strike if cornered. In this situation, racers typically vibrate their tails so rapidly that in dry grass they produce a sound reminiscent of the caudal whir of a rattlesnake. Everglades racers seldom find themselves cornered like this though, for they are quick to flee when encountered in the field—a manifestation of the nervous temperament that makes racers restless captives that seldom do well in confinement.

Abundance   Abundant in southern peninsular Florida, *C. c. paludicola* also occurs in a disjunct range well to the north in Brevard Co. near Cape Canaveral.

Size   Similar to that of the subspecies **Southern Black Racer (45)**.

Habitat   Despite its name, the Everglades racer is not a snake of the true Everglades marshes, for it is only rarely found in inundated sawgrass swale, though it is common in the hardwood hammocks, pinelands, and drained agricultural fields typical of the Everglades area. Elsewhere in South Florida, Everglades racers occupy a variety of habitats, both disturbed and undisturbed—urban parks, canals bordering sugar cane fields, and stands of melaleuca, pine, and cypress.

Prey   Racers are generalized predators, taking whatever smaller creatures are most seasonally available, including insects, birds and their eggs, frogs, lizards, rodents, and other snakes.

Reproduction   Identical to that of the **Southern Black Racer (45)**.

Coloring/scale form   The slender body and elongate head follow the same configuration as those of the southern black racer, but the dorsum is grayish brown, sometimes with a bluish cast. Unlike the dark red iris of the southern black racer the Everglades racer's iris is a distinctive paler orange or yellow. The venter is off-white, mottled with blue-gray, the 17 midbody rows of dorsal scales are smooth and glossy, and the anal plate is divided. Juveniles resemble those of the southern black racer but with both a slightly more pinkish ground color and more rusty dorsolateral patterning.

Similar snakes   The larger and longer-tailed **eastern coachwhip (43)** almost always has a lighter-hued posterior body with dark-edged caudal cross-hatching and 17 midbody rows of dorsal scales.

Behavior   I have found *C. constrictor* to be less wary when hidden in the thick branches of trees where, rather than flee, it is inclined to freeze, sometimes until actually touched.

47 Eastern Indigo Snake

Drymarchon corais couperi

Nonvenomous   First described by J. E. Holbrook in 1842, this beautiful reptile is perhaps the most impressive of all North American snakes. When encountered in the field, individuals may hiss, flatten their necks, and vibrate their tails in threat, but most allow themselves to be handled without aggression. The few that do bite, however, can inflict deep cuts.

Abundance   Threatened. Despite having been federally protected since 1978, as well as receiving legal protection from the state of Florida, *D. c. couperi* is vanishing. In the past, collecting for the pet trade heavily impacted the eastern indigo, but the most harmful factor in this animal's current decline is the accelerating deterioration of its habitat. As an essentially tropical animal living at the northern limit of its biological capacity, the indigo is unable to tolerate northern Florida's winter freezes without deep underground refuges. Due to the parallel decline of the gopher tortoise—also depleted by loss of habitat and commercial collecting—in whose burrows *Drymarchon* formerly found shelter, such retreats are now hard to find. In addition, as P. E. Moler of the Florida Game and Fresh Water Fish Commission has pointed out, the resinous wood industry's removal of thousands of the dead stumps beneath which indigos formerly found shelter has left these animals with greatly diminished opportunities to escape the cold. Cold is not the only reason indigos are dependent on tortoise burrows and stump holes, however, for according to Bogert and Cowles, *D. c. couperi* is extremely vulnerable to desiccation. Adapted to the always-moist tropics, these big reptiles need the humid subsurface conditions they find within tortoise burrows and other chthonic subterranean environments to withstand the dry late summer heat of north-central Florida.

Fragmentation of individual indigo snakes' home ranges is an even greater problem. Few indigenous serpents have suffered as much as *D.c. couperi* from the conversion of peninsular Florida's uplands to agriculture and residential subdivisions—where these big, unwary reptiles are quickly extirpated by landowners, dogs, and automobiles. Because of its need for space—the warm-weather range of adults averages over 370 acres, with adult males using much more territory—the eastern indigo requires preserves of at least 2,500 acres to maintain a stable population.

Nevertheless, despite its overall rarity, according to K. Enge, who monitors the state's commercial reptile trade for the Florida Game Commission, to a limited extent, "Indigos are now making a comeback in some agricultural areas due to reduced collecting pressure: (reptile) hunters are seeing quite a few along the canefield irrigation canals around Moore Haven."

Whipsnakes, Racers, and Indigo Snakes

Size   *Drymarchon corais couperi* is the largest nonvenomous snake in North America; adult males average 60 to 74 inches in length and 4 to 5.5 pounds in weight, while females average 60 to 72 inches and weigh about 3.5 pounds. The record is 103.5 inches.

Habitat   Although it was formerly numerous throughout the state in environments ranging from grassy prairie to longleaf pine forest to coastal scrub to tidal mangrove swamp, *D. c. couperi* is now uncommon in even the best natural habitats, occurring most often in undisturbed pine flatwoods, brushy riparian corridors, sandhills, and wet prairie hammocks. Adult indigos ordinarily occupy the flooded sawgrass prairies of extensive wetlands such as the Everglades only when moving between elevated hardwood hammocks, but juveniles apparently prefer wetland edges to upland environments. Microhabitat includes mammal burrows, including those of the nine-banded armadillo recently established in Florida, limestone solution holes, hollow logs, stump holes, and the deep cavities found beneath large live oaks and Australian pines.

Prey   One of the few snakes large and active enough to be easily observed in its foraging, eastern indigos patrol canal and pond banks, slide into and out of rodent burrows, then rapidly cross open ground on their way to the next patch of cover. Prey can include any vertebrate big enough to attract their attention and small enough to be swallowed. Wild-caught indigos have disgorged toads, a variety of other snake species, including southern and eastern hognoses, several kinds of water snakes, pigmy rattlers, aquatic turtles, and hatchling gopher tortoises. While not true constrictors, *Drymarchon* pin their prey to the ground with a muscular body coil, then immobilize it with bites from their powerful jaws. This tactic is effective in subduing even large pit vipers, whose venom seems to have no effect on the indigo. More preferred prey is pig frogs and corn snakes, which even newly captured *Drymarchon* will sometimes take directly from one's hands. In areas where indigos are plentiful, corn and rat snakes are generally found only aloft in the branches of trees, for although *D. c. couperi* is a surprisingly nimble climber when pursued, it apparently does not hunt in trees. The high incidence of frogs and other snakes in the diet of wild indigos makes them prone to the herpetofaunal-specific parasitic worms they acquire from these prey species and most wild caught individuals are heavily parasitized.

Reproduction   Egg-laying. Breeding takes place in late fall and winter, when the territoriality of adult males waxes to the extent that they sometimes inflict 6-inch-long razorlike fang cuts on each other's foreparts. Like many other reptiles, female indigos retain sperm[1] from autumnal pairings until early spring fertilization. Following 70 to over 100 days of incubation,

---

[1]Sometimes for long periods: one female *Drymarchon* deposited fertile eggs after 4 years of isolation.

the 4 to 11 oblong whitish eggs (as much as 3 inches in length and 1.3 inches in diameter, their leathery surfaces covered with fine pebbling) hatch into dorsally-blotched young, 18 to 26 inches long.

Coloring/scale form   Florida's most spectacular serpent, the adult indigo's thickly-muscled body is covered with blue/black dorsal scales so glossy that, on newly shed individuals, they seem almost iridescent. The chin and throat are usually reddish or white, with the red sometimes extending onto the forebody. The posterior venter exhibits a singular combination of cloudy orange and blue-gray. Like their brownish Central American *Drymarchon* relatives[2] many individuals have faint facial striping. Most of the 17 midbody rows of dorsal scales are smooth, but among *D. c. couperi* scutellation is sexually dimorphic: as males reach sexual maturity at 55 to 60 inches in length they may develop partial keels on a few of the vertebral scale rows. The anal plate is undivided.

Similar snakes   The **eastern coachwhip (43)** is a much slimmer, longer-tailed snake with a two-toned, dark forebody-lighter posterior body color division, a crosshatched caudal pattern, and a divided anal plate. The **southern black racer (45)** is also much more slender, with 15 posterior scale rows and a divided anal plate.

Behavior   The eastern indigo is seasonally territorial: during the warmer months male *D. c. couperi* range over hundreds of acres which, except in large uninhabited areas, places them in jeopardy from encounters with human beings. In winter, both sexes maintain smaller ranges of less than 50 acres near residence dens where the same individuals, marked by clipping subcaudal scales, have been recovered year after year. On their home terrain these animals seem to be familiar with every stick and bush in the neighborhood of their burrows, for if they are pursued they may make false runs in two or three different directions before doubling back toward their dens.

Indigo snakes' dramatic appearance has created a huge demand for captives, but *Drymarchon* are usually too restless to make satisfactory cage animals. Unable to settle into the lethargy that confinement requires, many rub their snouts raw trying to pry out of their enclosures, and almost all are so given to voiding musk and feces that handling them is seldom a pleasure. Besides being illegal to possess in captivity without a permit, the terrestrial indigo is also ill at ease off the ground (unlike captive arboreal snakes like the boas, which feel comfortable draped over one's limbs), and most individuals make such constant efforts to be free of human contact that it is clear they should have been left at large.

[2]Florida's population of *D. c. couperi* is a remnant of a Southwestern, desert-adapted Pleistocene fauna that once ranged eastward to the Atlantic, then became isolated in Florida by the colder winters associated with advancing Pleistocene glaciers.

Eastern Hognose Snake

Heterodon platirhinos

Nonvenomous   The eastern hognose is entirely harmless to humans. Its enlarged rear teeth, which introduce its mildly toxic saliva into its amphibian prey, are located too far back in its mouth to be used in defense.

Abundance   Found throughout Florida, *H. platirhinos* may be locally abundant, particularly in areas of sandy soil and heavy ground cover—conditions that favor its anuran prey.

Size   Most adults are 20 to 33 inches long; the record is 45.5 inches.

Habitat   Eastern hognoses live in a variety of sandy-substrate habitats, especially the central Florida uplands, sandhills, and scrub of the Lake Wales ridge area. Both mixed hardwood and upland pine forest are also inhabited, as are forest/grassland boundaries.

Prey   Eastern hognose snakes are largely scent hunters that locate prey beneath leaf litter and even buried in soil, then root it out with their upturned, plowshare-like rostral scale. This prey is almost always toads, for hognoses are extreme predatory specialists on these anurans.[1] Frogs are also a principal food, and lizards may occasionally be taken, but *H. platirhinos* has evolved specific physical attributes that allow it to feed on toads—creatures themselves adapted to swallowing air to balloon themselves too large to fit down a snake's throat.

These predatory adaptations include enlarged rear teeth and muscle-relaxing salivary toxins. After its flexible lower jaw has partially engulfed a toad and maneuvered the amphibian as far back into the mouth as possible, the hognose swings a pair of lance-shaped teeth forward (its genus name, *Heterodon,* means different-toothed). Hinged to the maxillary bone at the rear of the upper jaw, these long teeth puncture the amphibian's swollen body, introducing the snake's stringy, opalescent toxic saliva that soon leaves the toad too limp to continue its struggle.

Adult eastern hognoses also scavenge carrion (I have seen one trying to eat a road-killed leopard frog) but because they are disinclined to take the domestic mice that most captive snakes are fed, *H. platirhinos* was seldom maintained in confinement until it was discovered that many could be enticed to accept rodents by rubbing them with a live toad to impart its scent; as a result, both Florida hognose species are now bred in captivity.

---

[1]Toads are inedible by most carnivores due to the heart-suppressing digitaloid toxins they excrete from epidermal glands. Nevertheless, toads are eaten by many serpents, especially garter and ribbon snakes, but the toxicity of their skin secretions keeps anurans from forming the major portion of these reptiles' diet. In contrast, hognose snakes, which eat primarily toads, have adrenal glands (slender organs some .25 by 2 inches long in adults, located just ahead of the kidneys) that are some 10 times heavier in relation to body weight than the adrenals of other North American colubrid snakes, and produce sufficient adrenaline to largely neutralize the toads' digitaloid bufotoxins.

Reproduction   Egg-laying. Mating occurs March through May, followed, after 6 to 8 weeks, by deposition of 4 to 61 (average 22) 1.25 by .75 inch-long whitish eggs. The hatchlings measure 6.5 to 9.5 inches in length and typically experience their first shed while emerging from the egg. See **Southern Hognose Snake (49)**.

Coloring/scale form   *Heterodon platirhinos* is quite variable in dorsal coloring: individuals can be patterned with black, khaki green, or yellowish-to reddish-brown. In Florida, a light gray ground-colored color phase is common, and as these individuals age, they undergo an ontogenetic color change in which the juvenile patterning darkens until older adults are nearly solid black. Among all color morphs the underside of the tail is much lighter than the occasionally orange-blotched dark gray venter. So much variety in coloration means that the eastern hognose is best identified by its shape: stocky trunk, short head scarcely distinct from its wide neck, and pointed, upturned snout flanked by sharply-edged labial ridges. A prominent bulge over the little dark eyes is emphasized by a brown band that masks the fore-crown. The prefrontal scales touch, the heavily keeled dorsal scales are arranged in 23 to 25 midbody rows, and the anal plate is divided.

Similar snakes   The **southern hognose snake (49)** has an even more markedly upturned rostral scale, its prefrontal scutes are separated by small-er scales, and the underside of its tail is the same pale color as the rest of its venter. The **southern copperhead (64)** has unbroken dorsolateral bands, its slender neck is much narrower than its flat-crowned triangular head, and there is a dark pit between its nostril and its large, vertically slit-pupilled eye.

Behavior   The strongly keeled dorsolateral scales with which *H. platirhinos* is covered give it the traction to burrow with its muscular trunk, rooting through the earth with its wedge-like snout like a small plow, forcing loos-ened soil to the sides. In the open, the eastern hognose's deliberate pace makes it an easy target for predators and, in defense, it has developed an elaborate death-feigning ruse. This entails spreading its long ribs to flatten its body, hissing, and making feinting pseudo-strikes much like those of a pit viper, although the strikes are carried out with the mouth closed, and—unless one has recently handled a toad—even prodding its snout with a finger won't prompt *H. platirhinos* to bite. If its antagonist persists, the hognose may con-ceal its head under its tightly spiraled tail and, to make itself unappealing as a meal, writhe convulsively, regurgitate, defecate, discharge odorous musk from its cloaca and turn belly-up, its tongue hanging loosely from its slack-ened jaw. If placed right side up, some hognoses will even flop back over, righting themselves to crawl away only after the danger has passed.

In some rural areas the hognose is known, and even feared, as a "spread-ing adder."

Brown-blotched Terrestrial Snakes

49 Southern Hognose Snake

Heterodon simus

Nonvenomous Hognose snakes have so many bizarre habits, physical structures, and patterns of musculature that it has been suggested that the genus *Heterodon* be assigned subfamily distinction from other colubrids. If threatened, *Heterodon* simus may hiss, flatten its head and neck, and feign death, but it does not bite humans.

Abundance Uncommon to rare. Protected only in Alabama and Mississippi, *H. simus* is occasionally locally common in Florida, but it is not an abundant animal throughout most of its southeastern U. S. range. Similar in its size, dorsal pattern, and strongly upturned rostral scale to the western hognose species, *H. nasicus,* the southern hognose is a relict member of an ancient xeric-community fauna, and while presently found from the panhandle south through peninsular Florida (with the exception of a narrow strip along the northeastern Atlantic shore) to Lake Okeechobee, its old desert-dweller's orientation to silicaceous soil is evident in its greater abundance in Central Florida's sandhills, where *H. simus* is typically more numerous than the eastern hognose.

Size The smallest of the three North American *Heterodon,* the southern hognose averages only 20 to 21 inches in maximum length, with females being slightly larger than males. The record is 24 inches.

Habitat The southern hognose's primary habitat is sandhills, open-canopy, sandy-soiled pine/turkey oak woodland, and scrub. The stabilized dunes known as coastal strand are also home to southern hognoses. North-central Florida's scrub and sandhill uplands—biologically referred to as "island Florida" because during interglacial periods this area was cut off from the mainland by elevated sea levels—is home to other sand-adapted species like the short-tailed snake, the crowned snake and the eastern indigo snake.

Prey Predation by *H. simus* is even more narrowly focused on toads and frogs than is that of the eastern hognose; prey species are principally spade-foot, southern, and oak toads, although lizards and small mammals are also occasionally taken. *Heterodon* is able to prey on toads because enlarged adrenal glands allow them to metabolize the epidermal toxins that protect the anurans from most other predators. See **Eastern Hognose Snake (48), Prey.** Bill Griswold of Spring Hill, an authority on Florida's hognose snakes, reports that in captivity squirrel and green tree frogs, as well as mice scented with anuran skin secretions, are also accepted as prey.

Reproduction Egg-laying. No natural nests have been reported, but Griswold's records of captive reproduction among both *H. platirhinos* and *H. simus* document that courtship begins with the male nudging and caressing the female with his enlarged rostral. Breeding commences in mid-April and continues until mid-August (most other colubrids in Florida breed between March and May), and copulation—lasting up to 3 hours—entails an extremely large hemipenal bulge, which may indicate size/structure distinctions between the hemipenes of *H. simus* and other *Heterodon*. The clutches of 6 to 14 (average: 8) non-adherent eggs are deposited between July and late October and, after 55 to 60 days of artificial incubation in moist vermiculite, hatch into 6- to 7-inch-long young. Unlike eastern hognose neonates, which shed as they emerge from the egg, newborn southern hognoses do not shed until they are 3 to 5 days old.

Coloring/scale form   Unlike the eastern hognose, individual *H. simus* vary little in dorsal coloration, although at least one albino southern hognose snake has been discovered in the wild. Ground color is generally yellowish-brown, with dark vertebral blotches separated by smaller pale orange blotches; the tail is light- and dark-banded. (The undertail is the same sandy-gray hue as the anterior belly.) The prominent rostral scale is sharply upturned (*Heterodon* are anything but "hog" nosed), the prefrontal scales are separated by smaller scutes, and the keeled dorsal scales are usually arranged in 25 rows at midbody. The anal plate is divided.

Similar snakes   The **eastern hognose snake (49)** has a smaller and less upturned rostral scale, its prefrontals touch, the underside of its tail is lighter in color than its dark gray venter, and it occurs in a host of colors (including mottled olive green, orange-brown, and black) not found among southern hognoses. In Florida, many people mistakenly identify (and kill) southern hognose snakes as the **dusky pigmy rattlesnake (68)**. Besides having a small rattle, the pigmy rattler is a more grayish-brown reptile with a russet vertebral stripe and the pit vipers' characteristic configuration of a narrow neck and broad flat head marked by a dark pit between the nostril and the large, slit-pupiled eye.

Behavior   Most active during early summer, more often in early morning and evening when toads are abroad, during the day the southern hognose is able to scent out anurans hidden beneath ground cover and to root them from their buried nooks with its upturned rostral. Griswold reports that *H. simus* in his captive collection typically refuse food during the winter even when not in hibernation, so he artificially induces dormancy for 2 to 3 months (usually Thanksgiving to Valentine's Day) at a constant temperature of between 50 and 60°F.

Brown-blotched Terrestrial Snakes

50 Black Pine Snake
Pituophis melanoleucus lodingi

Nonvenomous   Like their close relatives the western bullsnakes, pine snakes are big, relatively slow-moving terrestrial foragers ill-suited for either flight or concealment. What members of the genus *Pituophis* have evolved, instead, is a dramatic tutelary display in which threatened individuals rear their forebodies off the ground and hiss loudly enough to be heard for several yards. The hiss is amplified by a unique physiological adaptation. Just in front of the airway at the base of its throat a flexible fin of cartilage protects the pine snake's glottal passage from the passage of ingested prey animals; when the snake expends its monumental exhalations, this flap buzzes so loudly in the outgoing airstream that it approximates the lethal-sounding whir of a big rattlesnake.

Abundance   *Pituophis melanoleucus lodingi* occurs in Florida only in an intergrade form exhibiting characteristics of the more easterly subspecies, the Florida pine snake, *P. m. mugitus*. These animals are only found in the panhandle west of the Escambia River. According to P. E. Moler of the Wildlife Research Laboratory of the Florida Game and Freshwater Fish Commission, three individuals from this part of the state approach the phenotype of *P. m. lodingi*: these adults are mostly black but, like the Florida pine snake, retain some of their juvenile pattern. Just to the east of the Escambia River, however, pine snakes are typical *P. m. mugitus*, the Florida pine snake.

Size   Most adults measure 36 to 60 inches in length; the record is 89 inches.

Habitat   Despite their name, pine snakes don't live in pine trees. Instead, pine snakes are primarily terrestrial, even fossorial residents of sandy-soiled pine and mixed hardwood forest communities. Juveniles have been found well above ground level, however, preying on nestling birds.

Prey   Pine snakes feed primarily on small vertebrates. Mice, birds and their eggs, reptile eggs, and young rabbits are reported as prey, but pocket gophers (*Geomys*) are pine snakes' principal—and usually habitat-determining—food species.

Reproduction   Breeding occurs in April and May; 4 to 8 whitish eggs (almost the size of hen eggs) are laid during June and July at the end of long subsurface tunnels. In September and October these hatch into 18- to 20-inch-long offspring.

Coloring/scale form   Among pure *P. m. lodingi* from Alabama, the adult dorsal ground color is black. Intergrade specimens with the Florida pine snake are so suffused with black pigment that the anterior vertebral blotches of the pure Florida pine are obscured and the dorsum is very dark brown to black. Hatchlings of both races are boldly blotched, and are not distinguishable by race until they pass about 30 inches in length. The venter is whitish to dark gray, with scattered black pigment. The 29 midbody rows of dorsal scales are heavily keeled, there are 4 prefrontal scales, and (as an adaptation to burrowing) the rostral scale is enlarged and extended upward between the internasals. The anal plate is undivided.

Similar snakes   Called pine snakes in the East, bullsnakes in the Midwest, and gopher snakes in the West, all members of the genus *Pituophis* are similar in body configuration and general marking. **Rat snakes (53—55)** have only 2 prefrontal scales and a divided anal plate. The **corn snake (52)** is distinguished by the dark-bordered, spearpoint-shaped marking on its crown; it also has but 2 prefrontal scales and a divided anal plate.

Behavior   Predation on pocket gophers, which have formidable defenses, is accomplished by the pine snake's singular hunting technique. Unlike generalized predators such as the rat snakes[1]—which, in a glass-walled observation arena, edge cautiously into an underground warren of rodent tunnels—*P. melanoleucus* virtually dives down such a burrow. Gophers are fast diggers, and if given a moment's warning will throw up a barricade of dirt, plugging their burrow behind them. A creeping rat snake encounters only a dead-end tunnel, but pine snakes are better adapted to overcome this obstacle. Aided by its conical skull and muscular neck, *P. melanoleucus* may twist its head sideways into a right-angle, then use it like a hoe to scoop dirt out of its path.

Yet, rather than excavate a gopher's two-inch barrier of dirt, a pine snake often turns away from a plugged burrow. If there is another route open, pine snakes evidently prefer to enter it rapidly, then employ the other predatory specialization they have developed for feeding on gophers. Constriction with a suffocating body coil isn't possible within the narrow walls of gopher tunnels, so to compensate for this pine snakes have been observed quickly forcing their way past startled gophers, then pinning them against the side of their burrows with a body coil—suffocating them without exposing the pine snake's head to the gopher's long yellow incisors.

---

[1]All *Pituophis* are thought to be rat snake descendants which, during the Pliocene, diverged from the *Elaphe* lineage by evolving morphological and behavioral adaptations to pursue and more effectively kill pocket gophers—a predator/prey relationship that dates back at least 8 million years.

51 Florida Pine Snake

Pituophis melanoleucus mugitus

Nonvenomous   Florida pine snakes do not bite unless they are attacked, but if harassed they are great bluffers. Before the sawmills moved into the South during the 1920s, *P. melanoleucus* was common, and attracted written comment on both its formidable size and the dramatic display in which it rears its forebody off the ground while hissing loudly enough to be heard for yards.

Abundance   Rare. The Florida pine snake is classified by the state as a threatened species of special concern; due to fragmentation of Florida's upland sandhill/pine/oak forest community, *P. m. mugitus* is now extirpated from much of its former range. Like other *Pituophis*, Florida pine snakes are long-lived—19 years is recorded—and breed readily in confinement, yet they are seldom propagated because there is a state possession limit of one specimen and captive-born offspring cannot be sold or traded. In favorable habitat, pine snakes' retiring habits (rodent prey is captured in subsurface burrows, where the serpents remain to digest their meal) allow pine snakes to avoid contact with humans except when dispersing to new hunting areas or during males' annual search for female pheromone trails.

Size   Most adults are 34 to 59 in.; the record is over 96 inches.

Habitat   Uncommon everywhere, Florida pine snakes are found more often in open, pine-turkey oak woodland and abandoned fields than in sandhill, scrub, or climax longleaf pine forest—the only other natural environments in which they regularly occur.

Prey   *P. m. mugitus* has been found living below ground in gopher colonies, where it even lays its eggs. See **Black Pine Snake (50)**. Pine snakes are also known to climb trees in search of birds' nests.

Reproduction   See **Black Pine Snake (50)**.

Coloring/scale form   Dorsal ground color is light tan, but dark pigment may obscure the forewardmost of the 25 to 31 dorsal blotches (juveniles have more distinctly blotched forebodies). The venter is gray, marked with varying amounts of black, there are 29 rows of keeled dorsal scales, 4 prefrontals, the rostral extends upward between the internasals, and the anal plate is undivided.

Similar snakes   See **Black Pine Snake (50)**.

Behavior   R. Franz's northern Florida field study revealed that *P. m. mugitus* had large home ranges, with a mean size of 130 acres, while males used up to 247 acres. These animals spent 85% of their time underground—mostly in gopher and tortoise burrows—but during droughts they moved into open areas adjacent to wetlands.

Corn Snake
Elaphe guttata guttata

Nonvenomous   Occasionally, wild corn snakes will rear up and strike, but this is mostly in bluff because their small teeth are not capable of seriously harming a large predator. Most *E. g. guttata* are docile though and, as the most commonly kept hobbyist's snake, thousands are bred in captivity every year. If given good care and gentle handling, virtually all remain tame throughout captive lives which can last as long as 22 years.

Abundance   Very common throughout the panhandle, peninsular Florida, and the Keys. Corn snakes from the lower Keys, however—a pinkish-orange color phase known as the rosy rat snake—comprise a threatened population of special concern.

Size   Adults are 18 to 44 inches long; the record is 72 inches.

Habitat   Like other rat snakes, *E. g. guttata* can occur in almost any terrestrial habitat—pinelands, hardwood hammocks, thickets of melaleuca, canal-bordering Australian pines, farmlands, and suburban neighborhoods. Most individuals are found in constricted micro-environments—within rockpiles, trash heaps, between dangling palm fronds, and in tree cavities (natural cavities are most common in "soft" hardwoods such as tupelo, red maple, and ash), around old buildings and within old wooden railroad trestles. During summer, newborns sometimes turn up in swimming pools.

Prey   Small rodents, lizards, birds, and frogs. Themselves a preferred prey of indigo snakes and coachwhips, *E. g. guttata* stay high in trees when these terrestrial predators are in the area.

Reproduction   Egg-laying. Breeding takes place April to June; 3 to 40 eggs are laid during the summer and hatch during July, August, and September. Only the largest females deposit clutches of more than 20.

Coloring/scale form   Named for the native American corn, or maize, which corn snakes' variegated orange-and-black dorsums suggest, *E. g. guttata* is a member of the rat snake genus *Elaphe* (corn snakes are also known as red rat snakes). Their natural reddish tints, which stand out boldly against some backgrounds, nevertheless probably function as camouflage in shade-dappled forest floored with russet pine needles. Corn snakes are found in many areas besides pinewoods, but their most common color manifestation seems to be a cryptic accommodation to the pine needle- and leaf-strewn substrate of the eastern pine-oak woodland that originally occupied most of the corn snake's range. Living largely to the west of the eastern forests, the subspecies great plains rat snake, *E. g. emoryi*, has the same dorsolateral patterning as the corn snake but, except for individuals found in the Louisiana pinewoods, it is a gray-brown snake. *E. g. emoryi* is still classified as a subspecies of the corn snake, but because its range has long been sepa-

Brown-blotched Terrestrial Snakes

rated from that of *E. g. guttata,* originally cut off by the old salt-water embayment of the lower Mississippi Valley, the two races have been proposed as separate species by J. T. Collins.

Most corn snakes have orange, gray, or tan ground-colored backs and sides with red to russet, prominently black-bordered vertebral blotches usually separated by no more than 3 rows of paler scales. Their most distinguishing marking, though, is a pair of black-edged brown lines that form a forward-pointing V on the crown; a similarly black-edged brown stripe runs across the snout, masking the eyes, and continues rearward past the supralabial scales onto the neck. Corn snakes' bellies are a black-and-white checkerboard, except for the underside of the tail, which is laterally dark-striped. The dorsal scales are weakly keeled, usually arranged in 27 (sometimes 29) midbody dorsal rows, and the anal plate is divided.

In a color morph known as "Miami phase," some *E. g. guttata* from the southeastern coast have a pale gray dorsolateral ground color which strikingly sets off their black-edged red vertebral blotches. To the west, extensive collecting near the southern end of Lake Okeechobee by Kenneth Krysko has shown that gray "anerythristic" corn snakes entirely devoid of red pigment make up approximately 20% of the local population, while elsewhere in peninsular Florida totally orange-and-white "amelanistic" individuals completely lacking black pigment have also been found.

Another variant population—precisely described in accounts from the 1930s—is the corn snakes living in the lower Florida Keys. Once thought to constitute a separate race, in its pure form this "rosy rat snake" variant of *E. g. guttata* is indeed brown- and rosy-speckled, with reduced black borders on its orangish dorsal blotches, minimal ventral checkerboarding, a faint or absent cephalic spearpoint, and a slimmer body and more elongated head than mainland corn snakes. Even individual Keys developed distinctive variants, yet these rat snakes have probably not been totally genetically isolated since the early Pleistocene, for most of the lower Keys are no more than ½ mile apart and mainland corn snakes have probably been carried there naturally on debris during storms and tidal changes.

Nevertheless, these unique, primarily terrestrial rat snakes evolved on the offshore Keys largely isolated from mainland corn snakes.[1] Their isolation has recently been broached, however, for as John Decker has pointed out,

---

[1]Appropriately, the orange-stemmed salt wort ground cover and maroon-trunked red mangroves that comprise much of the lower Keys' natural vegetation form an even more orangish background environment than the fallen pine needles of mainland forests—and with the constant presence of sharp-eyed predatory herons in the Keys, the area's diurnally active herpetofauna needs all the camouflage it can evolve.

hidden in pallets of sod and the burlapped root balls of landscape shrubbery trucked from nurseries near Homestead, mainland corn snakes have recently arrived on the Keys in such numbers that they have diluted the shallow gene pool of the original "rosy rat" so much that this variant may soon be bred out of existence in the wild. "Rosy rat phase" corn snakes are easy to raise, of course, but because corn snakes are illegal to collect on the lower Keys, few breeders risk propagating them.

Similar snakes   As juveniles, **gray rat snakes (53)** are similar, but lack the corn snake's black-edged brown cranial V. The brown band through their eyes stops at the corner of the mouth, their undertails are not usually dark-striped, and their brown vertebral blotches are neither dark-edged nor separated by 4 or more rows of paler scales. Both **eastern** and **southern hognose snakes (48, 49)** are entirely terrestrial and much stockier than the corn snake, with thick necks and distinctly-upturned rostral scales tipping their snouts. The similarly non-arboreal **mole kingsnake (57)** has smooth dorsal scales and an undivided anal plate.

The great natural variability among *E. g. guttata* has made it a favorite with reptile fanciers, who have used the corn snake's adaptively-maleable pigmentation to create an incredible palate of captive-bred color morphs.[2] Marketed, often at hundreds of dollars each, to the exotic animal trade under names such as "snow corn" (white, but with a trace of dorsal patterning and pink eyes), "blizzard corn" (white and patternless), and "butter corn" (lemon-butter yellow), these selectively-derived designer snakes have become the focus of a major husbandry enterprise.

Behavior   Primarily nocturnal, corn snakes are good burrowers, climbers, and swimmers (although they are seldom found in extensive wetlands). More than the closely related, equally arboreal black rat snake lineage of *E. obsoleta*, when not foraging corn snakes tend to hide—almost any penetrable crevice in a building, retaining wall, or loose-barked tree offers refuge for *E. g. guttata*.

---

[2]In 1973, R. D. Bartlett collected a female albino corn snake in Sarasota County. This animal was bred to a typical wild-type male, and although she died during egg-laying, her 5 heterozygous offspring were crossbred, with their descendants eventually producing the current myriad captive-raised lineages of "snow" corn snakes.

53 Gray Rat Snake
Elaphe obsoleta spiloides

Nonvenomous   This large and often beautiful serpent—known locally as "oak runner" or "white oak snake"—may bite to defend itself, but is considerably less aggressive than its close relative, the yellow rat snake.

Abundance   *Elaphe obsoleta spiloides* is common throughout the panhandle east into northern peninsular Florida. Immediately after hatching in late summer, the young are frequently found in both residential and rural areas.

Size   Most adults are 36 to 72 inches; the record is 84.25 inches.

Habitat   Almost every wooded terrestrial environment within its range offers habitat for *E. o. spiloides*—oak forest and pinelands, tree-lined riverbanks, hardwood hammocks and stands of cypress. Gray rat snakes are especially well adapted, however, to exploiting the increased rodent populations that occur along the borders of forest and disturbed areas such as cultivated fields and stock ponds. Even to humans, barns and sheds usually smell of mice, and to scent-hunting, agile-climbing *Elaphe*, farm outbuildings are a magnet.

Prey   Like other *Elaphe obsoleta*, gray rat snakes are both constrictors and generalized predators which, even as hatchlings, primarily take vertebrate prey—lizards in trees and frogs along margins of ponds. Adults feed more heavily on rodents, as well as birds and their eggs—a fact not lost on the avian community, because the surest way to find a rat snake coiled in the branches is to locate a group of agitated blue jays.

Reproduction   Egg-laying. Breeding takes place from April to July, with 5 to 27 eggs being deposited in mid to late summer. During September the pale gray, sharply brown-blotched hatchlings emerge.

Coloring/scale form   Most gray rat snakes have a gray ground color with anteriorly elongate dark dorsal blotches separated by 4 or more scale rows. A slightly different color morph, sometimes called the "white oak" phase, possesses a silvery ground color with dark brown or gray dorsolateral blotches. A third color phase, genetically influenced by the black ratsnake with which *E. o. spiloides* intergrades to the north of Florida, has a dark brown back with black vertebral blotches. The venter of most individuals is gray, marked with squarish dark blotches and a double row of black spots behind the vent. There are 2 prefrontal scales, the 25 (sometimes 27) midbody rows of dorsal scales are weakly keeled, and the anal plate is divided.

Similar snakes   Individuals from northwestern peninsular Florida were once thought to represent a separate race known as the Gulf Hammock rat snake, *Elaphe obsoleta "williamsi."* However, today the area is known to be occupied instead by intergrades between the gray rat snake and the subspecies **yellow rat snake (54)**. As they mature, the grayish intergrade baby *E. obsoleta* in this area undergo an ontogenetic color change to grayish-yellow, with the dark stripes of the yellow rat snake usually being confined to the forebody or abbreviated into elongate dorsolateral blotches. Juvenile **corn snakes (52)** are distinguished by the pair of black-edged brown lines that describe a V on their pale crowns; by the black-edged brown stripe that runs across the snout, masks the eyes, and continues past the upper labial scales onto the neck, by their dark-edged vertebral blotches, separated by no more than 3 rows of paler scales, and their laterally dark-striped undertails. The brown dorsal blotches of the entirely terrestrial **mole kingsnake (57)** are also usually edged with black, its dorsal scales are smooth, and its anal plate is undivided. The **Florida pine snake (51)** has a speckled crown, a dark-banded tail, 4 prefrontal scales (rat snakes have 2 prefrontals), and an undivided anal plate. Juvenile **racers (44, 45, 46)** have a predominantly solid-colored tail and an undivided anal plate, while young **water snakes (21, 22, 23, 24, 27)** have strongly keeled dorsal scales and, unlike the adults, seldom leave aquatic environments.

Behavior   Its adaptability to human-occupied areas and its wide-ranging search for rats and mice make *E. o. spiloides* the large serpent most likely to be found in suburban parts of northwestern Florida. (Gray rat snakes are the source of most of the calls police and fire departments receive about long, gray-brown serpents found hidden in garage rafters, attics, or abandoned automobiles and machinery.) Because these animals are usually cornered, their typical defensive posture—elevating the forequarters and making feinting strikes toward their assailant—appears so aggressive to those unaware of how much of the display is a bluff, evolved only to startle an assailant long enough for the snake to escape, that the animal is often misidentified as venomous and killed.

Part of the aboreal agility that gets *E. o. spiloides* into these situations derives from rat snakes' adaptively-stiffened ventral plates, whose backward-turned outer edges can be dug into furrowed tree bark: by using both lateral undulation and concertina movement (inching the ventral scutes ahead in successive waves of belly-muscle contraction), *Elaphe obsoleta* is able to ascend almost straight up a rough-trunked palm or Australian pine.

Once aloft, rat snakes are superlatively arboreal. Aided by some 50% more vertebrae than most terrestrial or aquatic serpents, they are able to stiffen their wirily-muscled bodies enough to bridge branch-to-branch gaps more than half their own length, then thread themselves through fronds and branches dozens of feet from the ground. Here, in broad daylight, both gray and yellow rat snakes are often seen draped along the branches. See **Evolution of Snakes,** Footnote # 5.

54 Yellow Rat Snake
Elaphe obsoleta quadrivittata

Nonvenomous   In the wild, *E. o. quadrivittata* (known rurally as the chicken snake) does not hesitate to strike at an aggressor, and if it makes contact tends to hang on and chew. Yet, like other rat snakes it tames readily and thrives in captivity, living up to 17 years with good care.

Abundance   The yellow rat snake is an abundant, even dominant (See **Everglades Rat Snake (55), Abundance**) statewide species, adaptable to a variety of habitats, although it is not common in the upper Keys.

Size   Adults generally measure 40 to 70 inches in length. The record yellow rat snake, collected in 1993 by Kenneth Krysko at Lake Okeechobee, is almost 90 inches.

Habitat   Like other *E. obsoleta,* the yellow rat snake is seldom found in open terrain. Primarily a climber, it most often inhabits cypress strands, pinelands, hardwood hammocks, melaleuca, and the margins of farms and other disturbed areas such as canal banks; microhabitat includes holes in palm and pine trees, hollows beneath loose tree bark, and the underpinnings of wooden trestles. See **Everglades Rat Snake (55).**

Prey   Birds and their eggs, rodents, lizards, and frogs.

Reproduction   Egg-laying. Similar to other *Elaphe obsoleta.*

Coloring/scale form   *E. o. quadrivittata* from peninsular Florida are boldly colored, their yellow backs and sides streaked with four dark stripes (*quadrivittata* means "four lined"). The belly is pale yellow and the tongue black. (All juveniles have a gray dorsum with dark vertebral and lateral blotches.) Individuals from northern peninsular Florida are more olive, with both dark stripes and dorsal blotches, while in the rare and often beautiful color morph known as "Deckert's phase," mangrove-living *E. o. quadrivittata* from the upper Keys may have dark golden brown to burnt orange backs and sides with dark stripes. The dorsal scales of these animals are sometimes silver-edged, and they are somewhat neotonic in retaining, as adults, the dark blotches of juveniles. There are 27 rows of weakly-keeled dorsal scales and the anal plate is divided.

Similar snakes   Very similar as a hatchling, the **gray rat snake (53)** remains a dark-blotched grayish brown as it matures, although intergrade forms with stripes as well as blotches occur in northeastern Florida.

Behavior   In south Florida, *E. o. quadrivittata* is often observed sunning itself—frequently just after a rain shower—on the dark-needled branches of canal-side Australian pines where its yellow dorsolateral coloring makes it particularly conspicuous.

55 Everglades Rat Snake

Elaphe obsoleta rossalleni

Nonvenomous   Cornered *Elaphe obsoleta* of all races may raise their forebodies and strike in self-defense, but unless seized or molested they do not bite humans.

Abundance   Rare. As recently as the 1970s, this subspecies was abundant around Lake Okeechobee and ranged southward to the tip of the peninsula. It is thought by herpetologists that in this seasonally flooded region it was adapted to the hardwood hammocks too wet for the more widely distributed yellow rat snake. Because much of the northern Everglades has been drained for agriculture and elevated roadway corridors built through the area, the more aggressive yellow rat snake has invaded the former territory of the Everglades race, genetically absorbing it to the extent that the bright orange Everglades rat snakes of only a few years ago are now almost nonexistent. Now, orange color variants are rare in the wild and the only rat snakes found within the Everglades are considered to be intergrades with yellow rat snake. See **Introduction.**

Size   Most adults are 36 to 72 inches; the record is nearly 90 in.

Habitat   Orange Everglades rat snakes were never restricted to the open river of submerged sawgrass and elevated hardwood hammocks of the Everglades/Big Cypress area (though they were good swimmers and were often found there), but also occurred in the Kissimmee prairie, among both strands of cypress and native pine, and in the introduced Australian pines lining roads and canal banks.

Prey   Like all rat snakes, *E. o. rossalleni* was a powerful constrictor as well as a generalized predator on birds, rodents, lizards, and frogs; with good care it thrived in captivity, where individuals have been maintained for up to 22 years.

Reproduction   Egg-laying. Similar to that of other *E. obsoleta.*

Coloring/scale form   Also known as the orange rat snake, adults of the beautiful pure *rossalleni* form can be spectacularly vivid. Four dark stripes are usually present, but may be faint, or even absent over much of the trunk. The belly is yellowish, the tongue (unlike that of the black-tongued yellow rat snake) is bright red, and even the eyes may be orange. The 27 rows of dorsal scales are weakly keeled; the anal plate is divided.

Similar snakes   See **Gray Rat Snake (53).**

Behavior   Like the long, muscular yellow rat snake, *E. o. rossalleni* is a good burrower and swimmer, but it is a truly distinguished climber.

Brown-blotched Terrestrial Snakes

56 Short-tailed Snake
Stilosoma extenuatum

Nonvenomous   This is a harmless little serpent that vibrates its tail in alarm and if molested, according to Conant and Collins, it "strikes with a sneeze-like hiss."

Abundance   Rare. Legally-protected by the state of Florida, *Stilosoma extenuatum* is a Florida endemic found only in north-central part of the state from Suwannee and Columbia counties south to Hillsborough, Orange, and Highlands counties. This rare reptile is the only species in its genus, moreover, a fact that makes protecting its habitat particularly important because if the short-tailed snake were to vanish, not only a species but the entire genus *Stilosoma* would disappear forever.

It is a strange genus, too, unique among North American snakes in the shape of its vertebrae, which are short and wide, with a long condylar neck and a condyle wider than it is high. Although externally the short-tailed snake resembles the kingsnakes, particularly the mole kings, W. Auffenberg concluded in 1963 that "On the basis of vertebral form only it is difficult to see how *Stilosoma* can be related to *Lampropeltis*."

Current immunological albumin-sequencing techniques for measuring reptiles' evolutionary kinship, however, suggest otherwise. They place the short-tailed snake as a comparatively recent, Pliocene evolutionary radiation of the kingsnake line, falling between the scarlet kingsnakes and the mole kingsnakes. From which of these *Lampropeltis* lineages *Stilosoma* emerged, however, is not evident. Pliocene fossils found near Gainesville show that *Stilosoma* was already present in the area at that time, and it has evidently continuously occupied this region since its origin.

Size   The short-tailed snake is a quite small reptile: 14 to 20 inches in length and pencil thin; the record is 25.75 inches.

Habitat   *Stilosoma extenuatum* is another of the rare, relict inhabitants of old "Island Florida"—the dry interior upland which, due to elevated sea levels during interglacial periods, was for long periods in fact an island. Here, the short-tailed snake's primary habitat is sandhill environments, including early successional sand pine scrub and xeric hammocks. This sandy-soiled, longleaf pine-turkey oak woodland is rapidly being depleted of its remaining evergreens by "timber management," which produces either degraded, turkey oak-only woodland or cutover open terrain whose well-drained soil is rapidly being converted to citrus groves, residential subdivisions, and golf courses.

The Ocala National Forest is the most extensive area still containing this animal's native habitat, and is for *Stilosoma* the prime natural area in need of protection. (This may not even require pristine tracts of woodland for, unlike many of Florida's larger and more active reptiles, according to H. Campbell and P. E. Moler, "In areas subject to unavoidable development, *S. extenuatum* may be able to coexist with man as long as development is not too intense. Zoning . . . to require one acre homesites which retain the native plant and animal species . . . may suffice, but care should be taken to preserve the invertebrate and small vertebrate fauna on which this species depends.")

Prey   In captivity this quasi-constrictor seems to be almost entirely ophiophagus, refusing skinks and taking only small, smooth-scaled snakes. Although no observation of predation in the wild has been recorded, it has been suggested by Mushinsky that in central Florida a single species of crowned snake, *Tantilla relicta*, may be the exclusive prey of *Stilosoma*.

Serpentine motion is clearly the triggering factor in eliciting the short-tailed snake's predatory response, moreover, because only live, wriggling snakes are attacked (dead specimens of the same species are ignored). Very small snakes are seized near the head and swallowed, while larger ones are loosely constricted. Yet, they are not killed by this constriction, for the body coils of *Stilosoma* seem capable only of temporarily restraining prey; its powerful jaws and side-to-side, kingsnake-like chewing motions are its principal ingestive strategy.

Reproduction   Egg-laying. No reproductive behavior is recorded.

Coloring/scale form   The slender, cylindrical gray body is patterned along the spine with a broad, often indistinct, orangish stripe broken by 50 to 80 dark vertebral blotches. A dark brown Y with a yellow-orange center marks the crown, and the internasal and prefrontal scales are often fused. The white venter is blotched with dark brown. As its name implies, the short-tailed snake's tail is in fact attenuated, comprising less than 10% of the animal's total length. The 19 midbody rows of dorsal scales are smooth, the anal plate undivided.

Similar snakes   The close relationship between *Stilosoma* and the *L. calligaster* kingsnakes is evident in the similar dorsal pattern and coloring, as well as in the Y-shaped cephalic marking of the **mole kingsnake (57)**, but the mole king is a much stockier snake, with a brownish ground color, which lacks an orangish vertebral stripe. The **corn snake (52)** has an orangish dorsum, a dark-edged spearpoint on its crown, a checkered belly, and a divided anal plate.

Behavior   Little is known; even in areas of prime habitat, short-tailed snakes are almost never seen because they so seldom appear above ground—mainly at night during either April or October. While it is mainly a burrower, in a trait extremely unusual for a fossorial snake, *S. extenuatum* also climbs well.

57 Mole Kingsnake
Lampropeltis calligaster
rhombomaculata

Nonvenomous   Although they are harmless to humans, some mole kingsnakes will strike in self-defense.

Abundance   Rare. Widely distributed across the southeastern U.S. from the Mississippi River to Chesapeake Bay, *L. c. rhombomaculata* is very seldom seen in Florida, even by herpetologists working in the field. Florida Game and Fish Commission biologist Kevin Enge and commercial reptile collector C. J. Longden agree that no more than 35 mole kingsnakes are known to have been found in the state during the last 25 years.

Size   Adults are 30 to 40 inches; the record is 47 inches.

Habitat   Secretive in nature, *L. c. rhombomaculata* inhabits a variety of terrestrial milieus, including upland pine/oak forest and its interface with agricultural areas or grassland.

Prey   Prey includes most smaller vertebrates, especially reptiles.

Reproduction   Egg-laying. No natural nests are recorded, and the hatchlings evidently live deeply fossorial lives for no wild newborns have been observed or collected. Captive-bred young are about 7 inches in length, and are willing to feed on small anoles, ground skinks, and small snakes.

Coloring/scale form   The light brown dorsal ground color is patterned (more sharply among juveniles) with an average total of 57 reddish-brown mid-dorsal markings (vertebral body blotches: av. 44; dark tail bands: av. 13). The rusty blotches and occasional partial striping of adults become less distinct with age, and old mole kingsnakes may be uniformly dusky brown. There is a dark Y-shaped marking on the crown, and the yellowish venter is checked or clouded with brown. The 21 to 23 midbody rows of dorsal scales are smooth, the anal plate undivided.

Similar snakes   The **short-tailed snake (56)** has a much more slender body and a silvery ground color. **Corn snakes (52)** have a dark-edged spearpoint on their crowns, some keeled dorsal scales, a divided anal plate, and a striped undertail.

Behavior   A primarily fossorial animal, *L. c. rhombomaculata* is occasionally encountered crossing roads after heavy spring and summer rainfall—a time when the completely saturated soil forces many burrowing serpents to seek drier ground. Because 19 of 25 Alabama specimens collected in this way were males, most were probably simultaneously engaged in the search for a reproductively receptive female's pheromone scent trail.

58 South Florida Mole Kingsnake

Lampropeltis calligaster occipitolineata

Nonvenomous　　This docile little snake does not bite humans.

Abundance　　Rare. Endemic to Florida, *L. c. occipitolineata* was only recognized as a subspecies in 1987, when it was described in the Bulletin of the Chicago Herpetological Society by R. Price. Until recently, fewer than 20 of these animals were known, most from a smattering of locations in Brevard and Okeechobee counties. New records of 19 additional South Florida mole kingsnakes from Okeechobee, De Soto, Glades, and Hendry counties have considerably extended its known range, suggesting that rather than occurring only in disjunct, localized populations, *L. c. occipitolineata* may instead occupy much of the grassy floodplain that stretches more than 40 miles to the north, northwest, and west of Lake Okeechobee.

Size　　*L. c. occipitolineata* is the same size as its northern subspecies the mole kingsnake.

Habitat　　South Florida mole kingsnakes have been found in cattle pastures, in oak hammocks, and in abandoned fields. The periodically-flooded grassland that formerly surrounded Lake Okeechobee is probably the South Florida mole kingsnake's primary habitat, however, for most of the few *L. c. occipitolineata* that have been recorded came from this environment. Three were discovered in new subdivisions, where a pair was found copulating beneath a sheet of plywood; nearby, another individual was spotted crawling out of a water-filled ditch.

Prey　　According to T. Walsh of the Central Florida Zoo, who has maintained this subspecies for 7 years, hatchling *L. c. occipitolineata* feed on anoles, ground skinks, and small snakes; adults take small rodents and snakes.

Reproduction　　Egg-laying. See **Mole Kingsnake (57)**.

Coloring/scale form　　The markings of this southern subspecies are similar to those of the mole kingsnake, except that adult *L. c. occipitolineata* retain the distinctly delineated dark brown dorsal blotches of juvenile mole kingsnakes of both races. *L. c. occipitolineata* averages 75 of these mid-dorsal blotches (body blotches: av. 58; dark tail bands: av. 17). Longitudinal dark lines may also streak the posterior sides of its head and anterior back, giving it the Latin name *occipitolineata*, or "eye-lined."

Similar snakes　　See **Mole Kingsnake (57)**.

Behavior　　This rare reptile's burrowing lifestyle is so secretive that it is almost never seen.

Brown-blotched Terrestrial Snakes

Eastern Kingsnake
Lampropeltis getula getula

Nonvenomous   Threatened eastern kingsnakes sometimes swell their necks and bite with determination. If treated gently, however, they soon calm down and become entirely at ease while being handled—unless one's hands smell of their prey, in which case they may try an exploratory nip. Because of this animal's great range of subtly to vividly contrasting dorsal patterns, its docile disposition, its willingness to breed in confinement, and the ease of feeding captive-bred young, *L. g. getula* is among the most popular captive snakes, and eastern kings bred in confinement have led captive lives of nearly 23 years—possibly double or triple the lifespan of wild individuals.

Abundance   Formerly abundant, the eastern kingsnake is presently only widespread over both northern peninsular Florida and the panhandle.

Size   Neonates are 5 to 8 inches in length, and about the diameter of a pencil; adult eastern kingsnakes are robust, cylindrically-bodied reptiles (as with most burrowing snakes, the head is no larger than the thick neck) usually 36 to 48 inches in length. The record is 82 inches.

Habitat   Found in pinelands, around hyacinth-filled ponds and canals, cypress strands, prairies and marshes—usually not far from water—*L. g. getula* also occurs on saline tidal flats and estuaries.

Prey   All *Lampropeltis* are primarily terrestrial, scent-oriented hunters that prey on a variety of smaller vertebrates. Other snakes, including members of their own species, as well as venomous pit vipers sometimes larger than themselves, are also devoured. (Eastern kingsnakes are largely immune to the venom of pit vipers. See **Florida Kingsnake (60), Prey.**) Kingsnakes overcome these formidable adversaries—which may strike and envenomate them repeatedly—by immobilizing the vipers with the powerful constriction for which the kingsnake's muscular body is adapted, while its robust neck and jaw muscles let it quickly work its way forward to the head of the serpent about to be swallowed. Small mammals, birds, fish, and frogs are also taken.

Another favorite food of *L. getula* is turtle eggs. Wright and Bishop reported in 1915 that local people regarded it commonplace to find a kingsnake waiting for a female turtle to deposit her eggs. More recently, in observations at the Savannah River Nuclear Plant in South Carolina, Knight and Loraine note that kingsnakes living in that area regularly search out turtle nests. They describe watching a box turtle obliviously excavating her nest cavity while an adult *L. getula,* its head and neck elevated for a better view, waited nearby. The kingsnake was captured and later regurgitated 4 turtle eggs, then after 3 days in captivity, defecated pieces of at least 10 additional *Sternotherus* and *Kinosternon* eggs, as well as three unbroken ones.

(Because of the small average clutch size of both turtle species, this means that 5 or 6 nests must have been robbed by this single kingsnake.) The three unbroken eggs were incubated and, despite their having passed through the digestive system of the kingsnake, after about 50 days hatched into normal baby stinkpot turtles (*S. odoratus*).

Reproduction   Egg-laying. Courtship among *L. g. getula* follows the typical pattern for colubrid snakes, with breeding occurring between March and June. Its clutches of 3 to 29 eggs can be deposited at any time throughout the summer, and after about 60 days of incubation—although this can vary markedly in the wild—the 5- to 8-inch-long young emerge.

Coloring/scale form   Kingsnakes from everywhere in Florida vary enormously in dorsolateral pattern and coloration, and in the past many of these color/pattern variants were thought to be separate races. Typical eastern kingsnakes possess black to deep-brown dorsums patterned with less than 30 narrow, white or yellow dorsal crossbands that split to form a chain-like pattern on their sides. Kingsnakes from the panhandle's Apalachicola Basin—which were once thought to be a separate subspecies known as "*L. g. goini*"—have much wider bands and blotches. Other kingsnakes found in the same area exhibit typical *L. g. getula* patterns, however, along with various combinations of blotched, striped, and patternless variants, and it is now recognized that both "goini" and the blotched and striped kingsnakes living in the same range are actually merely pattern variants of *L. g. getula*. There are usually 21 dorsal scale rows at midbody (some individuals have 23) and the anal plate is undivided.

Similar snakes   The subspecies **Florida kingsnake (60)** has a reduced, or less-distinct, pale dorsal pattern, with lighter-tipped dark scales appearing within the dark vertebral rectangles between its more than 40 pale vertebral crossbands. It usually has 23 midbody dorsal scale rows. Juvenile **racers (44–46)** have unpatterned tails and divided anal plates.

Behavior   *Lampropeltis getula getula* is a slow-moving, rather conspicuous serpent whose principal defense against large predators is to retire, rather deliberately, into holes or rodent tunnels. Even in wooded terrain, it is almost always encountered on the ground, although—surprisingly for a burrower—it can also swim very well, and even climb: Eichholz and Koenig found eastern kingsnakes ascending trees to prey on hatchling bluebirds inside nest boxes placed several feet above the ground.

60

Florida
Kingsnake
Lampropeltis getula floridana

Nonvenomous See **Eastern Kingsnake (59).**

Abundance The most numerous of the state's *Lampropeltis getula* subspecies, the Florida kingsnake is widespread from north-central Florida south to the tip of the mainland peninsula. Throughout a wide band, however—from Baker and Duval counties in the northeastern corner of the state through Alachua Co. south to Pinellas and Hernando counties on the Gulf Coast—eastern and Florida kingsnakes interbreed. In this area, members of the intergrade population produced by their genetic mixing may display characteristics of either, or a combination of, the markings and scutellation of both races.

Due to both habitat fragmentation brought about by residential and commercial development and to heavy hunting pressure from commercial reptile collectors, Kenneth Krysko, an authority on these animals, has found that the Florida kingsnake's numbers have drastically declined throughout peninsular Florida. Nevertheless, because of this animal's broad range and its abundance in the sugar cane fields around Lake Okeechobee, *L. g. floridana* is still not afforded legal protection. Krysko's solution would be "for this area to be managed for three months of each year by not permitting the collection of *L. getula* during March, April, and May, when breeding and egg laying takes place."

Size Florida kingsnakes are about the same size as their more northerly subspecies the **eastern kingsnake;** the record length is somewhat shorter, however, at 69.5 inches.

Habitat Similar to that of the **eastern kingsnake,** with the addition of the flooded stands of melaleuca found only in southern Florida.

Prey Like their northern subspecies, Florida kingsnakes are predatory generalists. During an extensive study of both races of *L. getula* living in Florida, Krysko identified in the natural diet of these large constrictors, Florida green water snakes, ribbon snakes, ringneck snakes, black racers, five-lined skinks, juvenile cottontails, hispid cotton rats, and turtle eggs. Other rodents, lizards, birds and their eggs, greater sirens, striped swamp snakes are also taken, as are members of their own species. Kingsnakes have also long been noted for their serenely powerful predation on venomous snakes: Archie Carr observed a Florida kingsnake eating an adult cottonmouth in a Lake Co. flatwoods pond and another devouring a coral snake on the shore of Lake Virginia in Orange Co. Kingsnakes can successfully exploit this ophiophagus predatory niche because their blood serum gives them immunity to the venoms of the many pit vipers frequently encountered by any snake-eating carnivore. (S. A. Weinstein found that of 6 kingsnake species whose blood was assayed for venom neutralizing properties, the eastern and Florida kingsnakes' blood serum "showed the broadest spectrum of neutralization of (pit viper) venoms . . .") Kingsnake blood antivenin did not work against the peptide-based neurotoxins of elapids, however, because the "venom-neutralizing serum proteins of *Lampropeltis* appear to be most effective against hemorrhagic and proteolytic venoms, with little or no neutralization capacities against venoms containing neurotoxic hypotensive peptides" like those of the coral snake.

Reproduction   Egg-laying. Breeding begins a bit earlier in the year than among Kingsnakes of the more northerly race—as early as February, combat rituals between rival males have been observed in the wild by Krysko, with breeding continuing until June. See **Eastern Kingsnake (59), Reproduction.**

Coloring/scale form   As with the subspecies eastern kingsnake, the great variation in dorsolateral color and pattern among *L. g. floridana* was originally thought to represent a number of different subspecies. For decades, yellow kingsnakes from south of Lake Okeechobee appeared in reference books as the subspecies *L. g. brooksi.* Yet, because the Florida king had been described first and indeed mentioned the Brooks form as a color phase in its initial description, by 1958 "*brooksi*" was combined with *L. g. floridana.* Individuals possessing both phenotypes are now known to occur throughout the Florida peninsula, including southern Dade County where the Brooks kingsnake was thought to be the only race, but is now regarded as merely a color variant of the Florida kingsnake. This error was aggravated by the pet trade, in which the more differently named types of kingsnakes one could offer for sale, the greater one's profits. The typical Florida kingsnake, however, is similar in appearance to the eastern king, except for having more than 40 vertebral crossbands whose enclosed dark dorsal scales are lightened anteriorly.

In some animals, this lightening leads to entirely pale-speckled dorsums. For example, all newborn *L. g. floridana* hatch with shiny black dorsums patterned with a very narrow yellowish-white crossbands which, in a chain-like configuration enclose dark vertebral rectangles. As these snakes mature, due to an ontogenetic pattern change the dark scales between the pale crossbands gradually lighten until, among some individuals formerly termed *L. g. brooksi,* or "Brooks kingsnakes," the crossbands completely disappear and the animal becomes entirely creamy- or yellow-speckled. The smooth dorsal scales are usually arranged in 23 rows at midbody (some individuals have 21), and the anal plate is undivided.

Similar snakes   The subspecies **eastern kingsnake (59)** has a shiny black to deep brown dorsum with less than 30 very narrow but distinct light-yellow crossbands that both enclose black vertebral rectangles and form a chain-like pattern on its sides; there are usually 21 midbody rows of dorsal scales. Juvenile **racers (44—46)** have no pattern on their tails, and divided anal plates.

Behavior   Local reptile hunters believe that in the vicinity of Lake Okeechobee kingsnakes feed solely on turtle eggs. Yet, while several Florida kings collected by Krysko near Lake Okeechobee had recently eaten turtle eggs, in captivity these adult *L. g. floridana* also fed readily on mice. (To some extent this predatory behavior may be learned rather than instinctual, for many newborn kingsnakes from southern Florida refuse to eat either nestling mice or small lizards.) As Krysko discovered, their innate feeding orientation is almost entirely ophiophagus. When he offered them a sliver of Florida green water snake flesh, it was immediately seized, and the same vigorous feeding behavior occurred when these reluctant-to-feed young snakes were presented with small red rat snakes and Florida water snakes. Therefore, contrary to popular belief, scent alone is probably not the principal mechanism that triggers these neonates' feeding response, for blocking olfaction does not inhibit attacks on prey. Nor is taste the activating mechanism because snakes' tongues have no taste buds. Instead, the chemical sense these hatchlings serpents probably use to recognize prey is vomerolfaction. (When a snake flicks its tongue, airborne molecules adhere to the sticky lingual surface and are carried into the mouth. These "scent particles" are then picked up by vomeronasal organs located in the roof of the mouth, where epithelia containing chemosensory neurons genetically programmed to respond to the chemical signature of particular prey species trigger the snake's feeding response.)

Such intense food preferences show that individuals from certain areas have an inherited orientation toward certain food species. These food animals constitute appropriate prey for *L. g. floridana* living in the marshlands adjacent to Lake Okeechobee because all are very abundant there. Florida green water snakes, in particular, are prolific breeders, depositing litters of up to 100 live offspring that disperse soon after birth—at a time that exactly coincides with young kingsnakes' first weeks of foraging.

Adult *L. g. floridana* captured in this area are also snake predators, as evidenced by numerous ophidian remains in their feces, but unlike the predatorily-naive hatchlings, mature Florida kingsnakes also feed readily on mice. For instinctual snake-eaters this may constitute learned behavior—a broadening of these kingsnakes' inbred vomeronasal images of appropriate food species to take advantage of the newly abundant small mammal prey recently provided by agricultural modification of their habitat.

Northern Scarlet Snake

Cemophora coccinea copei

Nonvenomous   *Cemophora coccinea copei* rarely bites, even when first handled in the field.

Abundance   Common. Northern scarlet snakes are locally abundant in pine flatwoods, wet prairies, bottomland forest, and coastal and inland sandhill habitat. Drift-fence surveys in their panhandle and northern peninsular Florida range regularly produce *C. c. copei* which, on late spring and early summer nights, are also often seen on roads through the Apalachicola National Forest.

Size   Adult scarlet snakes are 16 to just over 32 inches in length; the slim, rarely-seen hatchlings are 4.5 to 6 inches long.

Habitat   *Cemophora coccinea copei* is most often found in the sandy or loamy soil of pine, hardwood, and mixed forest communities, as well as on the borders of swamps and plowed fields.

Prey   Reptile eggs are this reptile's preferred food—in search of which *C. c. copei* apparently forages widely. To puncture the leathery shells of eggs too large to swallow whole it has developed enlarged upper posterior teeth. (One northern scarlet snake was discovered in the wild with its entire head inside a large *Pituophis* egg, lapping the contents.) These snakes may also occasionally take small lizards, snakes, and nestling rodents.

Reproduction   Egg-laying. See **Florida Scarlet Snake (62)**.

Coloring/scale form   Adult *C. c. copei* have a grayish or yellowish-white ground color, with red dorsal saddles bordered by black. The snout is orange-red and the most anterior black vertebral band usually touches the parietals. Yet the scarlet snake's appearance changes with age: hatchlings' ground color is off-white, their dorsal saddles are pink, extend but a short way down the sides, and are bordered below with black flecks. As they grow older, the youngsters' ground color yellows, and in an ontogenetic color change the black flecks gradually become the dark lower borders of steadily reddening dorsal blotches. Very old scarlet snakes have brown saddles on a ground color tarnished with gray. The venter is unmarked white, there are usually 6 supralabial scales, the 19 midbody rows of dorsal scales are smooth, and the anal plate is undivided.

Similar snakes   The subspecies **Florida scarlet snake (62)**, usually has 7 supralabial scales and its most anterior black band does not touch its parietal scales. See **Florida Scarlet Snake (62)**.

Behavior   Scarlet snakes are deep burrowers: *C. coccinea* has been unearthed up to 6 feet below the surface.

Red-and-black-banded Snakes

62 Florida Scarlet Snake
Cemophora coccinea coccinea

Nonvenomous The Florida scarlet snake does not bite humans.

Abundance Although it is rarely seen because of its secretive nature, Florida scarlet snakes are common in pine flatwoods, dry prairie, maritime hardwood hammock, and sandhill habitats from Marion County south to the tip of peninsular Florida.

Size Adults are 14 to 32 inches in length.

Habitat As a relict member of an ancient, xeric-adapted fauna that once stretched from the desert Southwest to Florida via a dry Gulf Coast corridor, *C. c. coccinea* is generally found in rather arid upland habitats, although it also inhabits limestone-sided irrigation canals in sawgrass prairies.

Prey Small snakes and lizards, newborn rodents, and reptile eggs.

Reproduction Egg-laying. Breeding occurs from March to June, with oviposition occurring May to August. The 3 to 8 eggs, 1 to 1.25 inches in length, hatch from July to October into 5.5- to 6-inch-long young that are colored quite differently from the adults. This is because an ontogentic color progression occurs over the course of the scarlet snake's life.

Coloring/scale form See **Northern Scarlet Snake (61), Coloring/scale form.** Among adults, the red dorsal saddles, which are found on both the back and the top of the tail, are bordered by black on a whitish- or yellowish-gray ground color. The snout is orange-red and the anterior-most black dorsal band usually does not touch the parietal scales on the head. The venter is uniformly pale, there are ordinarily 7 supralabial scales, the 19 midbody rows of dorsal scales are smooth, and the anal plate is undivided.

Similar snakes The **northern scarlet snake (61)** usually has 6 supralabial scales and its anterior-most black dorsal band touches its parietal scales. The **eastern coral snake (64)** has a round black snout, adjacent red and yellow bands that entirely circle its belly, a black- and yellow-banded tail, and an undivided anal plate. The **scarlet kingsnake's (63)** dorsal bands also encircle its venter.

Behavior Scarlet snakes are primarily burrowers seen above ground only well after dark; in summer, newborns are sometimes found in suburban swimming pools. In captivity, due to its strong preference for whole reptile eggs, *C. c. coccinea* is difficult to feed (typically refusing raw egg in a dish) and fares poorly except in the hands of a resourceful keeper. The longest-lived captive was maintained for over 6 years by D. C. McIntyre, who syringe-fed it 2 to 3 cc of stirred chicken egg every 2 weeks.

63 Scarlet Kingsnake
Lampropeltis triangulum elapsoides

Nonvenomous   Scarlet kingsnakes seldom bite when picked up in the field, but, like other *Lampropeltis*, occasional individuals may nip and hang on tenaciously. Commonly believed to be a coral snake mimic—although the biological validity of this interpretation of the scarlet kingsnake's brilliant dorsolateral coloring is uncertain—*L. t. elapsoides* is distinguished from the coral by both its red snout and cheeks and its black-bordered red dorsolateral bands: "Red touches black, friend of Jack."

Abundance   Scarlet kingsnakes are widespread throughout Florida, although these animals are rarely seen due to their retiring, semisubterranean habits. Especially in early spring when low-lying forest is flooded, *L. t. elapsoides* (which typically avoids wet ground) is found well above the surface, wedged beneath the loosened bark of longleaf pine stumps. Later in the year the scarlet kingsnake is primarily a fossorial, subsurface inhabitant of sandy loam, although it may appear at the surface under logs or construction debris during rainy weather. Once thought to be rare because its secretive nature limited its exposure to humans, it has survived major inroads into its habitat by timbering and land-clearing, and scarlet kingsnakes are now known to be locally abundant.

Size   Recorded up to 28 inches in length, but most adults measure only 14 to 20 inches.

Habitat   Scarlet kingsnakes are found in a variety of habitats throughout the state and even occur south into the Keys.[1] Data obtained from drift-fence surveys of the state's herpetofauna indicate that *L. t. elapsoides* is common, however, only in pine flatwood and wet prairie hammock habitat. It occurs less frequently in bottomland, mixed hardwood, and upland pine forest, in sandhills, and in the wind-pruned strip of stunted hardwoods, known as maritime hammock, which defines the border between marine-shore marshland and inland forest.

---

[1]Only two specimens have been reported from the Keys, one from Key Largo and one from Key West. The Key West specimen, which was collected before 1929, has been disregarded in the literature because it is more like mainland individuals in its ventral scale count (176) than the specimen from Key Largo (157). Yet other lower Keys species such as *Coluber constrictor* and *Elaphe guttata* also resemble their mainland populations more than they do upper Keys populations. This seeming anomaly exists because, although closer to the mainland, the upper Florida Keys are biologically less related to the mainland than are the lower Keys. This is because along with the islands of Florida Bay, the lower Keys were a dry land extension of the mainland during periods of lowered sea level. At this time the upper Keys, which were formed from a more recent coral reef, had not yet emerged. The old Key West specimen of *L. t. elapsoides* could, therefore, represent either a vanished population (island-living reptiles are extremely prone to extinction) or a current residual population of this very secretive species.

Prey   Much of the scarlet kingsnake's diet consists of smaller snakes that, along with its secondary prey of skinks and other small lizards, share the forest-floor microhabitat of leaf litter that most *L. t. elapsoides* occupy during their spring-through-autumn foraging period. Juvenile scarlet kingsnakes reportedly take earthworms and insects, and adults also prey opportunistically on nestling rodents.

Reproduction   Egg-laying. Breeding occurs from March to June, with the 2 to 9 elongate whitish eggs being deposited between May and August. During late summer and early autumn these hatch into very slender, 3- to 3.5-inch-long young.

Coloring/scale form   The scarlet kingsnake's pointed orange-red snout is distinctive, as is its dorsolateral pattern of wide scarlet, and narrow black and yellow bands (its red bands border only the black bands; the yellow bands touch only black bands). (Juveniles may have whitish bands in place of the yellow bands of adults.) Like the coral snake, all the dorsolateral bands circumscribe the entire body, including the venter. The smooth, glossy dorsal scales—the genus name *Lampropeltis* means "shining shield"— are arranged in 19 rows at midbody; the anal plate is undivided.

Similar snakes   Unlike *L. t. elapsoides,* the red and yellow bands of the eastern coral snake (**64**) touch. Coral snakes also have a stubby black snout, a yellow-and-black tail, and a divided anal plate. Among both northern and Florida scarlet snakes (**61, 62**) the red dorsolateral saddles do not reach the venter, which is unmarked white.

Behavior   Except for the limestone-lined banks of sugar cane irrigation fields, *L. t. elapsoides* is rare in extensive grassy wetlands, for this species is averse to both the openess and the inundation of huge marshes such as the Everglades. In the low-lying woods of the panhandle and northern peninsular Florida, scarlet kingsnakes occupy seasonally wet environments such as hydric hammocks and even hardwood swamps, but here they live within dead stumps well above the seasonally submerged ground.

To take advantage of these dry arboreal refuges, scarlet kingsnakes must be good climbers, and thus are frequently found among the dead fronds skirting palm trees, in the rafters of abandoned buildings, and among the supporting beams of old wooden railroad trestles. Often, scarlet kingsnakes are abroad in quite cool weather, for *L. t. elapsoides* seems to suffer less inhibition of movement due to chilly temperatures than most other Florida snakes. (In conditions so chilly that photographing other serpents—which slow down when they're cold—is easy, scarlet kingsnakes still present a fast-wriggling challenge.) This enables these reptiles to forage well into the fall, as well as adapting them to hunt effectively during the cooler hours of darkness.

Its nocturnal foraging, in fact, may be the reason for the scarlet kingsnake's bright coloring. Surprisingly, rather than mimicking the coral snake's bold dorsolateral pattern in a presumed oposematic deception, the scarlet king's contrasting colors may function as nocturnal camouflage. Although in daylight its bright bands rivet human attention, red looks gray at night—the only time that *L. t. elapsoides* appears in the open. With its crimson bands inconspicuous to color-visioned predators such as owls, the scarlet kingsnake's alternating black and pale yellow crossbands may have evolved as a cryptic approximation of light and dark shadows, a pattern that so fragments its serpentine image on the dappled patchwork of the nighttime forest floor that it virtually disappears.

But perhaps the best measure of the scarlet king's protective coloration is the very low apparent number of predator attacks on it. (Partial loss of the tail is a good measure of near-miss predation attempts on snakes, and few tail injuries are seen among dangerous serpents such as the coral snake, which is seldom molested by predators). Among a large group of non-venomous colubrids, however, tail injuries are common, and only the scarlet kingsnake showed no tail damage. This may confirm that *L. t. elapsoides* is indeed a coral snake mimic, with its bright dorsolateral bands serving as a predator-warning device; or it might simply mean that among both coral snakes and scarlet kingsnakes red- black- and yellow-banding serves as particularly effective nocturnal camouflage. See **Coral Snake (64), Behavior.**

Whatever its function in the nighttime woods, to human eyes the scarlet kingsnake's vivid pigmentation makes it a very attractive reptile. Adults do well in confinement—the captive longevity record is over 16 years—but the hatchlings' extremely small size makes them difficult to feed. After their first shed, at about 10 days of age, little scarlet kingsnakes will occasionally take lizard tails or pieces of newborn mice, but raising them is so much trouble that, unlike other gaudily-marked kingsnakes, *L. t. elapsoides* is usually bred only by specialists.

Red-and-black-banded Snakes

Elapidae

64

Eastern Coral Snake

Micrurus fulvius fulvius

Venomous "Red touches yellow, kill a fellow"—is generally too extreme a prognosis, but it is still the best way to quickly identify the coral snake, the only red, black, and yellow-banded snake in Florida whose red and yellow bands touch. Yet despite the rhyme, hardly anyone is harmed by a coral snake. Only about 1% of the venom poisonings in North America involve *Micrurus fulvius,* and many coral snake bites result in no envenomation at all. The coral's rigid little fangs, no more than ⅛ inch in length, are too short to penetrate shoe leather, but anywhere *M. fulvius* can make contact with bare flesh it has no trouble biting a larger animal. Coral snakes definitely do not need to find the end of a finger to nip, for their mouths can gape open to form a wide biting surface and their strong jaws are able to pinch out and puncture a fold of skin anywhere on the human body. Moreover, as hollow hypodermic needles, coral snake fangs are designed to instantly inject venom. The common myth is that these animals must chew to transmit their toxins, but restrained coral snakes typically twist sideways and in a flash deposit several drops of venom onto a glove or pinning stick.

Because its toxic components consist almost entirely of neurotoxically-destructive peptides, the venom of *M. fulvius* is more virulent than that of any snake in eastern North America. Approximately equal in potency to cobra toxins, the lethal dosage for a human adult is estimated to be as little as 5 to 10 milligrams, while the largest eastern coral snakes have been milked of up to 20 mg. See **Venom Table, page 45.**

Immediate pain usually accompanies a bite by *M. fulvius,* but because nervous system impairment may not manifest symptoms for several hours, in cases of definite envenomation, antivenin should be ready—and perhaps even be administered—before the onset of neurological problems because once symptoms appear it may be difficult to prevent further decline.

For the most part coral snakes are shy burrowers living beneath leaves and logs; if unmolested this little reptile is so nonaggressive toward humans that it poses almost no danger to anyone who has not handled it.

Abundance Common. Because coral snakes are not averse to human habitation, especially during their activity peaks in cool fall and spring weather, they are often encountered in suburban areas. In their study of 93 Alachua Co. *M. f. fulvius,* D. Jackson and R. Franz reported that the "red-, yellow-, and black-banded snakes found crossing driveways or crawling in yards . . . without exception proved to be coral snakes" because the coral's seldom-seen nocturnal look-alikes, the scarlet and scarlet kingsnakes, prefer unaltered natural terrain.

Size Eastern coral snakes grow larger than most people expect—the record is 51 inches. Very large *M. fulvius* are almost always female, for while the two sexes parallel each other in size during their first 3 years, the growth rate of males then declines. Females continue to grow at the same rate through at least their 4th year. In spite of the fact that females' tails are proportionately shorter, mean length of 125 individuals from northern peninsular Florida was 27 inches for males, 35 inches for females.

Habitat In Florida, *M. f. fulvius* lives primarily in wooded terrain: oak/hardwood hammocks, longleaf pine forest (both upland and seasonally-flooded flatwoods), and dry rosemary scrub. It is absent or rare in extensive wetlands. Thick ground cover of leaf litter, fallen logs, and pine or palmetto stumps is important as a hiding place and as habitat for the smaller snakes and lizards on which coral snakes prey.

Prey Chiefly small snakes; in the field I spotted a 26-inch-long female *M. fulvius* in the process of envenoming a young rat snake (*E. obsoleta*). The rat snake—which was nearly an inch longer than the coral snake—was immobilized and swallowed, but later, perhaps due to the stress of being captured itself, the coral snake disgorged its prey. Skinks, other slender-bodied lizards, and small amphisbaenians are also taken, although much less frequently than ophidian prey. Cannibalism has also been reported.

Reproduction Egg-laying. Of western *M. fulvius,* herpetologist H. Quinn notes that "No other North American snake has been reported to breed from late summer to late spring, then lay its eggs in midsummer."

In Florida, Jackson and Franz found that male and female coral snakes follow seasonally differing sexual cycles. Females undergo early spring vitellogenesis, developing their eggs between March and May, while males' testicular enlargement and spermatogenesis occurs in autumn. Because viable sperm is stored by males throughout the year most breeding occurs in late spring, with the single clutch of up to 13 (but usually less than 8) white, sausage-shaped eggs, 1.6 by .65 inches in diameter, being laid between late May and the end of July. Some two months later the eggs hatch into 6.5- to 7.5-inch-long young, identical to the adults but rarely seen in the wild because during their first year they are apparently exclusively fossorial; a number of yearling coral snakes emerge each fall. At this time, female *M. f. fulvius* are engaged in a seasonal activity peak, foraging heavily to replace the fat stores depleted by their summertime egg-laying, and throughout this period may breed with young, newly sexually-mature males that—unlike older and larger males—are also active during the cooler months.

Coloring/scale form Lined with 15 midbody rows of smooth dorsal scales, the coral's equally broad red and black bands are separated by bright yellow rings. Black speckles, spots, or large blotches are often present within the red bands, while aberrant color morphs with much wider red than black bands are known. Only black and yellow bands are found on the tail and forward of the nape. The dorsolateral bands entirely circle the venter, whose subcaudal scales occur in a double row. The anal plate is divided.

Similar snakes   Both races of **scarlet snakes (61, 62)**, as well as the **scarlet kingsnake (63)** have elongate orange snouts. Red bands occur all the way to their tailtips, and their black crossbands do not touch their yellow ones ("Red touches black, venom lack").

Behavior   Whether the coral snake's bold patterning actually functions as a warning signal is still an area of controversy. Its vivid dorsal hues are inconspicuous to the largely color-blind mammalian carnivores that feed on small terrestrial serpents, but the sharp contrast between the coral's yellow and black body bands seems to deter some predators: opossums, which readily take snakes as food, usually hesitate before a coral snake.

As a primarily diurnal reptile, however, *M. fulvius* is seldom active during the nocturnal foraging period of most mammalian carnivores. Jackson and Franz found that during all weather conditions coral snakes' above-ground activity peaks in late morning and again in the afternoon, so most of its predators are likely to be color-visioned diurnal birds of prey. During these periods, the coral snake's bright dorsal pigmentation is plainly visible, yet successful predation on *Micrurus* (as well as on red- and black-ringed *Lampropeltis*) is known among various hawks and falcons, which typically immediately decapitate ophidian prey. Yet, if the coral snake is not quickly incapacitated, the raptor may become the victim. A red-tailed hawk that landed in a meadow near Gainesville with a 3-foot-long female coral snake in its talons "became progressively uncoordinated and unresponsive and finally collapsed [due to] flaccid paralysis typical of the neurotoxic effects of elapid venom" according to K. Brugger of the U.S. Fish and Wildlife Service, who witnessed the hawk's death. The red-tail had 6 small fang punctures in its tarsus and 9 in its posterior.

Perhaps the best measure of the effectiveness of coral snakes' presumably aposematic dorsal coloring, however, is the probable level of predator attacks on it. As F. Gehlbach pointed out in 1972, partial loss of the tail is a good measure of near-miss predation attempts on snakes, and few tail injuries occur among dangerous species seldom molested by predators. In spite of the characteristic defensive maneuver in which *M. fulvius* tucks its foreparts under its body while extending its curled, yellow-and-black tailtip in imitation of its similarly pigmented, about-to-strike head, coral snakes rarely have damaged tails. Only two of 134 individuals seen by Jackson and Franz were missing parts of their tails, while of the 26 other species of non-venomous colubrid snakes examined for predation-caused injuries, only the scarlet kingsnake, a possible mimic of *M. fulvius*, showed no tail damage.

Viperidae

65

Southern Copperhead
Agkistrodon contortrix contortrix

Venomous   Throughout its broad distribution across the southeastern U.S., as well as within its limited Florida Panhandle range, the southern copperhead often occurs in suburban neighborhoods adjacent to creeks and woodlands. Yet, records of the Antivenin Institute of America show that during a 10-year period, regardless of the kind of treatment, not a single death resulted from 308 copperhead bites in several southern states. This is because *A. contortrix* seldom strikes unless it is stepped on or handled, it has short (⅜ in. maximum length) fangs, and its venom is only about half as destructive as that of most rattlesnakes. Sherman Minton estimated the lethal dosage for a healthy human adult at well over 150 mg, but since the largest copperheads can be milked of only 40 to 70 mg and no viperid can inject more than a third of its milkable capacity in a single bite, *A. contortrix* is considerably less dangerous than timber or eastern diamondback rattlesnakes. In past years, when medical treatment was less effective, copperhead envenomations occasionally caused the loss of a digit, and a severe bite could still be fatal to a small child. See **Venom Table,** page **45.**

Abundance   In both dry and moist woodlands *A. c. contortrix* may be fairly common, although during the day copperheads are usually hidden beneath logs or debris left by humans in forested areas.

Size   The largest of the copperhead subspecies, an *A. c. contortrix* from the southeastern U.S. reached a record size of 52 inches, although most adults measure 24 to 36 inches.

Habitat   *Agkistrodon contortrix contortrix* is almost always found in tree-shaded areas where fallen litter and woodpiles offer terrestrial shelter; in Florida this animal is found mostly in Gadsden, Calhoun, and Liberty counties, where it occupies bottomland forest and mixed pasture/upland hardwoods forest more often than longleaf pine forest.

Prey   Copperheads generally feed on whatever prey is seasonally most available. At times, this means large insects such as cicadas. In spring, large numbers of puddle-spawning frogs are taken, and throughout the year small rodents are a staple. When excited by nearby prey, young copperheads vibrate their yellowish- or grayish-green tailtips in an unconscious but tantalizing imitation of a wriggling caterpillar—a maneuver which may lure small frogs and toads within striking range.

Reproduction   Live-bearing. Courtship begins with the male advancing to touch the female with his snout and, if she does not move away, rubbing her body with his chin. If she is receptive the female will remain stationary, often flattening her body, waving or vibrating her tail, and eliminating waste

Mocassins

as a preliminary to mating. This is initiated only when she gapes open the cloaca to receive the male's hemipene, after which copulation can last for several hours. Breeding occurs in both late fall and spring, with spermatozoa from autumn pairings remaining viable throughout the female's winter retirement to fertilize the first ova she produces in spring. (Vernal breeding by a female carrying sperm from a previous autumn pairing can produce a litter sired by two males.) Born during the latter part of July and all of August, the 4 to 8 neonates are 7.5- to 10-inches long, with paler pigmentation than their parents.

Coloring/scale form   Thirteen to 20 pale-centered brownish dorsolateral bands, which are broad at the belly line and cinched or contorted—thus the Latin, *contortrix*—into a narrow hourglass shape over the spine, line the back. A pair of dark spots generally dot the rear of the tan, wedge-shaped crown, while prominent supraocular scales form the upper part of a sharply-angled intersection between the crown and the flat, undercut cheeks. Just behind the nostril is the dark heat-sensor pit. Posterior to the vertically-slit pupil of the coppery eye the supralabials are marked with a pale, rearward-pointing V whose upper border is defined by a dark line from the eye to the rear corner of the jaw. The venter is slightly mottled off-white, with (for ⅔ of its length) a single row of subcaudal scales. Arranged in 23 to 25 rows at midbody, the dorsal scales are weakly keeled and the anal plate is undivided.

Similar snakes   The **eastern hognose snake (48)** is often mistaken for the southern copperhead, for this short, heavy-bodied, somewhat similarly patterned serpent inhabits the same tree-shaded environments as the copperhead and like it, shows little fear of people. The hognose's raised forehead, small, round-pupiled dark brown eyes, proportionately thick neck, and sharply upturned snout are distinctive, however, as is its divided anal plate and double row of subcaudal scales. Juvenile **Florida cottonmouths (67)** are similar, but are gray-brown, with a wide, pale-outlined dark band across their cheeks.

Behavior   Unlike rattlesnakes, which are usually quickly eliminated from urbanized areas, copperheads readily adapt to the presence of man and frequently do well in wooded suburbs, where they are most often seen at dawn or dusk. Here, these small vipers are generally so non-aggressive that the shock of unexpectedly finding one in a woodpile or trash heap is usually the only harm that comes from the encounter. In this sort of microhabitat *A. contortrix* preys on the resident mice, but usually does so at such a leisurely rate that nests of baby rodents have been found within inches of a well-fed copperhead—its lethargy having failed to excite the parent into moving her brood.

66 Eastern Cottonmouth

Agkistrodon piscivorus piscivorus

Venomous The eastern cottonmouth is similar in both defensive behavior and venom toxicity to the subspecies Florida cottonmouth.

Abundance Common (as an intergrade with the Florida cottonmouth) in the western panhandle.

Size Similar in size to the **Florida cottonmouth (67)**.

Habitat Almost any heavily vegetated, still-water aquatic environment—especially wooded streams—can serve as habitat for *Agkistrodon piscivorus*.

Prey Any vertebrate small enough to swallow; for large cottonmouths this means prey up to the size of adult swamp rabbits.

Reproduction Live-bearing. Reproduction follows the usual viperid pattern of slow growth, delayed maturation, and low reproductive frequency, although to a slightly lesser extent than with other large pit vipers because the more favorable foraging opportunities of their aquatic milieu affords female cottonmouths a better chance than terrestrial vipers of acquiring the body fat necessary for pregnancy. Unlike most terrestrial viperids—sit-and-wait predators that typically experience lower hunting success than the more actively foraging cottonmouth—some female *A. piscivorus* are able to breed annually. Maternal attendance of the young for a short while after birth has also been reported by C. H. Wharton, who interpreted it as "guarding behavior," although a parent's presence with young is not considered to be active guarding unless actual defense occurs.

Coloring/scale form Adult eastern cottonmouths have a more yellowish ground color than the Florida race, with narrower dark dorsolateral bands and less distinct whitish facial markings, but in north-central Florida eastern and Florida cottonmouths occur only as intergrades. In this area, individuals morphologically typical of either race are sympatric with specimens showing intermediate characteristics of both subspecies. (Old animals of both subspecies, as well as intergrades, may be entirely black or dark gray.) There are 25 rows of keeled dorsal scales at midbody, most of the subcaudal scales occur in a single row, and the anal plate is undivided.

Similar snakes For similarities with water snakes, see **Florida cottonmouth (67)**. Juvenile **southern copperheads (65)** are lighter brown and have dark-edged beige cheeks unlike the cottonmouth's dark labial scales.

Behavior See **Florida Cottonmouth (67)**.

Mocassins

67 Florida Cottonmouth
Agkistrodon piscivorus conanti

Venomous   Despite the cottonmouth's formidable reputation, very few people are bitten by these reptiles—the mortality rate for the entire U.S. is less than one person per year. Envenomation by *Agkistrodon piscivorus* may be serious in terms of tissue death, however, for while its toxins are less potent than those of *Crotalus* rattlesnakes—S. Minton estimates the lethal dose for a healthy human adult as about 150 mg—their hemorrhagic effects are pronounced. Cottonmouths can also be quite large, with proportionately wide jaws, up to ⅜-inch-long fangs, and venom-storage lumens which have yielded, from the largest individuals, over 1000 mg of venom. See **Venom Table, page 45.**

Abundance   *Agkistrodon piscivorus conanti* is still very common in some areas—old-time hide hunters sometimes took over 300 in a single night. Most "cottonmouth" sightings, however, are actually of *natricine* water snakes. Where cottonmouths *are* abundant, their unique musky scent is sometimes noticeable in still, humid air.

Size   The record Florida cottonmouth measured 74.5 inches, and the heavy-bodied proportions of *A. piscivorous* would have made that individual an enormous snake. Most *A. p. conanti* are much smaller, with the majority of adults attaining around 38 inches in length. Males are longer, and up to twice as heavy as females.

Habitat   *Agkistrodon piscivorus conanti* may be found almost anywhere in Florida except cities. Although cottonmouths generally live within a half-mile of permanent fresh, brackish, or salt water, dry forest and grassland are sometimes occupied, while in spring, flooded prairies are prime foraging sites. As the only aquatic pit viper, cottonmouths primarily frequent aquatic habitats, but they also do well in entirely dry environments. Salt marshes and the low-lying saline barrier islands bordering peninsular Florida are particularly good cottonmouth habitat, and *A. p. conanti* occurs there in very high densities. Yet, cottonmouths are absent from the lower Keys, and even on the mainland their populations tend to vary, with large areas of apparently prime habitat being entirely devoid of these reptiles.

Prey   Frogs are probably this pit viper's most frequent prey, but *A. piscivorus* is an indiscriminate feeder whose diet alters with the availability of prey. At various times this can include fish, hatchling alligators, cottontails and swamp rabbits, water birds, and sizable water snakes, as well as smaller cottonmouths. Game fish species such as Florida largemouth bass and bluegills are generally too fast for the cottonmouth to capture, and only sick or dead ones are taken (like other aquatic serpents, cottonmouths feed readily on carrion, however, and are often drawn to injured or dead fish dangling from fishermen's stringers, giving rise to the popular notion of their competition for game fish).

Reproduction   Live-bearing. Breeding follows the pattern of most pit vipers—adult males initiate contact by following a female's pheromone scent trail, engaging in dominance behavior such as rearing the forebody in threat if they encounter another male engaged in the same pursuit. Actual fighting seldom occurs, however. Courtship involves dorsal tongue-flicking by the male, as well as rubbing his chin on the female's back before attempting copulation. The 3 to 12 young are born during August and September, with the newborns being so stoutly proportioned that gravid cottonmouths average only 5 or 6 offspring per litter; similarly-sized female water snakes ordinarily deposit dozens of much more slender young.

Juvenile cottonmouths are more brownish and clearly patterned than adults, with distinct dark dorsal bars and lateral blotches. Their tails have grayish-green tips which, in a predatory technique shared with their relatives the copperheads, are used by juvenile cottonmouths in caudal luring. In this instinctive hunting technique, motionless young *Agkistrodon* wriggle their tailtips in excitement upon seeing prey. This response may entice small lizards, frogs, and toads (which apparently take the yellowish caudal tip for a worm or caterpillar) within striking range.

Coloring/scale form   Sometimes displayed in open-jawed threat, the white interior of the mouth is the source of this reptile's common name. Of its scientific designation, *Agkistrodon piscivorus conanti*, "*Agkis*" is a mistranslation of "*ancil*," meaning forward; "*odon*" refers to the cottonmouths' fangs; and "*piscivorus*" means fish-eating. The cottonmouth is therefore a forward-fanged fish eater. "*Conanti*" refers to Roger Conant, the eminent herpetologist for whom the Florida race is named.

Adult Florida cottonmouths are dark gray-brown, with broad, often dimly-defined paler dorsolateral bands. These animals' apparently dull dorsal coloring sometimes results from a film of water-deposited sediment and algae. Clean-water-living cottonmouths have more distinct patterning and lighter brown lower sides. Very old individuals are almost entirely dark gray or black, yet even among obscurely-patterned specimens, the Florida cottonmouth's slightly paler upper labial scales and the light longitudinal line between its crown and the sides of its head are noticeable.

There are 25 rows of keeled dorsal scales at midbody and the scales beneath the tail occur in a pattern by which *Agkistrodon* can be identified even from their shed skins, because for ⅔ of the tail's length the subcaudal scales occur in a single row. The posterior third of the undertail has a double row of scales like that of nonvenomous snakes. The anal plate is undivided.

Mocassins

Similar snakes   The heavy bodies and aquatic habitat of Florida's large water snakes (21–28) often cause them to be mistaken for cottonmouths. Water snakes lack the cottonmouth's dark, heat-sensing facial pit between the eye and nostril and have clearly visible round pupils. In daylight, the pupils of the cottonmouth's big gray eyes are black slits; at night in the beam of a light they are more rounded for the moment it takes them to close against the glare. *A. piscivorus* also behaves differently from water snakes. Most individuals flee when approached, although on land some hold their ground and gape open-mouthed, twitching their tailtips. Water snakes neither gape in threat nor twitch their tails. Also, unlike water snakes, the cottonmouth swims in a leisurely way, its whole body floating buoyantly with the head high; water snakes swim by squirming rapidly along, their bodies drooping below the surface when they stop.

Behavior   Cottonmouths can be very pugnacious when annoyed, yet *A. piscivorus* is not nearly as ferocious as popularly envisioned. One example of their mythical fierceness is the scary, nest-of-cottonmouths story prompted by the masses of harmless water snakes periodically concentrated in drying creeks and ponds during late summer. The most popular outgrowth of this erroneous observation concerns the water-skier (or television series river-fording cowboy) killed by a flurry of bites after falling into a nest of moccasins. Various retellings of this purported event have circulated in boating circles for decades, but no water-skier (or horseman) has ever suffered multiple envenomation from tumbling into a nest of cottonmouths.

Agkistrodon piscivorus does not "nest," for one thing, and packed groups would last no longer than it took the larger cottonmouths to swallow the smaller ones. Further, although some cottonmouths show little fear of humans, none attack—alone or en masse—and even their characteristic open-mouthed gape is actually a rather passive defensive gesture because, unless the mouth itself is touched, wide-jawed cottonmouths often fail to strike even when prodded elsewhere on their bodies.

Can a cottonmouth bite underwater? Of course, that's how they catch fish. Apparently it's *only* fish, though; in the water, cottonmouths swim away if annoyed. In the water, cottonmouths do not gape in threat, because water resistance against a wide-spread mouth—a position necessary for biting—would make a defensive strike almost impossible. Without something solid to press against, a swimming cottonmouth would be pushed backward by the force of its own strike.

This is all rather hypothetical, though, because unlike water snakes *A. piscivorus* is not a true aquatic animal and seldom forages underwater. (In observation tanks cottonmouths take fish by cornering them in shallow water or—rarely—by seizing them with a short lateral grab as the fish accidentally brush against the cottonmouth's sides.) Indeed, cottonmouths spend little time submerged; mostly they forage along banks and shorelines, bask on top of floating aquatic vegetation, and swim slowly across the surface—diving, briefly, only if they are attacked.

68 Dusky Pigmy Rattlesnake

Sistrurus miliarius barbouri

Venomous   Despite the fact that pigmy rattlers are pugnacious, quick-to-strike little serpents with moderately potent venom (about the same toxicity as that of the southern copperhead), *S. miliarius* is far less dangerous than the state's larger rattlesnakes. The pigmy rattler's diminutive fangs (no more than 5/32 inch across the curve) limit it to superficial penetration of the human body, while, even when their venom glands are artificially milked to depletion, the largest *S. miliarius* yield no more than 35 milligrams (dry weight) of venom. This is more than twice as much as the snake could expel on its own, but it is still less than half the probable lethal dose for an adult human being. For this reason envenomation by pigmy rattlers is seldom serious (a severe envenomation could still be fatal to a small child, however), rarely causing the extensive tissue necrosis characteristic of envenomation by *Crotalus*-genus rattlesnakes. See **Venom Table, page 45.**

Abundance   Pigmy rattlesnakes are common throughout Florida, and locally abundant. In biologically generous marsh/palmetto grassland environments—particularly the Everglades—*S. m. barbouri* is one of the most numerous serpents. Yet these animals are less often encountered than their numbers would suggest because they are almost always well hidden beneath ground cover. Primarily because of habitat appropriation by human development, pigmy rattlesnakes are now spottily distributed.

Size   Adult *S. m. barbouri* are short, plump, and seldom more than 20 inches long. The record is 31 inches.

Habitat   Primary habitats include both wet and dry areas: mesic pine flatwoods, bottomland hardwood forest, wet sawgrass and marl prairies, hardwood hammocks and xeric sandhills, scrub, and maritime hammocks.

Prey   Because much of the warm-blooded prey taken by larger vipers is too big for pigmy rattlers, the typical food of juvenile crotalids—amphibians, lizards and small snakes, and even insects—constitutes much of the diet of adult *S. miliarius*. Thirteen dusky pigmy rattlesnakes from southern Georgia contained 4 large centipedes, 3 ground skinks, 1 six-lined racerunner, 1 ringneck snake, and 2 deer mice.

Reproduction   Live-bearing. Pit vipers tend to have slow growth and maturation rates, as well as low levels of reproduction. Female rattlesnakes living in cooler climates, subject to shorter seasonal activity and viperids' typically low-productivity, sit-and-wait style predation, are seldom able to marshall sufficient resources to give birth every year. Yet, even pigmy rattlers active year-round in subtropical southern Florida follow this reproductive cycle. As T. Farrell and M. Pilgrim report, only about half of adult Florida females become gravid every year. Primarily autumn breeders, when males have been observed in combat rituals, over 90% of *S. m. barbouri* births in the southern parts of the state take place (after winter-long sperm storage by the female) during August. One captive pair of *S. miliarius* bred throughout September, with the female giving birth some 8.5 months later to three, ¹⁄₁₀-oz., 5.3-inch-long young with pale yellow tailtips.

Prior to parturition, females cease feeding and move to the sunniest parts of their territories to bask, thereby elevating their body temperature and accelerating the development of the young. Like other pit vipers, pigmy rattlesnakes have large abdominal cavities compared to most terrestrial snakes, but because their neonates are also large, 26 litters of *S. m. barbouri* ranged from 2 to only 11. (Because the size of the individual offspring is generally determined by the minimal dimensions it needs to survive, smaller snake species typically give birth to fewer young than larger species.)

Coloring/scale form   The agile movements of the dusky pigmy rattler do not suggest the conventional heavy-bodied, slow-crawling "rattlesnake" image, nor does its black-spotted gray dorsum lined with a russet vertebral stripe. The pigmy rattlesnake's sides are spotted with a triple row of small dark blotches above its faintly stippled whitish venter, and because *S. miliarius* has such a miniscule rattle—no longer than the width of its head—a myth has arisen of the rattle-less ground rattlesnake. The strongly keeled dorsal scales are arranged in 23 to 25 rows at midbody, the crown is covered with 9 large scale plates, and the anal plate is undivided.

Similar snakes   Except as newborns, **timber (69)** and **eastern diamondback rattlesnakes (70)** are much larger. Numerous small scales cover the center of their broad crowns, while the timber rattler has a black tail and jagged, dark brown dorsal chevrons. The diamondback's dorsum is marked with white-edged diamonds. The **southern hognose snake (49)** is sometimes mistaken for the pigmy rattler, but it lacks a rattle and has both a sharply upturned snout and small, dark eyes with round pupils.

Behavior   Entirely terrestrial and seldom seen in the open, pigmy rattlesnakes, if disturbed, often rattle their tails from beneath ground cover or fallen palmetto fronds. If exposed, they may flatten their bodies and snap sharply sideways without coiling. The strike never spans more than a few inches, though, because *S. miliarius* does not raise its forebody into the elevated defensive posture that enables larger rattlesnakes to strike up to half their body length.

69 Timber Rattlesnake
Crotalus horridus

Venomous   It is thought—with the support of both laboratory and field evidence—that the venom of some *Crotalus horridus* from Florida and South Carolina may contain a larger percentage of neurotoxically-active peptide components than the venom of timber rattlers from the northern and central U.S. Immediate, serious, systemic reactions to timber rattlesnake envenomation have been caused by a number of bites from the Southeast. I have also occasionally encountered the same sort of immediate shock and near-lethal systemic failure in timber rattlesnake envenomations from East Texas, and the data from the Southeast may only reflect the fact that more people have been bitten in this part of the country.

Because only a small percentage of these envenomations have been serious, however, the most significant attribute of *Crotalus horridus* venom seems to be its great variability. More than 20 years ago S. Minton established this by obtaining from a pair of gravid female timber rattlers, captured on the same day on a single northern hilltop, one venom sample whose toxins were 5 times as powerful as the other's. An average lethal dose for a human adult might be about 100 mg., and between 100 and 400 mg. of venom has been obtained from the largest specimens, with the snake able to inject perhaps 30% of that amount on its own. See **Venom Table, page 45.**

Abundance   In most of its broad range (particularly that in Florida) the timber rattler has suffered massive habitat loss to human development. At the same time, hunting for the pet and hide trades—including the summertime collection of gravid females—has removed large numbers of *C. horridus* from the wild, further diminishing whole regional communities of this slow-reproducing species. As a result, in most of its limited Florida range (where it is known as the **canebrake rattlesnake**), *C. horridus* is uncommon near human-populated areas, although it is still found in the Osceola National Forest.

Size   Most adult timber rattlers range from 30 to 48 inches in length; the record is just over 74 inches.

Habitat   In the central and northeastern U.S. the timber rattler is known as a predominantly upland animal of wooded, rocky ridges. Yet throughout the southern states, including northern Florida, *C. horridus* rarely occurs in upland forest, occurring most often in the dense thickets of moist riparian corridors. Cypress swamps and wet prairie habitats are also occasionally occupied.

Except for a few large areas of bottomland forest, timber rattlers' territories are now artificially segmented by the presence of man, but in less restricted environments radio-telemetry-equipped individuals maintain home ranges varying from the 10 or fewer acres used by quiescent gravid females to as much as several hundred acres for wide-roaming males.

Rattlesnakes

Prey   Prey is almost entirely warm-blooded, and primarily mammalian. Smaller *C. horridus* take mostly white-footed mice, while in the stomachs of 30 large individuals collected in Louisiana were 10 rabbits, 8 mice, 6 rats, and 1 fox squirrel.

Yet, there are exceptions to this preference for ectothermic prey. One 3-foot-long specimen captured by herpetologist C. McIntyre refused small mammal prey for weeks. Just as McIntyre was ready to release it for fear it would starve, he accidentally discovered its sole food requirement was birds—a diet on which the snake subsequently thrived for years. Moreover, cannibalism has also been observed among *C. horridus*. The answer probably lies in the fact that research suggests pit vipers can acquire a singular prey preference by successfully killing a particular food animal early in life—an event which may then register in the snake's predatory behavior an unchanging image of what constitutes appropriate prey.

Reproduction   Live-bearing. An average brood numbers just over 10, born in late summer.

Coloring/scale form   The black tail, cinnamon vertebral stripe, and dark dorsolateral chevrons are definitive, while the dull whitish or yellowish venter may be smudged along its edges with patches of darker pigment. Both ontogenetic variation and sexual dimorphism—the latter rare among snakes—occurs in *C. horridus*. As these vipers age, their bodies darken, obscuring the beautiful contrast between their creamy youthful ground color, black dorsolateral chevrons, and reddish vertebral stripe. Males are generally more grayish than females, so the oldest and largest males are far less colorful than young females.

Among Florida *C. horridus,* more individuals have 25 mid-body rows of keeled dorsal scales than among northern and western populations, where 23 rows is most common. Like that of other rattlesnakes, the anal plate is undivided.

Similar snakes   Herpetological opinion is divided over whether the southern form of the timber rattlesnake constitutes a separate subspecies **canebrake rattler,** *C. h. atricaudatus,* or is instead a geographically determined color variant. Those who define the southern canebrake as a full subspecies do so on the basis of its paler dorsal ground color, its 25 midbody rows of dorsal scales, and its different microhabitat of moist bottomland. Northern timber rattlers are generally regarded as upland animals of dry wooded ridges, although this may be true only of the wintering den-sites where most specimens have been captured. Perhaps the best approach to the controversy is that of W. S. Brown, whose monograph on the timber rattlesnake recognizes 3 major intraspecific populations: the northeastern variant (which includes both predominantly black and yellow color phases; the southern variant (the classic, vertebrally russet-striped *C. atricaudatus*), and the western variant (from eastern Kansas and Missouri, where both "canebrake" and classically marked timber rattlesnake color morphs intergrade).

The **eastern diamondback rattlesnake (70)** occupies drier environments such as open pinewoods, sandhills and maritime hammock; it is distinguished by its chocolate- and white-edged vertebral diamonds, its brownbanded tail, and its white-bordered dark postocular stripe. As an adult, the **dusky pigmy rattlesnake (66)** is only the size of a newborn timber rattler; it has a tiny rattle, a gray ground color with dark dorsal and lateral spots, and a narrow crown, both striped with chocolate and—unlike the small-scaled crown of the timber rattler—capped with 9 large scale plates.

Behavior   Because *C. horridus* is thinly dispersed in even the richest natural habitat, as a sedentary nocturnal forager it is seldom seen—although before spring foliage has cut visibility in the woodland understory an occasional individual is sometimes found basking in a patch of sunlight at the base of a tree or next to a fallen log.

This propensity for coiling next to logs has been noted since 1900, but only recently have studies shown it to be part of a sophisticated hunting strategy. Because timber rattlesnakes feed primarily on alert rodents and lagomorphs, they must maximize contact with these highly mobile creatures beyond chance encounters on the forest floor. Fallen logs are important byways for small woodland mammals, and timber rattlers have been observed moving from one log to another, apparently investigating them for evidence of prey animals' scent trails by repeated tongue-flicking along the logs' upper surface. Quickly passing over trunks lacking strong rodent scent, *C. horridus* typically coils next to a well-used small-mammal avenue, resting its head on the trunk's upper surface. Here its eyes and heat-sensing pits can survey both directions along its prey's line of travel, while its sensitive throat can detect even the miniscule vibrations of a white-footed mouse's approaching footsteps. Only actively hunting timber rattlers engage in this behavior, moreover: males and non-gravid females typically hunt in this way but heavily pregnant females, which have no room in their bellies for prey (and have thus foregone feeding) do not coil with their chins on logs.

Telemetry has shown that few large rattlesnakes average more than one meal per month. Yet, as low-metabolism ectomorphs, this is a schedule to which they are well-adapted, and the sedentary lifestyle this feeding schedule requires is so compatible with captive conditions that timber rattlesnakes have lived as long as 30 years in confinement.

70 Eastern Diamondback Rattlesnake
Crotalus adamanteus

Venomous   The most dangerous venomous snake in the state, *C. adamanteus* often holds its ground instead of retreating when threatened. Adults' large size and agility gives them a striking range that can exceed 3 feet, and their broad heads and voluminous venom glands, as well as their proportionally long fangs, allow eastern diamondbacks to deliver a large quantity of venom well below the surface. Feeding on sizeable prey like rabbits (which if not dropped quickly may run so far that their bodies are difficult for the snake to find) may accustom these reptiles to delivering a substantial amount of venom, for among prey animals, death often occurs within 60 seconds of the strike. In addition to its hemorrhagic properties, eastern diamondback venom contains a significant proportion of neurotoxically-active peptide fractions which, even in creatures as large as human beings, can result in systemic failure. The lethal dose is probably somewhat less than 100 mg for a healthy human adult, with the largest eastern diamondbacks being milked, in the old reptile-show days, of nearly 900 mg. Pit vipers can deliver less than a third their total venom capacity in a bite, but even this amount constitutes far more than the amount needed for a deadly envenomation. Almost all of Florida's rare snakebite fatalities (about 1 per year) are the result of bites by *Crotalus adamanteus*. See **Venom Table, page 45.**

Yet, despite their abundance in some areas these rattlers are involved in surprisingly few hostile encounters with human beings. This is due partly to the diamondback's propensity for remaining out of sight below ground in rodent and gopher tortoise burrows, and partly because even when closely approached most eastern diamondbacks do not behave aggressively. While radio-tracking *C. adamanteus* in northern Florida, biologist W. Timmerman made 743 visits to locate his transmittered snakes, often accidentally stepping very close to their hiding places. Yet in only nine instances did such a close approach trigger a rattle, and none of the snakes struck.

Abundance   Increasingly uncommon. Eastern diamondback rattlesnakes occur throughout Florida, including its saline offshore keys, yet *C. adamanteus* is now in decline. It is a decline initiated decades ago by human predation that began on a major scale with rattlesnake roundups. Though the eastern diamondback was never as abundant as the western diamondback, *Crotalus atrox,* on which Texas' and Oklahoma's huge reptile carnivals are based, the Florida roundups obtained their sacrificial snakes in the same way—pumping gasoline into "gopher holes." Besides flushing out poisoned though still-living rattlesnakes, this practice decimated a variety of burrow-living wildlife, including the protected gopher tortoises that originally dug the tunnels. Tunnel-gassing is now illegal in Florida but, along with rattlesnake roundups, it still occurs in Georgia and Alabama.

Current human predation on *C. adamanteus,* however, is prompted primarily by the commercial trade in rattlesnake skins. For over a quarter of a century the Ross Allen Reptile Insititute shipped eastern diamondback rattlesnakes (more than 50,000 in all) out of the state, and a network of hide-hunters and commercial collection points still exists in Florida. Although *C. adamanteus* is far less numerous today, between 1990 and 1992, the state's largest snakeskin dealer exported some 10,000 eastern diamondback hides each year.[1]

The major problem facing *C. adamanteus* is much more serious than exploitation by hide hunters, however. Eastern diamondback rattlesnakes face the same overwhelming threat as does most of Florida's vertebrate wildlife, which is loss of its native habitat to residential development. Small reptiles such as ringneck and brown snakes can burrow unharmed in neighborhood lawns, garter snakes thrive in suburban plantings, and cryptic nocturnal species like corn snakes adapt to disturbed environments; but big, dangerous serpents like the eastern diamondback are quickly exterminated in human-occupied areas. Building is now proceeding so rapidly everywhere in Florida that the occasional *Crotalus adamanteus* that turns up on the fringes of urban areas has simply been overtaken by the asphalt glacier of human commerce.

Size   A beautiful and impressive reptile at any size, the eastern diamondback presently averages 32 to 48 inches in adult length, while a 6-foot-long individual is a rarity. R. Allen's records show a decline in the average diamondback's length from more than 5 feet during the 1930s to just over 4 feet in the 1960s. Because a 5-foot rattlesnake is a much larger and heavier animal than a 4-footer, this reflects a major reduction in the average size of the population, and because the largest females produce the most offspring, the diminished dimensions of female *C. adamanteus* due to human-caused mortality makes for a less fecund population. Yet, if undisturbed, these animals can grow much larger. Old male *C. adamanteus* are the largest and heaviest snakes in North America—the record measured 8 feet, 3 inches in length, with a midbody diameter of 4.5 inches and a crown 3.25 inches wide.

Habitat   Eastern diamondbacks can occur almost anywhere in both mainland Florida and its offshore saltwater keys, but the prime habitats for *Crotalus adamanteus* are open upland pine forest, pine-palmetto flatwoods, sandhills, and coastal maritime hammocks. Timbering has not impacted

---

[1]Florida's recent requirement for filing reports on hide transactions has meant that most of the reported diamondback hides are fallaciously designated as coming from Georgia.

these reptiles as negatively as might be expected: when mature longleaf pines were logged out of the Ocala and Osceola National forests the cut-over areas that grew up in palmetto scrub were more productive of rodents and therefore improved as habitat for eastern diamondbacks.

Prey   Large pit vipers tend to be generalized predators of a variety of warm-blooded animals. Adult eastern diamondbacks' most-favored prey is probably marsh rabbits and cottontails, but squirrels, gophers, and cotton rats, as well as quail and other birds are also taken.

Like other large rattlesnakes, *C. adamanteus* is both an active forager and a sit-and-wait ambush predator. At times eastern diamondbacks employ the same hidden-site hunting tactics as *C. horridus,* and because this technique seldom produces more than a dozen meals a year, diamondbacks are adapted to the same long non-feeding periods between kills. (Newborns are off to a good start, for example, if they manage to kill a single mouse between their late-summer birth and their first winter dormancy—an amount of food more than sufficient to sustain them until spring.)

Reproduction   Live-bearing. The reproductive capacity of large pit vipers such as the eastern diamondback is partially determined by these creatures' slow growth. *C. adamanteus* requires at least two years to reach reproductive maturity, and its subsequent low breeding frequency is the result of females' inability to acquire the body fat necessary for pregnancy more often than every other year.

Many females, in fact, only gain enough fat to reproduce every third or fourth year. This attenuated reproductive cycle makes receptive female *C. adamanteus* a scarce resource. During the late summer breeding season, males become both territorial and aggressive toward rivals, and dominance-establishing "combat dances"— in which competing males try to raise their bodies above the foreparts of other males—are well known. Because males radically increase their travel time on the surface at this season, commercial hide hunting also peaks, with traders bringing in some 50% more males than females.

(The necessity for male crotalids to aggressively pursue seldom-available females has given rise to the myth of rattlesnakes not only mating for life, but waiting in ambush for those who have killed their mates. After dispatching a rattler the rural tradition is to hang it, as a sort of grim trophy, over a fence. If the carcass is that of a reproductively receptive female, opening its body cavity disperses the potent olfactory pheromone signals by which male rattlers locate potential breeding partners. In folklore, however, the rattler found coiled beneath the body the next morning is assumed to be a bereaved, revenge-seeking mate.)

It is not entirely clear why viperids lack the ability to reproduce more frequently. Part of the reason may be that to complete gestation of their large, well-developed young, gravid female *C. adamanteus* forego hunting by moving to optimally-warm basking sites with low prey availability. This can occur many weeks before parturition and, as predominantly ambush hunters with lower foraging success than snakes that actively seek prey, post-partum female eastern diamondbacks typically require more than a year to rebuild the fat reserves consumed by giving birth. Such intense effort makes for great parental investment in the 7 to 24 (mean: 14) plump, 7- to 10-inch-long offspring, born in late summer, and there are accurate accounts of at least the appearance of maternal protection. Neonate *C. adamanteus* remain near their birth site—typically a tortoise or rodent burrow whose humid interior minimizes the desiccation to which they are prone—at whose entrance an adult eastern diamondback, presumably a female, has often been observed for days in succession. After their first shed at about 10 days of age the young are less vulnerable to drying and venture away from their natal shelter, but during their first week the mother's nearby resting from parturition probably deters predators and unintentionally affords her young enhanced odds of survival. (Maternal protection of eggs and young is well known among reptiles, but the protective role of female *C. adamanteus* seems to be entirely passive.)

Coloring/scale form   Less-vividly patterned than diamondbacks from the Carolinas, Florida *C. adamanteus* have more gray than yellow in their ground color but display the same white-edged chocolate vertebral diamonds—which posteriorly enclose the back's ground color, then fuse into brown crossbands. The tail is olive, ringed with black. There is a white-edged dark postocular stripe, the venter is pale yellow, and the crown is capped with small scales between its lateral postocular plates. The 27 to 29 midbody rows of dorsal scales are keeled and the anal plate is undivided. Aberrantly-colored *C. adamanteus* are also well known. Albino or leucistic yellow individuals are periodically found west of Gainesville, and for years "Snowflake," an albino eastern diamondback, was the showpiece of Glades Herp in Ft. Myers.

Similar snakes   The **timber rattlesnake (69)** has a tan crown, a rusty mid-dorsal stripe, blackish dorsolateral chevrons, and an entirely black tail. Even the largest **dusky pigmy rattlesnakes (68)** are only the size of a juvenile diamondback, with a tiny rattle, small dark dorsal and lateral blotches on a gray ground color, and a dark-striped crown capped with 9 large scales unlike the small-scaled crown of the eastern diamondback.

Behavior   Young eastern diamondbacks are preyed upon by raptors, mammalian carnivores, hogs, and ophiophagus serpents, but adult *C. adamanteus* need only fear man. In the wild they are reported to reach 10 years in age, which is an extremely long life for a wild snake, although captives have lived nearly 23 years.

Glossary

Adhesive-shelled eggs—Eggs with a sticky surface that causes them to adhere in a cluster when laid (the shells soon dry out, but the eggs remain stuck together).

Aestivation—Dry- and/or hot-weather-induced dormancy of many reptiles and amphibians.

Allopatric—Having a separate or discrete range.

Amelanistic—Color phase almost entirely lacking black pigment.

Amphiuma—Large, eel-like aquatic salamander with small legs and no external gills.

Anal plate—Scale covering the cloacal vent.

Anaphylaxis—Antigen-antibody reaction caused by sensitivity to a foreign protein such as antivenin; capable in extreme cases of producing severe shock, respiratory impairment, coma, and death.

Anchor coil—The lowermost loop of the body of a coiled snake; this serves the animal as a foundation from which to strike.

Anerythristic—Color phase almost entirely lacking red pigment.

Annelid—Segmented worm or leech; most commonly the earthworm.

Anterior—Toward the head.

Antibody—A globulin produced in reaction to the introduction of a foreign protein.

Antiserum—The fluid portion of the blood of an animal previously infused with a reactive foreign protein.

Antivenin—Crystallized serum produced from the antibodies of animals infused with venom; able to partly neutralize venom's effects on the victim's tissue by blocking the toxic enzymes' access to their target cells.

Antivenin Index—A compendium of antivenins is available in the United States (including those for non-indigenous snakes) from the Arizona Poison Center at the University of Arizona Medical School in Tuscon. Antivenin for indigenous North American pit viper and coral snake venoms is produced by Wyeth Laboratories in Philadelphia.

Anuran—Frog or toad.

Aposematic—Warning signal: sound, posture, coloration, etc.

Arachnid—Eight-legged invertebrate: spiders, scorpions, mites, and ticks.

Arthropod—Segmented invertebrate with jointed legs: insects, arachnids, and crustaceans.

Azygous scale—A single scale (that is, not one of a bilateral pair).

Belly line—The horizontal line of intersection between the belly and the lower sides of the body.

Brumation—Winter dormancy of reptiles and amphibians.

Caudal—Pertaining to the tail.

Cephalic—Pertaining to the head or crown.

Chemoreception—The perception of chemical signals—most often by means of scent particles—apprehended by the smell/taste mechanism of olfactory and veromonasal glands. See **Jacobson's organ.**

Chin shields—The central scales on the underside of the lower jaw.

Chthonic—Below or within the earth.

Cloaca—Lower chamber of the digestive, urinary, and reproductive systems of birds, reptiles, and amphibians, which opens to the outside through the anus, or vent.

Colubrid—A member of the largest worldwide family of snakes, *Colubridae;* most North American species are harmless.

Compartment syndrome The pressure of extreme edema, which after severe envenomation may rarely cut off blood flow to a limb, causing the death of its tissue. Some authorities believe this to be a cause of local necrosis that warrants surgical alleviation by fasciotomy; most maintain that necrosis is due almost exclusively to the enzymatic, digestive action of the venom itself.

Congeneric—Within the same genus. (Species belonging to the same genus are congeneric.)

Conspecific—Within the same species. (Subspecies, or races, of a single species are conspecific.)

Corticosteroid—Steroid (often used to treat venom poisoning) that originates in the adrenal cortex and whose effects include the enhancement of protein replacement, the reduction of inflammation, and the suppression of the body's immune responses.

Crepuscular—Active at dusk or dawn.

Crossband—Among snakes, a pigmented strip running from side to side across the back.

Crotalid—A pit viper; a member of the family *Viperidae*, subfamily *Crotalinae*. In the United States: rattlesnakes, the cottonmouth, and the copperhead.

Cryotherapy—Treatment of an injury with cold. Dangerous when a snakebitten extremity is radically chilled, because this can cause tissue death. (A cold pack on the wound may slightly reduce pain; another on the forehead may help to offset the nausea that often accompanies pit viper poisoning.)

Cryptic—Serving to conceal or camouflage.

Debridement—The surgical removal of (venom-saturated) tissue.

Depauperate—Diminished in species diversity.

Dichromatism—The presence of two or more color phases within a species or subspecies.

Diel—Daily or daytime.

Disjunct—Geographically separate.

Distally—Toward the periphery, or sides, of the body.

Diurnal—Active during the day.

Dorsal—Pertaining to the back.

Dorsolateral—Pertaining to the back and sides: either (a) the entirety of the back and sides or, (b) the juncture of the back and sides.

Dorsum—The back and upper sides.

Duvernoy's gland—A gland that produces some of the venom of rear-fanged colubrid snakes; named for the French anatomist D. M. Duvernoy, who first described it.

Ecdysis—The shedding of a reptile's outer skin. See **Exuviation.**

Ecotone—Transition zone between differing biological communities, such as the border between forest and meadow.

Ectotherm—Animal whose temperature is almost entirely determined by its environment.

Edema—Swelling of tissue due to the release of fluids (primarily from the vascular and lymphatic systems) into the interstitial tissue spaces.

Egg-bearing—Reproduction by means of eggs deposited outside the body. See **Oviparous.**

Elapid—A rigidly front-fanged, venomous serpent of the family *Elapidae*, such as the coral snake. Elapids are characterized by a large proportion of neurotoxically active venom fractions.

Endemic—Only found in a particular area.

Endotherm—Internally heat-regulating animal.

Envenomation—Infusion of venom.

Enzyme—Organic agent capable of producing the metabolic breakdown of tissue into its component proteins.

Exuviation—A shed: the sloughing of the entire outer covering, or *stratum corneum*, of a snake's body. This process first occurs a few days after birth, then takes place every few weeks to months (more often if the snake has been injured; less often as the snake grows older) throughout the animal's annual foraging period. This process can occupy from ten minutes to several hours. Rattlesnakes add a new basal rattle segment with each exuviation; the terminal segments are periodically broken off.

Fasciotomy—Surgical incision into the fascial band enclosing a muscular compartment. This is usually done in an attempt to prevent tissue destruction from excessive hydraulic pressure caused by the fluid released by the venom's perforation of the capillary walls and pumped into the tissues by the heart. Fasciotomy is of questionable value except as an emergency measure to save a limb in immediate danger of general necrosis due to vascular constriction.

Form—Subspecies or race.

Fossorial—Adapted to burrowing; subterranean.

Frontal scale—Scales located on the crown, or top of the head between the eyes.

Genotype—Genetic makeup of an individual.

Gravid—Pregnant.

Hemotoxic—Poisonous or destructive to blood, blood cells, or the vascular system.

Hemipene—The bi-lobed, therefore Y-shaped, penis of serpents and lizards.

Hibernation—Dormancy during winter.

Holotype—The specimen from which the description of a species or subspecies is derived.

Hydric—Well watered; wet.

Hydrophytic—Plant life adapted to living in standing fresh water.

Hypovolemic shock—Shock due to a loss of fluid from the circulatory system; in snakebite, this occurs when the arteriole and venule walls are perforated by venom enzymes.

Infralabial scales—The scales that line the lower jaw.

Indigenous—Native to an area; not introduced.

Infrared perception—Apprehension of the infrared band of the light spectrum.

Intergradation—The gradual genetic alteration of one subspecies into another across a geographical continuum.

Intergrade—Intermediate individual or population that often exhibits some combination of the characteristics of two or more species or subspecies.

Internasal scales—Scales just posterior to the rostral scale on top of the snout, anterior to the prefrontals.

Jacobson's organ—Double-sided sensory organ located in the roof of the mouth of serpents and some lizards into which the tips of their forked tongues are pressed. When a snake flicks its tongue, molecules that adhere to its sticky surface are carried into the mouth when the tongue returns to its sheath, and placed in ducts in the roof of the mouth. These ducts lead to veromonasal epithelia containing the chemosensory neurons that have evolved highly specific, inherited selective recognition of the chemical signature of appropriate prey species.

Keel—Small longitudinal ridge creasing the centerline of a dorsal scale.

Labial scales—Large scales lining the outer edges of the upper and lower jaws: **supralabial scales** line the upper jaw; **infralabial scales** line the lower jaw.

Lacertilian—Pertaining to lizards.

Lateral—Pertaining to the sides.

Lecithotrophy—Yolk-nourished embryos.

Leucistiphosis—The nourishment of embryos by means of yolks

Leutic—Still, i.e., non-flowing, water.

Ligature—Binding a limb with a circulation-impairing band such as a tourniquet.

Littoral—Pertaining to the margins of bodies of water; shoreline.

Live-bearing—Reproduction by means of fully-formed young born in membranous sheaths that are immediately discarded. See **Ovoviviparous** and **Oviparous.**

Loreal scale—Scale between the preocular and nasal scales.

Lumen—Venom-generating and storing gland.

Lysis—The breakdown or metabolism of cells or tissue by a peptide or enzyme.

Matrotrophy—Nourishment of embryos by nutrient exchange from the mother's blood.

Maxillary bones—Paired bones at the front of the upper jaw that in anterior-fanged venomous snakes carry the fangs. In the pit vipers, the maxillary bones are able to rotate outward, individually swinging the fang tips forward.

Mesic—Moderately watered; moist.

Midventral—The center of the belly.

Milieu—Environment or habitat.

Morph—Short for morphological; of variant appearance. For example, a color phase.

Morphological—Pertaining to an animal's appearance (as opposed to its genetic make-up).

Natricine—Large water snakes of the genus *Nerodia.*

Nasal scales—Scales through which the nostrils open.

Necrosis—Death of bone or soft tissue.

Neotenic—Retention of the juvenile form or coloring into adulthood.

Neurotoxic—Destructive primarily by impairing neuromuscular function; ophidian neurotoxins block the acetylcholine receptor sites of the upper spinal ganglia.

Non-indigenous—Not native to an area: therefore, introduced.

Nuchal—Pertaining to the neck.

Ocular—Pertaining to the eye.

Ocular scale—Scale covering the eye.

Ontogenetic—A change in morphology due to aging.

Ophidian—Pertaining to snakes.

Ophiophagous—Feeding on snakes.

Oviparous—Egg-bearing or laying: producing young by means of eggs that hatch outside the body.

Oviposition—Egg-laying.

Ovoviviparous—Live-bearing. Producing young by means of membranous eggs, whose membrane-encased embryos remain within the mother's body until hatching, at which time they are deposited as fully developed offspring.

Paraphyletic—Genus or species-level groups of organisms which, due to unusual habits, morphology or physiology, have emerged from their ancestral families, and rather than replacing them, now exist alongside their progenitors in slightly different niches.

Parietal scales—Pair of large scales located on the rear of the crown, or top of the head.

Parotid gland—Organ that secretes saliva in mammals and most of the venom in pit vipers and elapids.

Parthenogenesis—Reproduction by the development of an unfertilized egg.

Phenotype—Physical characteristics of an organism.

Pheromone—Chemical substance released by an animal that influences the behavior of others of the same species. Among snakes, pheromones are, as far as is known, mostly hormone-derived scents excreted by breeding-condition females as a location/tracking indicator for reproductive males.

Placentophosis—Nourishment of embryos by nutrient exchange from the mother's blood.

Plate—Large scales covering the crown, or top of the head, as well as the venter, or belly.

Polyvalent antivenin—An antivenin produced from a combination of antibodies and therefore useful against the venom of an entire genus of snakes. Wyeth's polyvalent antivenin is a single crystallized serum developed to treat the bites of all North American pit vipers: rattlesnakes, copperheads, and cottonmouths.

Posterior—Toward the tail.

Postocular scales—Scales bordering the posterior edge of the eye.

Preocular scales—Scales bordering the anterior edge of the eye.

Proteinase—Proteolytic, or tissue-dissolving, enzyme.

Proteolysis—Destruction of tissue due to the inability of venom-weakened cell walls to withstand their internal fluid pressures.

Race—Subspecies.

Range—The area thought to be the entire geographic distribution of an organism.

Relict population—Contemporary remnant group of a species formerly found over a broader range.

Riparian—Along the banks of streams or rivers.

Rostral scale—Scale covering the tip of the snout, frequently enlarged among burrowing species.

Ruderal—Agricultural.

Scute—Large scale plate.

Scutellation—Scalation: the arrangement of scales.

Serosanguinous—Swollen with blood.

Sexual dimorphism—A phenotypic difference (in coloring, pattern, size, configuration, or other trait) according to gender.

Siren—Large aquatic salamander shaped like an eel but possessing forelegs and external gills.

Spermatogenesis—Generation of spermatozoa.

Squamata—The Order of Classification comprising snakes and lizards.

Subcaudal scales—The scales lining the undersurface of the tail posterior to the cloacal opening, or vent.

Subocular scales—Small scales separating the lower edge of the eye from the supralabial scales.

Subspecies—A group or cluster of local populations that, to a significant degree, differs genetically or taxonomically from adjacent groups or clusters.

Supralabial scales—The scales that line the upper jaw.

Supraocular scales—The scales on the sides of the crown above the eyes.

Sympatric—Overlapping or corresponding ranges; occurring in the same area.

Syntopic—Overlapping or corresponding microhabitats; occurring in the same pond, or beneath the same log.

Temporal scales—Scales along the side of the head behind the postocular scale(s) and between the parietals and the supralabials.

Terminal segment—Among *Sistrurus* and *Crotalus,* the terminal rattle segment. Because rattles break off periodically, there are rarely more than 8 or 10 segments in a series no matter how old the snake. See **Exuviation.**

Thermoregulation—Control of body temperature—usually by an ectotherm—by moving toward or away from warmer or cooler areas.

Variant—Individual or population difference, most often in color or pattern; not judged to be of sufficient genetic magnitude to warrant recognition as a subspecies or race.

Venom fractions—The approximately three dozen discrete toxic proteins—principally peptides and enzymes—that make up reptile venoms. Most of these fractions can be isolated from the venom mix by electrophoresis and dialysis.

Vent—The posterior opening of the cloaca.

Venter—The belly.

Ventral—Pertaining to the belly.

Ventral scales—The transversely elongate scale plates, or scutes, that line the underbody of most snakes.

Ventrolateral—On the outer edge of the venter and the lower sides of the body.

Vertebral—Along the spine.

Vitellogenesis—Generation of ova.

Viviparous—Live-bearing. Among snakes this means retaining the developing young (in their membranous egg-sacs) within the body cavity of the mother until their deposition-and-hatching, which occur simultaneously.

Vomeronasal organ—Snakes' tongues are devoid of taste buds; their sensory function is to carry scent particles into the mouth, for the primary chemical sense that snakes use to orient themselves in their environment and to detect prey is vomerolfaction. This is mediated by the vomeronasal, or Jacobson's organ, named after its descriptor. See **Jacobson's organ.**

Xeric—Arid.

Bibliography

Abell, Jr., J. M., M.D. 1974. Snakebite: Current treatment concepts. *University of Michigan Medical Center Journal* 1 (40):29–31.

Abrahamson, W. G., and D. C. Hartnett. 1990. R. L. Myers and J.J. Ewell (eds.) *Ecosystems of Florida*. Orlando: Central Florida University Press.

Aldridge, R. D. 1992. Oviductal anatomy and seasonal sperm storage in the southeastern crowned snake (*Tantilla coronata*). *Copeia* 1992 (4): 1103–1106.

_____ and R. D. Semlitsch. 1992. Female reproductive biology of the southeastern crowned snake (*Tantilla coronata*). *Amphibia-Reptilia* 13: 209–218.

_____, and _____. 1992. Male reproductive biology of the southeastern crowned snake (*Tantilla coronata*). *Amphibia-Reptilia* 13: 219–225.

Allen, F. M., M.D. 1938. Mechanical treatment of venomous bites and wounds. *Southern Medical Journal* 31 (12): 1248–1253.

_____. 1939. Observations on local measures in the treatment of snake bite. *American Journal of Tropical Medicine* 19: 393–404.

Allen, E. R., and W. T. Neill. 1950. The coral snake. *Florida Wildlife* 5 (5): 14–15.

_____, and _____. 1953. The short-tailed snake. *Florida Wildlife* 6 (11): 8–9.

Anderson, P. K. 1961. Variation in populations of brown snakes, genus *Storeria*, bordering the Gulf of Mexico. *American Midland Naturalist* 66 (1): 235–247.

Arnold, S. J. 1972. Species densities of predators and their prey. *American Naturalist* 106: 220–236.

Ashton, Jr., R. E., S. R. Edwards, and G. R. Pisani. 1976. *Endangered and Threatened Amphibians and Reptiles in the United States*. Lawrence, Kan.: Society for the Study of Amphibians and Reptiles, Herpetological Circular no. 5.

_____, and P. S. Ashton. 1988. *Handbook of Reptiles and Amphibians of Florida. Part 1. The Snakes*. Miami: Winward Publishing, Inc.

Auffenberg, W. 1955. A reconsideration of the racer (*Coluber constrictor*) in the eastern United States. *Tulane Zoological Studies* 2 (6): 89–155.

_____. 1963. The fossil snakes of Florida. *Tulane Zoological Studies* 10 (3): 131–216.

Baker, R. S., G. A. Mengden, and J. J. Bull. 1972. Karyotypic studies of thirty-eight species of North American snakes. *Copeia* 1972: 257–265.

Ballinger, R. E., and J. D. Lynch. 1983. *How to Know the Amphibians and Reptiles*. Dubuque, Iowa: Wm. C. Brown Publishers.

_____. 1981. Florida environments and their herpetofaunas. Part I: environmental characteristics. Florida State Museum, Florida Herpetology No. 2.

Bartlett, R. D. 1988. *In Search of Reptiles and Amphibians*. New York: E. J. Brill.

Bechtel, B. H. 1978. Color and pattern in snakes. *Journal of Herpetology*. April, 1978: 521–532.

_____. 1980. Geographic distribution of two color mutants of the corn snake (*Elaphe guttata guttata*). *Herpetological Review* 11 (2): 30–40.

_____ and E. Bechtel. 1989. Color mutations in the corn snake (*Elaphe guttata guttata*): Review and additional breeding data. *The Journal of Heredity* 80 (4): 272–276.

_____. 1995. *Reptile and Amphibian Variants*. Florida: Krieger Publishing Company.

Behler, J. L., and F. W. King. 1979. *The Audubon Society Field Guide to North American Reptiles and Amphibians*. New York: Alfred A. Knopf.

Bellairs, A. 1970 *The Life of Reptiles*. 2 vols. New York: Universe Books.

_____, and J. Attridge. 1975. *Reptiles*. London: Hutchinson.

_____, and C. B. Cox (eds.) 1976. *Morphology and Biology of Reptiles*. London: Academic Press.

_____, and G. Underwood. 1951. The origin of snakes. *Biological Reviews of the Cambridge Philosophical Society* 26: 193–237.

Bernardino, Jr., F. S., and G. H. Dalrymple. 1992. Seasonal activity and road mortality of the snakes of the Pa-hay-okee wetlands of Everglades National Park, USA. *Biological Conservation* 62, 71–75.

Blanchard, F. N. 1924. The snakes of the genus *Virginia*. Papers of the Michigan Academy of Arts, Science, and Letters 3 (3): 343–365.

_____. 1936. Eggs and natural nests of the eastern ringneck snake (*Diadophis punctatus edwardsii*). Papers of the Michigan Academy of Science, Arts, and Letters 22: 521–532.

_____. 1937. Data on the natural history of the red-bellied snake (*Storeria occipitomaculata*) in Northern Michigan. *Copeia* 1937: 151–162.

———. 1938. Snakes of the genus *Tantilla* in the United States. Field Museum of Natural History (Zoology) 20 (28): 369–376.

———. 1942. The ring-neck snakes, genus *Diadophis*. Bulletin of the Chicago Academy of Science 7 (1): 1–142.

Blaney, R. M. 1971. An annotated checklist and biogeographic analysis of the insular herpetofauna of the Apalachicola Region, Florida. *Herpetologica* 27: 406–430.

Blem, C. R., and L. B. Blem. 1990. Lipid reserves of the brown water snake (*Nerodia taxispilota*). *Comparative Biochemistry and Physiology* 97A (3): 367–372.

Bloom, F. E. 1981. Neuropeptides. *Scientific American* 245 (October, 1981): 148–168.

Bogert, C. M. 1949. Thermoregulation in reptiles, a factor in evolution. *Evolution* 3: 195–211.

Bonilla, C.A., and M. K. Fiero. 1971. Comparative biochemistry and pharmacology of salivary gland secretions. II.: Chromatographic separation of the basic proteins from North American rattlesnake venoms. *Journal of Chromatography* 56: 253.

Boulenger, G. A. 1973. *Contributions to American Herpetology: Collected Papers.* Facsimile Reprints. (Index 1977). New York: Society for the Study of Amphibians and Reptiles.

Bowler, J. K. 1977. Longevity of reptiles and amphibians in North American collections. Society for the Study of Amphibians and Reptiles, Herpetological Circular no. 6.

Boxall, J. 1982. Pressure/immobilization first aid treatment of snake bite. *Medical Journal of Australia* 1: 155.

Bragg, A. N. 1960. Is *Heterodon* venomous? *Herpetologica* 16: 121–123.

Braswell, A. L., and W. M. Palmer. 1984. *Cemophora coccinea copei*. *Herpetological Review* 15 (2): 49.

Brattstrom, B. H. 1955. The coral snake "mimic" problem and protective coloration. *Evolution* 9: 217–219.

———. 1964. Evolution of the pit vipers. Transactions of the San Diego Society of Natural History 13: 185–265.

———. 1965. Body temperature of reptiles. *American Midland Naturalist* 1965: 376–422.

Brinton, D. G. 1968. *Myths of the New World*, 3rd ed. New York: Haskell House.

Brisbin, I. L. and C. Bagshaw. 1993. Survival, weight changes, and shedding frequencies of captive scarlet snakes (*Cemophora coccinea*) maintained on an artificial liquid diet. *Herpetological Review* 24 (1): 27–29.

Brodie, III, E. D, and P. K. Ducey. 1989. Allocation of reproductive investment in the redbelly snake (*Storeria occipitomaculata*). *The American Midland Naturalist*. 122 (1): 51–58.

Brown, W. S. and H. S. Fitch, reviewer. 1994. *Biology, Status and Management of the Timber Rattlesnake* (book review). *The Journal of Wildlife Management* 58 (1): 186–187.

Burden, S. J., H. C. Hartzell, and D. Yoshikami. 1975. Acetylcholine receptors at neuromuscular synapses: phylogenetic differences detected by snake a-neurotoxins. *Proc. Nat. Acad. Sci.* USA 72: 3245–3249.

Burger, J., R. T. Zappalorti, J. Dowell, T. Georgiadia, J. Hill and M. Gochfeld. 1992. Subterranean predation on pine snakes (*Pituophis melanoleucus*). *Journal of Herpetology* 26 (3): 259–263.

Burghardt, G. M. 1970. Chemical perception in reptiles. In *Advances in Chemoreception Communication by Chemical Signals*, p. 241–308. Johnson, J. W., Jr., Moulton, D. G., Turk, A. (eds.) New York: Appleton-Century-Crofts.

Burkett, R. O. 1966. Natural history of the cottonmouth moccasin (*Agkistrodon piscivorus*). University of Kansas. Publications of the Museum of Natural History 17 (9): 435–491.

Butler, J. A., T. W. Hull, and R. Franz. 1995. Neonate aggregations and maternal attendance of young in the eastern diamondback rattlesnake (*Crotalus adamanteus*). *Copeia* 1995 (1): 196–198.

Campbell, H. W. and S. P. Christman. 1982. The herpetofaunal components of Florida sandhill and sand pine scrub associations. N. J. Scott, Jr. (ed.) *Herpetological Communities*. U.S. Fish and Wildlife Service, Wildlife Resources Report No. 13.

Campbell, J. A. and E. D. Brodie, Jr. (eds.) 1992. *Biology of the Pit Vipers*. Tyler, Texas: Selva.

Carmichael, P., and W. Williams. 1991. *Florida's Fabulous Reptiles and Amphibians*. Florida: World Publications.

Carpenter, C. C. 1979. A combat ritual between two male pigmy rattlesnakes (*Sistrurus miliarius*). *Copeia* 1979 (4): 638–642.

Carr, A. F. 1940. A contribution to the herpetology of Florida. University of Florida Publications, Biol. Ser. 3 (1).

_____. 1963. *The Reptiles*. Life Nature Library. New York: Time-Life.

_____ and C. J. Goin. 1959. *Guide to the Reptiles, Amphibians, and Freshwater Fishes of Florida*. Gainsville: University of Florida Press.

Chenowith, W. L. 1948. Birth and behavior of young copperheads. *Herpetologica* 4: 162.

Chiszar, D., C. W. Radcliffe, and R. Overstreet. 1985. Duration of strike-induced chemosensory searching in cottonmouths (*Agkistrodon piscivorus*) and a test of the hypothesis that striking prey creates a specific search image. *Canadian Journal of Herpetology* 63: 1057–1061.

Christman, S. P. 1988. Endemisn in Florida's interior sand pine scrub. Florida Game and Freshwater Fish Commission, Nongame Wildlife Program Final Report.

Clark, Jr., D. R., and R. R. Fleet. 1976. The rough earth snake (*Virginia striatula*): Ecology of a Texas population. *Southwestern Naturalist* 20 (4): 467–478.

Clausen, H. J. 1936. Observations on the brown snake (*Storeria dekayi*) with special reference to habits and birth of young. *Copeia* 1936: 98–102.

Cloudsley-Thompson, J. L. 1971. *The Temperature and Water Relations of Reptiles*. London: Merrow Publishing.

Cohen, P., W. H. Berkley, and E. B. Seligmann, Jr. 1971. Coral snake venoms: in vitro relation of neutralizing and precipitating antibodies. *American Journal of Tropical Medical Hygiene.* 20: 646–649.

Cohen, W. R., W. Wetzel, and A. Kadish. 1992. Local heat and cold application after eastern cottonmouth moccasin (*Agkistrodon piscivorus*) envenomation in the rat: Effect on tissue injury. *Toxicon* 30 (11): 1383: 1386.

Collins, J. T. 1990. *Standard Common and Current Scientific Names for North American Amphibians & Reptiles.* Lawrence, Kansas: University of Kansas, Museum of Natural History.

_____. 1993. *Amphibians and Reptiles in Kansas.* 3rd. ed. Lawrence, Kan.: University of Kansas Museum of Natural History.

Collins, J. T., and S. L. Collins. 1993. *Reptiles and Amphibians of Cheyenne Bottoms.* U. S. Fish and Wildlife Service.

Conant, R. 1956. A review of two rare pine snakes from the Gulf coastal plain. *American Museum Novitates* 1781: 17–21.

Conant, R., and J. T. Collins. 1991. *A Field Guide to Amphibians and Reptiles of Eastern and Central North America.* 3rd ed. Boston: Houghton Mifflin Co.

Cook, D. G. and F. J. Aldridge. 1984. *Coluber constrictor priapus. Herpetological Review* 15 (2): 49.

Cook, F. R. 1964. Communal egg laying in the smooth green snake. *Herpetologica* 20: 206.

Cooper Jr., W. E., D. G. Buth and L. J. Vitt. 1990. Prey odor discrimination by injestively naive coachwhip snakes (*Masticophis flagellum*). *Chemoecology* 1: 86–89.

Coulter, A. R., J. C. Cox, S. K. Sutherland, and C. J. Waddell. 1978. A new solid-phase sandwich radioimmunoassay and its application to the detection of snake venom. *Journal of Immunological Methodology* 23: 241–252.

Cowles, R. B., and R. L. Phelan. 1958. Olfaction in rattlesnakes. *Copeia* 1958: 77–83.

Craighead, F. C. 1974. Hammocks of South Florida. In: Gleason, P. J. (ed.) *Environments of South Florida: Present and past II. Miamo Geol. Soc. Mem. No. 2,* Coral Gables, Fla.

Crews, D., and W. R. Gartska. 1982. The ecological physiology of a garter snake. *Scientific American* 247 (5): 158–168.

Cunningham, E. R., et al. 1979. Snakebite: role of corticosteroids as immediate therapy in an animal model. *American Surgery* 45 (12): 757–759.

Curtis, L. 1949. The snakes of Dallas County, Texas. *Field and Laboratory* 17 (1): 1–13.

_____. 1952. Cannibalism in the Texas coral snake. *Herpetologica* 8: 27.

Dalrymple, G. H., F. S. Bernardino, Jr., T. M. Steiner, and R. J. Nodell. 1991. Patterns of species diversity of snake community assemblages, with data on two Everglades snake assemblages. *Copeia* 1991: 517–521.

Dalrymple, G. H., T. M. Steiner, R. Nodell and F. S. Bernardino, Jr. 1992. Seasonal activity of the snakes of Long Pine Key, Everglades National Park. *Copeia* 1991: 294–302.

Danzig, L. E., and G. H. Abels. 1961. Hemodialysis of acute renal failure following rattlesnake bite, with recovery. *Journal of the American Medical Association* 175: 136.

Ditmars, R. L. 1936. *The Reptiles of North America*. Garden City, New York: Doubleday and Co., Inc.

Dodd, Jr., C. K. 1992. Biological diversity of a temporary pond herpetofauna in north Florida sandhills. *Biodiversity and Conservation* 1: 125–142.

_____. 1993. Population structure, body mass, activity, and orientation of an aquatic snake (*Seminatrix pygaea*) during a drought. *Can. J. Zool.* 71: 1281–1288.

Dodd, Jr., C. J., and B. G. Charest. 1988. The herpetofaunal community of temporary ponds in north Florida sandhills: species composition, temporal use, and management implications. pp. 87–97. In R. C. Szaro et al., (tech. coords.) Proc. Symp. Manage. Ambhibs., Reptiles, and Small Mammals in N. Am. USDA For. Serv. Gen. Tech. Rep. RM-166.

Donald, J. A. and J. E. O'Shea. 1990. Neural regulation of the pulmonary vasculature in a semi-arboreal snake (*Elaphe obsoleta*). *Journal of Comparative Physiology B*. 159: 677–685.

Dowling, H. G. 1950. Studies of the black swamp snake (*Seminatrix pygaea*, Cope, with descriptions of two new subspecies. Museum of Zoology, University of Michigan Miscellaneous Publication No. 76.

Dowling, H. G., and L. R. Maxon. 1990. Genetic and taxonomic relations of the short-tailed snakes, genus *Stilosoma*. *Journal of Zoology* 221: 77–85.

Drummond, H. 1983 Aquatic foraging in garter snakes: A comparison of specialists and generalists. *Behaviour* 86: 1–30.

_____. 1985. The role of vision in the predatory behavior of natricine snakes. *Animal Behavior* 33: 206–215.

Duellman, W. E., and A. Schwartz. 1958. Amphibians and reptiles of southern Florida. Bulletin of Florida State, Museum of Biological Sciences. 3: 181–324.

Dundee, H. A., and D. A. Rossman. 1989. *The Amphibians and Reptiles of Louisiana*. Baton Rouge: Louisiana State University Press.

Dunn, E. R. 1954. The coral snake mimic problem. *Evolution* 2: 97–102.

Dyrkacz, S. 1982. Striped pattern morphism in the prairie kingsnake (*Lampropeltis c. calligaster*). *Herpetological Review* 13 (3): 70–71.

Edgren, Richard A. 1948. Notes on a litter of young timber rattlesnakes. *Copeia* 1948: 132.

_____. 1952. A synopsis of the snakes of the genus *Heterodon,* with the diagnosis of a new race of *Heterodon nasicus*. Chicago Academy of Sciences, Natural History Miscellanies, no. 112.

_____. 1955. The natural history of the hognosed snakes, genus *Heterodon:* A review. *Herpetologica* 11: 105–117.

_____. 1957. Melanism in hog-nosed snakes. *Herpetologica* 13: 131–135.

Eichholz, M. W., and W. D. Koenig. 1992. Gopher snake attraction to birds' nests. *Southwestern Naturalist* 37 (3): 293–298.

Emery, J. A., and F. E. Russell. 1961. Studies with cooling measures following injection of *Crotalus* venom. *Copeia* 1961: 322–326.

Enge, K. M. 1991. Herptile Exploitation. Annual Performance Report. Florida Game and Freshwater Fish Commission. Tallahassee, Fl.

_____. 1992. The basics of snake hunting in Florida. *Florida Wildlife* 46 (1): 2–8.

_____. 1993. Herptile use and trade in Florida. Florida Game and Freshwater Fish Commission, Nongame Wildlife Program Final Performance Report. Tallahassee.

_____. Habitat Occurrence of Florida's Amphibians and Reptiles. Technical Report. Nongame Wildlife Program. Florida Game and Freshwater Fish Commission. Tallahassee.

Ernst, Carl H. 1992. *Venomous Reptiles of North America.* Washington: Smithsonian Institution Press.

Etheridge, R. E. 1950. Color variants in snakes from the southeastern United States. *Copeia* (4): 321.

Farrell, Terrence M., Peter G. May and Melissa A. Pilgrim. 1995. Reproduction in the rattlesnake (*Sistrurus miliarius barbouri*) in Central Florida. *Journal of Herpetology* 29 (1): 21–27.

Fearn, H. J., C. Smith, and G. B. West. 1964. Capillary permeability responses to snake venom. *Journal of Pharmaceutical Pharmacology* 16: 79–84.

Fischer, F. J., H. W. Ramsey, J. Simon, and J. F. Gennaro, Jr. 1961. Antivenin and antitoxin in treatment of experimental rattlesnake venom intoxication (*Crotalus adamanteus*). *American Journal of Tropical Medicine* 10: 75–79.

Fitch, H. S. 1960. Autecology of the copperhead. University of Kansas Publications, Museum of Natural History 3 (4): 85–288.

_____. 1963. Natural history of the racer (*Coluber constrictor*) University of Kansas Museum of Natural History Publication 5 (8): 351–468.

_____. 1970. Reproductive cycles of lizards and snakes. University of Kansas Museum of Natural History Miscellaneous Publication 42: 1–247.

_____. 1975. A demographic study of the ringneck snake (*Diadophis punctatus*) in Kansas. University of Kansas Museum of Natural History Miscellaneous Publication No. 62.

_____. 1982. Resources of a snake community in prairie-woodland habitat of northeastern Kansas. In N. J. Scott, Jr. (ed.) *Herpetological Communities.* U. S. Fish and Wildlife Service, Wildlife Resources Report No. 13.

_____. 1985. Variation in clutch and litter size in New World reptiles. University of Kansas Museum of Natural History Miscellaneous Publication No. 76.

_____ and R. R. Fleet. 1970. Natural history of the milk snake (*Lampropeltis triangulum*) in northeastern Kansas. *Herpetologica* 26: 387–395.

Florida Natural Areas Inventory. 1990. Guide to the natural communities of Florida. Florida Department of Natural Resources. Tallahassee.

Foley, G. W. 1971. Perennial communal nesting in the black racer (*Coluber constrictor*). *Herpetological Review* 3: 41.

Ford, N. B. 1978. Evidence for species specificity of pheromone trails in two sympatric garter snakes. *Herpetological Review* 9: 10.

_____. 1979. Aspects of pheromone trailing in garter snakes. Ph.D. dissertation, Miami University (Ohio).

_____. 1981. Seasonality of pheromone trailing in two species of garter snakes. *Southwestern Naturalist* 26 (4): 385–388.

Fox, W., and H. C. Dessauer. 1962. The single right oviduct and other urogenital structures of female *Typhlops* and *Leptotyphlops*. *Copeia* 1962: 590–597.

Franz, R., K. C. Dodd, Jr., and A. M. Bard. 1992. The Non-Marine herpetofauna of Edgmont Key, Hillsborough County, Florida. *Florida Scient.* 53 (3): 179–183.

Frazer, J. G. 1892. *The Golden Bough*. New York: Macmillan.

Funderburg, J. B., and D. S. Lee. 1968. The amphibian and reptile fauna of pocket gopher (*Geomys*) mounds in central Florida. *Journal of Herpetology* 1: 99–100.

Gamow, R. I., and John F. Harris. 1973. The infrared receptors of snakes. *Scientific American* 228 (5): 94–102.

Gans, C. 1970. How snakes move. *Scientific American* 222 (6): 82–96.

_____, T. Krakauer, and C. V. Paganelli. 1968. Water loss in snakes: Interspecific and intraspecific variability. *Comparative Biochemical Physiology* 27: 757–761.

_____ and F. Billet (eds.) 1970–present. *Biology of the Reptilia*. New York: John Wiley & Sons.

Garfin, S. R., et al. 1979. Role of surgical decompression in the treatment of rattlesnake bites. *Surgical Forum* 30: 502–504.

Garton, S. G., E. W. Harris, and R. A. Brandon. 1970. Descriptive and ecological notes on *Natrix cyclopion* in Illinois. *Herpetologica* 26: 454–461.

Gehlback, F. R. 1970. Death-feigning and erratic behavior in leptotyphlopid, colubrid, and elapid snakes. *Herpetologica* 26: 24–34.

_____. 1972. Coral snake mimicry reconsidered: The strategy of self-mimicry. *Forma et Functio* 5: 311–320.

_____ and J. Baker. 1962. Kingsnakes allied with *Lampropeltis mexicana*: Taxonomy and natural history. *Copeia* 1962: 291–300.

_____, J. F. Watkins II, and J. C. Kroll. 1971. Pheromone trail-following studies of typhlopid, leptotyphlopid, and colubrid snakes. *Behavior* 40 (pts. 3–5) 282–294.

Geiser, S. W. 1948. *Naturalists of the Frontier*. Dallas: Southern Methodist University Press.

Gill, K.A., Jr. 1970. The evaluation of cryotherapy in the treatment of snake envenomation. *Southern Medical Journal* 63: 552–556.

Gillingham, J. C. 1976. Reproductive behavior of the rat snakes of eastern North America, *Elaphe*. *Copeia* 1979: 319–331.

_____. 1976. Early egg deposition by the southern black racer (*Coluber constrictor priapus*). *Herpetological Review*. 7 (3): 115.

Gingrich, W. C., and J. C. Hohenadel. 1956. Standardization of polyvalent antivenin. In E. E. Buckley and N. Proges (eds.), *Venoms* 381–385. Amer. Assoc. Advanc. Sci., Washington, D.C.

Githens, T. S., and N. O'C. Wolff. 1939. The polyvalency of crotalidic antivenins. III. Mice as test animals for study of antivenins. *Journal of Immunology* 37: 47–51.

Glass, T. G., Jr. 1969. Cortisone and immediate fasciotomy in the treatment of severe rattlesnake bite. *Texas Medicine* 65: 41.

_____. 1976. Early debridement in pit viper bites. *Journal of the American Medical Association* 235: 2513.

Glenn, J. L., and R. C. Straight. 1977. The midget faded rattlesnake (*Crotalus viridis concolor*) venom: Lethal toxicity and individual variability. *Toxicon* 15: 129–133.

_____ and _____. 1978. Mojave rattlesnake *Crotalus scutulatus scutulatus* venom: variation in toxicity with geographic origin. *Toxicon* 16: 81–84.

_____ and _____. 1982. *Rattlesnake Venoms: Their Action and Treatment*. New York: Marcel Dekker.

Gloyd, H. K. and R. Conant. 1990. *Snakes of the Agkistrodon Complex*. Oxford, Ohio: Society for the Study of Amphibians and Reptiles.

Godley, J. S. 1980. Foraging ecology of the striped swamp snake (*Regina alleni*) in southern Florida. *Ecological Monographs* 50: 411–436.

_____. 1982. Predation and defensive behavior of the striped swamp snake (*Regina alleni*). *Florida Field Naturalist* 10 (2): 31–36.

Goin, C. J. 1943. The lower vertebrate fauna of the water hyacinth community in Northern Florida. G. Proc. Fla. Acad. Sci. 6 (34): 143–153.

Goldstein, R. C. 1941. Notes on the mud snake in Florida. *Copeia* 1941: 49–50.

Greene, Harry W. 1973. The food habitats and breeding behavior of New World coral snakes. Master's thesis, University of Texas at Arlington.

_____. 1992. The ecological and behavioral context for pit viper evolution. In *Biology of the Pit Vipers*. J. A. Campbell and E. D. Brodie, Jr. (eds.) Tyler, Texas: Selva.

Greene, H. W., and R. W. McDiarmid. 1981. Coral snake mimicry: does it occur? *Science* 213: 1207–1212.

Grobman, Arnold B. 1978. An alternative solution to the coral snake mimic problem. *Journal of Herpetology* 12 (1): 1–11.

Groves, F. 1960. The eggs and young of *Drymarchon corais couperi*. *Copeia* 1960: 51–53.

_____ and R. J. Assetto. 1976. *Lampropeltis triangulum elapsoides*. *Herpetological Review*. 7 (3): 115.

Grudzien, T. A. and P. J. Owens. 1991. Genic similarity in the gray and brown color morphs of the snake *Storeria occipitomaculata*. *Journal of Herpetology*. 25 (1): 90–92.

Haast, W. E., and R. Anderson. 1981. *Complete Guide to Snakes of Florida*. Miami: Phoenix Publishing.

Hall, H. P., and J. F. Gennaro. 1961. The relative toxicities of rattlesnake (*Crotalus adamanteus*) and cottonmouth (*Agkistrodon piscivorous*) venom for mice and frogs. *Anat. Rec.* 139: 305–306.

Hall, P. M. 1993. Reproduction and behavior of western mud snakes (*Farancia abacura reinwardtii*) in American alligator nests. *Copeia* 1: 210–222.

Haller, R. 1971. The diamondback rattlesnakes. *Journal of Herpetology* 5 (3): 141–146.

Hamilton, W. J., Jr., and J. A. Pollack. 1955. The food of some crotalid snakes from Fort Benning. Georgia Natural History Miscellanies, no. 140.

Hardy, D. L. 1981. *Rattlesnake Envenomation in Southern Arizona.* Tuscon, Ariz.: Arizona Poison Control System, University of Arizona Health Sciences Center.

_____. 1982d. Overview of rattlesnake bite treatment. Address given November 5–6, 1982, at the Second Annual Southwestern Poison Symposium, Scottsdale, Arizona.

Hawthorne, K. 1972. Rat Snakes: Genus *Elaphe. Herpetologica* 9: 11–16.

Heatwole, H. 1977. Habitat selection in reptiles. In C. Gans and D. W. Tinkle, (eds.) *Biology of the Reptilia,* vol. 7, pp. 137–155. New York: Academic Press.

Heckman, C. W. 1960. Melanism in *Storeria dekayi. Herpetologica* 16: 213.

Hellman, R. E., and S. R. Telford, Jr. 1956. Notes on a large number of redbellied mud snakes, (*Farancia a. abacura*), from northcentral Florida. *Copeia* 1956: 257–258.

Holman, J. A. 1962. A Texas Pleistocene herpetofauna. *Copeia* 1962: 255–162.

Holman, J. A., and W. H. Hill. 1961. A mass unidirectional movement of *Natrix sipedon pictiventris. Copeia* 1961: 498–499.

Huheey, J. E. 1959. Distribution and variation in the glossy water snake (*Natrix rigida*). *Copeia* 1959: 303–311.

Iverson, J. B. 1979. Reproductive notes on Florida snakes. *Florida Scientist* 41: 201–207.

Jackson, D. R., and Richard Franz. 1981. Ecology of the eastern coral snake (*Micrurus fulvius*) in northern peninsular Florida. *Herpetologica* 37: 213–228.

Jackson, D. 1929. Treatment of snake bite. *Southern Medical Journal* 22: 605–608.

_____. 1931. First aid treatment for snake bite. *Texas State Journal of Medicine* 23: 203–209.

Jayne, B. C. 1985. Swimming in constricting (*Elaphe g. guttata*) and non-constricting (*Nerodia fasciata pictiventris*) colubrid snakes. *Copeia* 1985 (1): 195–208.

Jayne, B. C., and J. D. Davis. 1991. Kinematics and performance capacity for the concertina locomotion of a snake (*Coluber constrictor*). *The Journal of Experimental Biology* 1991 (156): 539–556.

Jones, J. M., and P. M. Burchfield. 1971. Relationship of specimen size to venom extracted from the copperhead (*Agkistrodon contortrix*). *Copeia* 1971: 162–163.

Jones, K. B., W. G. Whitford. 1989. Feeding behavior of free-roaming *Masticophis flagellum:* An efficient ambush predator. *Southwestern Naturalist* 34: 460–467.

Justice, D. W. and R. E. Herrington. 1988. Life history notes: *Elaphe guttata* (corn snake). *Herpetological Review* 19: 35.

Kapus, E. J. 1964. Anatomical evidence for *Heterodon* being poisonous. *Herpetologica* 20: 137–138.

Kardong, K. V. 1975. Prey capture in the cottonmouth snake. *Journal of Herpetology* 9 (2): 169–175.

Keenlyne, K. D. 1972. Sexual differences in feeding habits of *Crotalus horridus horridus*. Journal of Herpetology 6 (3–4): 234–237.

Kennedy, J. P. 1959. A minimum egg complement for the western mud snake (*Farancia abacura reinwardti*). *Copeia* 1959: 71.

_____. 1965. Territorial behavior in the eastern coachwhip (*Masticophis flagellum*). *Anatomical Record* 1965: 151–499.

Kiester, A. R. 1971. Species density of North American amphibians and reptiles. *Systematic Zoology* 20: 127–137.

King, R. B. 1993. Determinants of offspring number and size in the brown snake (*Storeria dekayi*). *Journal of Herpetology* 27 (2): 175–185.

Klauber, L. M. 1940a. The rattlesnakes, genera *Sistrurus* and *Crotalus*. Chicago Academy of Science Special Publication 4: 1–266.

_____. 1956. *Rattlesnakes: Their Habits, Life Histories and Influence on Mankind.* 2 vols. Los Angeles: University of California Press.

Knight, J. L. and R. K. Loraine. 1986. Notes on Turtle Egg Predation by *Lampropeltis getulus* (Linnaeus) (Reptilia: Colubridae) on the Savannah River Plant, South Carolina.

Knight, R. L. and A. W. Erickson, 1976. High incidence of snakes in the diet of red-tailed hawks. *Raptor Res.* 10: 108–111.

Kofron, C. P. 1978. Foods and habitats of aquatic snakes (Reptilia, Serpentes) in a Louisiana swamp. *Journal of Herpetology* 12: 543–554.

_____. 1979a. Female reproductive biology of the brown snake (*Storeria dekayi*) in Louisiana. *Copeia* 1979: 463–466.

_____ and J. R. Dixon. 1980. Observations on aquatic colubrid snakes in Texas. *Southwestern Naturalist* 25: 107–109.

Kroll, J. C. 1976. Feeding adaptations of hognose snakes. *Southwestern Naturalist* 20 (4): 537–557.

Krysko, K. L. 1995. Resolution of the controversy regarding the taxonomy of the kingsnake, *Lampropeltis getula*, in Southern Florida. Unpublished master's thesis, Florida International University.

Lawler, H. E. 1977. The status of *Drymarchon corais couperi* (Holbrook), the eastern indigo snake, in the southeastern United States. *Herpetol. Rev.* 8: 76–79.

Lawson, R., A. J. Meier, P. G. Frank and P. E. Moler. 1991. Allozyme variation and systematics of the *Nerodia fasciata-Nerodia clarkii* complex of water snakes (Serpentes-Colubridae). Copeia (3): 638–659.

Laszlo, J. 1977a. Notes on thermal requirement of reptiles and amphibians in captivity: the relationship between temperature ranges and vertical climate (life) zone concept. Proceedings from the American Association of Zoological Parks and Aquariums Regional Conference, 1977, Wheeling, West Virginia.

Layne, J. M., and T. M. Steiner. 1984. Sexual dimorphism in occurrence of keeled dorsal snakes in the eastern indigo snake (*Drymarchon corais couperi*). *Copeia* 1984 (3): 776–778.

Lazell, Jr., J. D., 1989. *Wildlife of the Florida Keys: A Natural History.* Covelo, Calif: Island Press.

Levell, J. P. 1995. *A Field Guide to Reptiles and the Law.* Excelsior, MN: Serpent's Tale Natural History Book Distributors.

Lipske, M. 1995. The private lives of pit vipers. *National Wildlife* 33 (5): 14–21.

Loennberg, E. 1984. Notes on the reptiles and batrachians Collected in Florida in 1892 and 1893. Proc. U. S. Nat. Museum 17: 317–339.

Lovich, J. E., and E. O. Wilson. 1967. *The theory of island biogeography.* Princeton: Princeton University Press.

Mara, W. P. 1992. The eastern indigo snake: One of nature's finest. *Tropical Fish Hobbyist* 41 (2): 164.

_____. 1995. Observations on scarlet snakes (*Cemophora coccinea*). *Tropical Fish Hobbyist* 43 (7): 128.

Markel, R. G., and R. D. Bartlett. 1995. *Kingsnakes and Milksnakes.* New York: Barron's.

Martin, W. F., and R. B. Huey. 1971. The function of the epiglottis in sound production (hissing) of *Pituophis melanoleucus. Copeia* 1971: 752–754.

Martof, B. S., W. M. Palmer, J. R. Bailey, and J. R. Harrison III. 1980. *Amphibians and Reptiles of the Carolinas and Virginia.* Chapel Hill, N.C.: University of North Carolina Press.

Marvel, B. 1972. A feeding observation on the yellow-bellied water snake (*Nerodia erythrogaster flavigaster*). Bulletin of the Maryland Herpetological Society 8 (2): 52.

Mattison, C. 1988. *Keeping and Breeding Snakes.* London: Blanford Press.

McCollough, N. E., and J. R. Gennaro, Jr. 1963. Evaluation of venomous snake bite in the southern United States. *Journal of the Florida Medical Association* 49: 959–972.

McDowell, S. B., and C. M. Bogert. 1954. The systematic position of *Lanthanotus* and the affinities of the anguinomorphan lizards. Bulletin of the American Museum of Natural History 105: 1–142.

McEachern, M. J. 1991. *A Color Guide to Corn Snakes Captive-Bred in the United States.* Lakeside, CA: Advanced Vivarium Systems, Inc.

Meade, G. O. 1934. Feeding *Farancia abacura* in captivity. *Copeia* 1934: 91–92.

_____. 1935. The egg-laying of *Farancia abacura. Copeia* 1935: 190–191.

_____. 1937. Breeding habits of *Farancia abacura* in captivity. *Copeia* 1937: 12–15.

_____. 1940a. Maternal care of eggs by *Farancia. Herpetologica* 2: 15.

_____. 1941. The natural history of the mud snake. *Science Monthly* 63 (1): 21–29.

Means, D. B. 1985. Radio-tracking the eastern diamondback rattlesnake. *National Geographic Society Res. Rep.* 18: 529–536.

Mertens, R. 1960. *The World of Amphibians and Reptiles.* London: George C. Harrap & Co.: New York: McGraw Hill.

Meshaka, Jr., W. E. 1994. Clutch parameters of *Storeria dekayi,* Holbrook (Serpentes: Colubridae) from Southcentral Florida. *Brimleyana* 21: 73–76.

Miller, D. A., and H. R. Mushinsky. 1990. Foraging ecology and prey size in the mangrove water snake (*nerodia fasciata compressicauda*). *Copeia* 1990: 1099–1106.

Minton, Jr., S. A., 1953. Variation in venom samples from copperheads (*Agkistrodon contortrix mokeson*) and timber rattlesnakes (*Crotalus horridus horridus*). *Copeia* 1953: 212–215.

_____. 1954. Polyvalent antivenin in the treatment of experimental snake venom poisoning. *American Journal of Tropical Medicine and Hygiene* 3: 1077–1082.

_____. 1956b. Some properties of North American pit viper venoms and their correlation with phylogeny. In E. E. Buckley and N. Porges, (eds.) *Venoms*, pp. 145–151. American Association for the Advancement of Science, publication no. 44.

_____. 1957. Snakebite. *Scientific American* 196 (1): 114–122.

_____. 1974. *Venom Diseases.* Springfield, Illinois: Thomas.

_____ and M. R. Minton. 1969._____ *Venomous Reptiles.* New York: Charles Scribner's Sons.

_____ and S. K. Salanitro. 1972. Serological relationships among some colubrid snakes. *Copeia* 1972: 246–252.

_____ and D. Simberloff. 1987. The peninsula effect: habitat-correlated species declines in Florida's herpetofauna. *Journal of Biogeography* 14: 551–568.

Moler, P. E. 1992. *Rare and Endangered Biota of Florida. Volume III. Amphibians and Reptiles.* Gainesville: University of Florida Press.

Mount, R. H. 1975. *The Reptiles and Amphibians of Alabama.* Auburn, Ala.: Auburn University Agricultural Experimental Station.

Mullin, S. J. 1994. Life history characteristics of *Nerodia clarkii compressicauda* at Placido Bayou, Florida. *Journal of Herpetology* 28 (3): 371–372.

Mullin, S. J. and H. R. Mushinsky. Foraging ecology of the mangrove salt marsh snake, (*Nerodia clarkii compressicauda*): Effects of vegetational density. *Amphibia-Reptilia* 16 (2): 167–175.

Murphy, J. B., and B. L. Armstrong. 1978. *Maintenance of Rattlesnakes in Captivity.* Lawrence, Kan.: University of Kansas Press.

Murphy, J. B., L. A. Mitchell, and J. A. Campbell. 1979. Miscellaneous notes on the reproductive biology of reptiles. *Journal of Herpetology* 13 (3): 373–374.

Mushinsky, H. R., and J. J. Hebrard. 1977. Food partitioning by five species of water snakes in Louisiana. *Herpetologica* 33: 162–166.

Mushinsky, H. R. 1984. Observations of the feeding habits of the short-tailed snake, (*Stilosoma extenuatum*) in captivity. *Herpetological Review* 15 (3): 67–68.

Mushinsky, Henry R., and Brian W. Witz. 1993. Notes on the peninsula crowned snake, *Tantilla Relicta,* in periodically burned habitat. *Journal of Herpetology* 27 (4): 468–470.

Myers. 1961. An exceptional pattern variant of the coral snake (*Micrurus fulvius,* Linnaeus). *Quarterly Journal of Florida Academy of Science* 24: 56–58.

Myers, C. W. 1965. Biology of the ringneck snake (*Diadophis punctatus*) in Florida. Bulletin Florida State, Museum of Biological Sciences 10: 43–90.

_____. 1967. The pine woods snake (*Rhadinea flavilata*, Cope). Bulletin Florida State, Museum of Biological Sciences 11: 47–97.

Neill, W. T. 1964. Rainbow snake. *American Midland Naturalist* 71 (2).

_____. 1956. Secondarily injested food items in snakes. *Herpetologica* 12: 172–174.

_____ and E. R. Allen. 1955. Metachrosis in snakes. *Quarterly Journal of the Florida Academy of Sciences* 18 (3): 207–215.

Newman, E. A., and P. H. Hartline. 1982. The infrared "vision" of snakes. *Scientific American* 246 (3): 116–127.

Odum, W. E., C. C. McIvor, and T. J. Smith, III. 1982. The ecology of the mangroves of south Florida: A community profile. U.S. Fish and Wildlife Services Office of Biological Services. FWS/OBS-81/24.

Oxer, H. F. 1982. Australian work in first-aid of poisonous snakebite. *Annals of Emergency Medicine* 11: 228.

Palmer, William M. 1971. Distribution and variation of the Carolina pigmy rattlesnake, *Sistrurus miliarius miliarius*. North Carolina Journal of Herpetology 5 (1): 39–44.

Parker, H. W., and A.G.C. Grandison. 1977. *Snakes: A Natural History*. London: British Museum of Natural History; Ithaca, N.Y.: Cornell University Press.

Parker, W. S., and W. S. Brown. 1980. Comparative ecology of two colubrid snakes, *Masticophis t. taeniatus* and *Pituophis melanoleucus deserticola*, in north Utah. Milwaukee Public Museum Publication, Biological Geology 7. 104pp.

Parrish, Henry M. 1963. Analysis of 460 fatalities from venomous animals in the United States. *American Journal of Medical Science* 245 (2): 35–47.

_____. 1966. Incidence of treated snakebites in the United States. Public Health Reports 81: 269–276.

_____. 1980. *Poisonous Snakes in the United States*. New York: Vantage Press.

Parrish, H. M., and M. S. Khan. 1967. Bites by coral snakes: Report of eleven representative cases. *American Journal of Medical Science* 253: 561–568.

Peam, J., J. Morrison, N. Charles, and V. Muir. 1981. First-aid for snakebite. *Medical Journal of Australia* 2: 293–295.

Perkins, C. B. 1940. A key to the snakes of the United States. Bulletin of the Zoological Society of San Diego, no. 16.

Perlowin, D. 1994. *The General Care & Maintenance of Garter Snakes & Water Snakes*. Lakeside, CA: Advanced Vivarium Systems, Inc.

Perz, S. G. 1994. Optimal foraging by Patch and Prey Selection in *Thamnophis sirtalis similis*. *Journal of General Psychology* 121 (2): 121–130.

Peters, J. A. 1964. *Dictionary of Herpetology*. New York: Hafner Publishing.

Pinou, T., C. A. Hass, and L. R. Maxon. 1995. Geographic variation of serum albumin in the monotypic snake genus *Diadophis* (Colubridae: Xenodontinae). *Journal of Herpetology* 29 (1): 105–110.

Pisani, G. R., J. T. Collins, and S. R. Edwards. 1973. A re-evaluation of the subspecies of *Crotalus horridus*. Kansas Academy of Sciences 75 (3): 255–263.

Platt, D. R. 1969. Natural history of the eastern and western hognose snakes *Heterodon platyrhinos* and *Heterodon nasicus*. University of Kansas, Publications of the Museum of Natural History 18 (4): 253–420.

Plummer, M. V. 1981. Habitat utilization, diet, and movements of a temperate arboreal snake (*Opheodrys aestivus*). *Journal of Herpetology* 15 (4): 425–432.

_____. 1983. Annual variation in stored lipids and reproduction in green snakes (*Opheodrys aestivus*). *Copeia* 1983 (3): 741–745.

_____. 1990. Nesting movements, nesting behavior, and nest sites of green snakes (*Opheodrys aestivus*) revealed by radiotelemetry. *Herpetologica* 46: 190–195.

Plummer, M. V., and H. L. Snell. 1988. Nest site selection and water relations of eggs in the snake (*Opheodrys aestivus*). *Copeia* 1988 (1): 58–64.

Plummer, M. V., and J. D. Congdon. 1994. Radiotelemetric study of activity and movements of racers (*Coluber constrictor*) associated with a Carolina Bay in South Carolina. *Copeia* 1994 (1): 20–26.

Porter, K. R. 1972. *Herpetology*. Philadelphia: W. B. Saunders Co.

Pough, F. H. 1964. A coral snake "mimic" eaten by a bird. *Copeia* 1964: 223.

Quinn, H. R. 1979. Reproduction and growth of the Texas coral snake (*Micrurus fulvius tenere*). *Copeia* 1979: 453–463

Rawat, S., G. Laing, D. C. Smith, D. Theakston and J. Landon. 1993. A new antivenom to treat eastern coral snake (*Micrurus fulvius fulvius*) envenoming. *Toxicon* 32 (2): 185–190.

Redi, Francesco. 1664. *Osservazioni Intorno alle Vipere*. Florence.

Reichling, S. B. 1995. The taxonomic status of the Louisiana pine snake (*Pituophis melanoleucus ruthveni*) and its relevance to the evolutionary species concept. *Journal of Herpetology* 20 (2): 186–198.

Riches, R. J. 1976. *Breeding Snakes in Captivity*. St. Petersburg, Fla.: Palmetto Publishing.

Richmond, N. D. 1952. *Opheodrys aestivus* in aquatic habitats in Virginia. *Herpetologica* 8: 38.

Riemer, W. J. 1957. The snake *Farancia abacura*: An attended nest. *Herpetologica* 13: 31–32.

Robertshaw, D. 1974. *Environmental Physiology*. Baltimore: University Park Press.

Romer, A. S. 1966. *Vertebrate Paleontology*. 3rd ed. Chicago: University of Chicago Press.

_____. 1967. Early reptilian evolution reviewed. *Evolution* 21: 821–833.

Rosenberg, M. J. 1981. *Medical Treatment of Venomous Snakebite*. Cleveland: Cleveland Museum of Natural History.

Rossi, J. V. 1992. *Snakes of the United States and Canada, Keeping Them Healthy in Captivity. Vol. 1: Eastern Area*. Florida: Krieger Publishing Company.

_____ and R. Rossi. 1993. Notes on the captive maintenance and feeding behavior of a juvenile short-tailed snake (*Stilosoma extenuatum*). *Herpetological Review* 24 (3): 100–101.

_____ and _____. 1995. *Snakes of the United States and Canada, Keeping Them Healthy in Captivity. Vol. 2: Western Area.* Florida: Krieger Publishing Company.

Rossman, D. A. 1963b. The colubrid snake genus *Thamnophis:* A revision of the *sauritus* group. *Bulletin of the Florida State Museum of Biological Sciences* 7 (3): 99–178.

Rossman, D. A., and R. L. Erwin. 1980. Geographic variation in the snake *Storeria occipitomaculata* (Storer) (Serpentes: Colubridae) in southeastern United States. *Brimleyana* 4: 95–102.

Ruben, J. A. 1977. Morphological correlates of predatory modes in the coachwhip (*Masticophis flagellum*) and rosy boa (*Lichanura roseofusca*). *Herpetologica* 33: 1–6.

Russell, F. E. 1961. Injuries by venomous animals in the United States. *Journal of the American Medical Association* 177: 903–907.

_____. 1966. Shock following snakebite. *Journal of the American Medical Association* 198: 171.

_____. 1967. Pharmacology of animal venoms. *Clin. Pharmacol. Ther.* 8: 849–873.

_____. 1969. Treatment of rattlesnake bite. *Journal of the American Medical Association* 207: 159.

_____. 1980. *Snake Venom Poisoning.* Philadelphia: J. B. Lippincott.

_____ and J. A. Emery. 1959. Use of the chick in zootoxicologic studies on venoms. *Copeia* 1959: 73–74.

_____, R. W. Carlson, J. Wainschel, and A. H. Osborne. 1975. Snake venom poisoning in the United States: Experiences with 550 cases. *Journal of the American Medical Association* 233: 341.

Schmidt, K. P., and D. D. Davis. 1941. *Field Book of Snakes of the United States and Canada.* New York: G. P. Putnam's Sons.

Semlitsch, R. D., and G. B. Moran. 1984. Ecology of the redbelly snake (*Storeria occipitomaculata*) using mesic habitats in South Carolina. *American Midland Naturalist* 111: 33–40.

_____, J. H. K. Pechmann, and J. W. Gibbons. 1988. Annual emergence of juvenile mud snakes (*Farancia abacura*) at aquatic habitats. *Copeia* 1988: 243–245.

Seigel, R. A., and H. S. Fitch. 1984. Ecological patterns of relative clutch mass in snakes. *Oecologia* 61: 293–301.

Seigel, R. A., and Joseph T. Collins (eds.) 1993. *Snakes: Ecology and Behavior.* New York: McGraw-Hill, Inc.

Sexton, O. J., P. Jacobson and J. E. Bramble. 1992. Geographic variation in some activities associated with neartic pit vipers. In *Biology of the Pit Viper.* J. A. Campbell and E. D. Brodie (eds.) Tyler, Texas: Selva Press.

Slavens, F. L. 1980. *Inventory of Live Reptiles and Amphibians in North American Collections.* Seattle, Wash.: Frank L. Slavens.

Smith, C.. 1992. Rattle length in *Crotalus horridus atricaudatus.* Bulletin of the Maryland Herpetological Society 28 (3): 77.

Smith, H. M. 1941b. A review of the subspecies of the indigo snake (*Drymarchon corais*). *Journal of the Washington Academy of Sciences* 31 (11): 466–481.

Smith, H. M., and F. N. White. 1955. Adrenal enlargement and its significance in the hognose snakes (*Heterodon*). *Herpetologica* 11: 137–144.

Smith, N. G. 1969. Avian predation of coral snakes. *Copeia* 1969: 402–404.

Smith, R. L. 1977. *Elements of Ecology and Field Biology*. New York: Harper & Row.

Smith, S. M. 1975. Innate recognition of coral snake pattern by a possible avian predator. *Science* 187: 759–760.

Snyder, C. C., J. E. Pickins, R. P. Knowles, et al. 1968. A definitive study of snakebite. *Journal of the Florida Medical Association* 55: 330–338.

Stewart, J. R. 1989. Facultative placentotrophy and the evolution of squamate placentation: quality of eggs and neonates in *Virginia striatula*. *American Naturalist*. 133 (1): 111–137.

———. Development of the extraembryonic membranes and histology of the placentae in *Virginia striatula* (Squamata: Serpentes). *Journal of Morphology* 205 (1): 33–43.

Stinner, J. N., and D. L. Ely. 1993. Blood pressure during routine activity, stress, and feeding in black racer snakes (*Coluber constrictor*). *American Journal of Physiology* 1993 (264).

Strecker, J. K. 1927. Chapters from the life history of Texas and amphibians. Part two. Contrib. Baylor University Museum No. 10.

Sutherland, S. K. 1977. Serum reactions, an analysis of commercial antivenoms and the possible role of anticomplexity activity in de novo reactions to antivenoms and antitoxins. *Medical Journal of Australia* 1: 613–615.

———. 1980. Venom and antivenom research. *Medical Journal of Australia* 2: 246–250.

———. 1981. When do you remove first-aid measures from an envenomed limb? *Medical Journal of Australia* 1: 542–544.

———, and A. R. Coulter. 1981. Early management of bites by eastern diamondback rattlesnakes (*Crotalus adamanteus*): Studies in monkeys. *American Journal of Tropical Medicine and Hygiene* 30 (2): 497–500.

———, ———, and R. D. Harris. 1979. Rationalization of first-aid measures for elapid snakebite. *Lancet* 1: 183–186.

Teather, K. L. 1991. The relative importance of visual and chemical cues for foraging in newborn blue-striped garter snakes (*Thamnophis sirtalis similis*). *Behaviour* 117 (3–4): 255–261.

Telford, S. R., Jr. 1948. A large litter of *Natrix* in Florida. *Herpetologica* 4: 184.

———. 1955. A description of the eggs of the coral snake (*Micrurus f. fulvius*). *Copeia* 1955: 258.

Tennant, A. 1984. *The Snakes of Texas*. Austin: Texas Monthly Press, Inc.

———. 1985. *A Field Guide to Texas Snakes*. Austin: Texas Monthly Press, Inc.

Thomas, R. G., and F. H. Pough. 1979. Effects of rattlesnake venom on digestion of prey. *Toxicon* 17 (3): 221–228.

Thompson, S. 1936. *Index of Folk Literature*. Bloomington, Ind.: Indiana University Press.

Tinkle, D. W. 1957. Ecology, maturation, and reproduction of *Thamnophis sauritus proximus*. *Ecology* 38 (1): 69–77.

_____. 1960. A population of *Opheodrys aestivus*. *Copeia* 1960: 29–34.

Timmerman, W. W. 1989. Home range, habitat use and behavior of the eastern diamondback rattlesnake. Master's Thesis, University of Florida.

_____. 1994. Big snakes in trouble. *Florida Wildlife*. 48 (5): 12–14.

Trapido, H. 1940. Mating time and sperm viability in *Storeria*. *Copeia* 1940: 107–109.

Truitt, J. O. 1968. *A Guide to the Snakes of South Florida*. Miami: Hurricane House Publishers, Inc.

Underwood, G. 1957. *Lanthanotus* and the anguinomorphan lizards: A critical review. *Copeia* 1957: 20–30.

_____. 1967. *A Contribution to the Classification of Snakes*. London: British Museum of Natural History.

Van Hyning, O. C. 1931. Reproduction of some Florida snakes. *Copeia* 1931: 59–60.

Van Mierop, L.H.S. 1976. Poisonous snakebite: A review. *Journal of the Florida Medical Association* 63: 191–209.

Visser, J., and D. S. Chapman. 1978. *Snakes and Snakebite*. London: Purnell & Son.

Vosjoli, P. de. 1995. *Basic Care of Rough Green Snakes*. Santee, CA: Advanced Vivarium Systems, Inc.

Wade, D., J. Ewel, and R. Hofstetter. 1980. Fire in South Florida ecosystems. U. S. Dep. Agric. For. Serv., Gen. Tech. Rep. SE-17, Southeast. For. Exp. Stn., Asheville, N.C. 125pp.

Watt, C. H., Jr. 1978. Poisonous snakebite treatment in the United States. *Journal of the American Medical Association* 240: 654.

Weinstein, S., C. DeWitt, and L. A. Smith. 1992. Variability of Venom-neutralizing Properties of Serum from Snakes of the Colubrid Genus *Lampropeltis*. *Journal of Herpetology* 26 (4): 452–461.

Werler, John E. 1948. *Natrix cyclopion cyclopion* in Texas. *Herpetologica* 4: 148.

Wharton, C. H. 1960. Birth and behavior of a brood of the cottonmouth, *Agkistrodon piscivorus leucostoma*, with notes on tail-luring. *Herpetologica* 16: 125–129.

_____. 1966. Reproduction in the cottonmouths, *Agkistrodon piscivorus*, of Cedar Keys, Florida. *Copeia* 1966: 149–161.

_____. 1969. The cottonmouth moccasin on Sea Horse Key, Florida. Bulletin of Florida State, Museum of Biological Sciences 14: 227–272.

Williams, K. L., and L. D. Wilson. 1967. A review of the colubrid snake genus *Cemophora*. *Tulane Studies in Zoology and Botany* 13 (4): 103–124.

_____. 1970b. The racer (*Coluber constrictor*) in Louisiana and eastern Texas. *Texas Journal of Science* 22 (1): 67–85.

Wilson, L. D., and L. Porras. 1983. The ecological impact of man on the south Florida herpetofauna. University of Kansas, Museum of Natural History, Special Publication No. 9.

Wingert, W. A., T. R. Pattabhiraman, R. Cleland, P. Meyer, R. Pattabhiraman, and F. E. Russell. 1980. Distribution and pathology of copperhead (*Agkistrodon contortrix*) venom. *Toxicon* 18: 591–601.

Witwer, M. T. and A. M. Bauer. 1995. Early breeding in a captive corn snake (*Elaphe guttata guttata*). *Herpetological Review* 26 (3): 141.

Wolfe, S. H., J. A. Reidenauer, and D. B. Means. 1988. An ecological characterization of the Florida panhandle. U. S. Fish and Wildlife Services Biological Report 88 (12).

Wright, A. H., and W. D. Funkhauser. 1915. A biological reconnaissance of the Okeefinokee Swamp in Georgia. Proc. Academy of Natural Science Philadelphia 1915: 107–195.

_____, and A. A. Wright. 1957. *Handbook of Snakes of the United States and Canada.* 2 vols. Ithaca, N.Y.: Comstock Publishing.

Ya, P. M., T. Guzman, and J. F. Perry, Jr. 1961. Treatment of bites of North American pit vipers. *Southern Medical Journal* 52 (2): 134–136.

Young, R. A. 1992. Effects of Duvernoy's gland secretions from the eastern hognose snake (*Heterodon platirhinos*) on smooth muscle and neuromuscular junction. Toxicon 30 (7): 775–779.

Zegel, J. C. 1975. Notes on collecting and breeding the eastern coral snake, *Micrurus fulvius fulvius.* Bulletin of the Southeastern Herpetological Society 1 (6)L10.

Zug, D. A., W. A. Dunson. 1979. Salinity preference in freshwater and estuarine snakes (*Nerodia sipedon* and *N. fasciata*). *Florida Sci.* 42: 1–8.

Zug, G. R. 1993. *Herpetology, and Introductory Biology of Amphibians and Reptiles.* London: Academic Press.

Zweifel, R. G., G. R. Zug, C. J. McCoy, D. A. Rossman, and J. D. Anderson (eds.) 1963–present. *Catalogue of American Amphibians and Reptiles.* New York: Society for the Study of Amphibians and Reptiles.

Index